RELIGION IN AMERICAN LIFE

edited by JANET PODELL

THE REFERENCE SHELF

Volume 59 Number 5

THE H. W. WILSON COMPANY

New York   1987

THE REFERENCE SHELF

The books in this series contain reprints of articles, excerpts from books, and addresses on current issues and social trends in the United States and other countries. There are six separately bound numbers in each volume, all of which are generally published in the same calendar year. One number is a collection of recent speeches; each of the others is devoted to a single subject and gives background information and discussion from various points of view, concluding with a comprehensive bibliography. Books in the series may be purchased individually or on subscription.

Library of Congress Cataloging in Publication Data

Main entry under title:

Religion in American life / edited by Janet Podell.

    p. cm. — (The Reference shelf ; v. 59, no. 5)
    Bibliography: p.
    1. United States—Religion—1960- I. Podell, Janet. II. Series.
BL2525.R466   1987   291'.0973—dc19   87-30279
ISBN 0-8242-0752-1

Printed in the United States of America

CONTENTS

PREFACE

Calvin Coolidge was only half right when he said, "The business of America is business." True, ours is a society that glorifies commerce and engages in it in the most enthusiastic and obsessive way. But it is no less obsessive about another matter—one that in less paradoxical cultures is often thought to be antithetical to commerce: religion. The colony of Virginia was founded by commercial interests, the Massachusetts Bay colony by religious dissidents, so that this dual heritage has been with us from the beginning.

Americans, on the whole, are among the most serious religionists in the world. As far back as the 1730s and 40s, the colonies were rocked by an explosion of spiritual fervor that made hundreds of converts for evangelical groups and resulted in a shifting of political power away from the established churches. This was the first Great Awakening, the revival that produced the Shakers, the Universalists, and the Freewill Baptists. Since then there have been other mass revivals, giving birth to other sects, and the continuous importation of religious traditions from other continents by immigrants.

We are now, arguably, in the midst of another Great Awakening, as the articles in the first section of this volume suggest. The expectation that modernity would dry up the wellsprings of religious feeling and turn the United States into a mainly secular society has been proved unrealistic. According to recent Gallup polls, fully 90 percent of all Americans declare a preference for a particular religion, although they may not be formally affiliated; even those who are "unchurched" are likely to pray privately (75 percent). The United States is thus an anomaly among industrialized nations, where material wealth and access to education usually lead to the opposite situation—a decline in religious observance. The intensity of religious feeling in the United States is apparently genuine, and perhaps this is due partly to the lack of an official religion, which eliminates the inevitability of widespread hypocrisy.

What distinguishes the United States even more is its immense diversity of religious life. To the large number of religious groups now active—all the world's major religions and denominations and probably most of its minor ones, together with indigenous groups—must be added those that have already passed into obscurity, including many failed Utopian communities and discredited millennial sects. Socially, this diversity has been made possible by the intermittent willingness of the United States to accept refugees, dissenters, and other bearers of alien cultures, and to make room for domestic nonconformists; legally, it has been made possible by the neutrality of government toward religion and the Constitution's guarantee of freedom of conscience. Portraits of six contemporary religious communities are given in Section II of this volume.

While the guarantee of religious liberty in the First Amendment prevents the United States from being a Christian nation in the legal sense, it is certainly Christian in a cultural sense. The failure to make this important distinction has helped give rise to the confusion surrounding the bid for political dominance of the Christian right wing. When, for example, the Christian conservatives claim to advocate the "moral" or "religious" position on ethical issues such as abortion, they find it convenient to overlook the existence of other religions with other moral positions that are equally legitimate in the eyes of the law. On the other hand, when secularists seek to protect public policy from "contamination" by any religious influence—ultimately, to separate voters from their identities as believers—they find it convenient to overlook the fact that many of the great reform movements in American history, including abolition and temperance, were led by religious believers in obedience to their consciences. The challenge of maintaining mutual tolerance and an impartial government is taken up in Section III, which examines the attitudes toward religious liberty of the creators of the Bill of Rights and of some of their modern-day descendants.

Even in a society as comparatively tolerant as this, religious freedom is not held to be absolute. The courts have held repeatedly that some activities practiced by members of some religious groups—polygamy and child slavery, for example—are not protected by the First Amendment. Subjects of current controversy include tax exemption for religious groups that engage in political lobbying, use of religion to promote fascist ideologies, the status of cults, protection of minority rights versus the public interest, and attempts by one group to assert the sole validity of its doctrines and to dominate other groups. These are among the issues examined in the final section of this volume.

The editor wishes to thank the authors and publishers who kindly gave permission to reprint the material in this collection. Special thanks are given to Diane Podell of the B. Davis Schwartz Memorial Library, C. W. Post Center, Long Island University, for research assistance.

JANET PODELL

November 1987

I. A NATION WITH THE SOUL OF A CHURCH

EDITOR'S INTRODUCTION

American religious life has undergone radical changes since midcentury. At the beginning of the Cold War, the mainline Protestant churches were in the ascendant; prejudice against Roman Catholics and Jews (the majority of whom were immigrants or the children of immigrants) was common; anything outside the Judeo-Christian tradition was for exotic tastes only. Few people would have expected that the coming years would bring a civil rights movement led by black ministers, the election of a Catholic president, the ordination of women, the embrace by college students of Zen Buddhism and "born-again" Christianity. Nor do things show any sign of settling down in the 80s, as Wade Clark Roof and William McKinney show in an article from the *Annals of the American Academy of Political and Social Science*, "Denominational America and the New Religious Pluralism."

The demographic changes laid out by Roof and McKinney are the subject of an insightful analysis by Peter L. Berger in the second article, "Religion in Post-Protestant America," reprinted from *Commentary*. The United States, Berger notes, is "an India, with a little Sweden superimposed"—that is, an intensely religious society dominated by a nonreligious professional elite. That is not a comfortable combination, and it helps to explain the acrimony of the current debate over the role of religion in politics and public policy-making.

In addition to spiritual conviction, religious identity is influenced by a variety of factors, including ethnicity, gender, familial expectation, socioeconomic status, region of residence, and level of education. College students are prime candidates for the religious "switching" described by Roof and McKinney, because the process of education presents a challenge to their assumptions that naturally affects their religious assumptions as well. The five students described in the third selection, an article from *The Pennsylvania Gazette*, have found different ways to affirm their connections to particular traditions. In addition, the article describes how a multiplicity of religions can successfully coexist on

the campus of a secular university—in some ways a microcosm of
the nation.

DENOMINATIONAL AMERICA AND THE NEW
RELIGIOUS PLURALISM[1]

In a time when religious news is dominated by controversies
over which candidate for public office is the better Christian, by
popular television preachers and calls for restoring the nation's
morality, and by esoteric cults and strange new religious movements, denominational religion receives little attention. The religious traditions that once shaped so much of America's way of life
now seem distant—matters of individual concern, for sure, but
of limited social significance. There is a vague awareness that Jimmy Carter is a born-again Southern Baptist, Marie Osmond a
Mormon, and Michael Jackson a Jehovah's Witness, but these affirmations seem to be little more than personal idiosyncrasies, interesting raw material for *People* magazine feature articles.

Religion, after all, is personal, a matter of one's opinion, a private matter with which neither church nor state has the right to
interfere. A Gallup poll finds that 81 percent of the American
population feels "an individual should arrive at his or her own religious beliefs independent of any church or synagogue" and that
78 percent feels "a person can be a good Christian or Jew without
attending a church or synagogue." That trends have moved in the
direction of greater religious privatism in this century is hardly
disputable. Indeed, viewing the American religious scene circa
1985, one might well make the case for the triumph of what Ernst
Troeltsch in 1911 called mysticism, that radically individualistic
form of religion that, as he said, envisions "a new situation altogether, in which it will no longer become necessary to connect religion with the decaying churches." Troeltsch went on to say,

It creates no community, since it possesses neither the sense of solidarity
nor the faith in authority which this requires, nor the no less necessary

[1]Reprint of an article by Wade Clark Roof, professor of sociology at the University of Massachusetts at Am-
herst, and William McKinney, Director of Educational Programs and Professor of Religion and Society at Hartford
Seminary. *The Annals of the American Academy of Political and Social Science.* 480:24–38. Jl. '85. Copyright © 1985 by
The American Academy of Political and Social Science. Reprinted by permission of Sage Publications, Inc.

.fanaticism and desire for uniformity. It lives in and on communities which have been brought into existence by other ruder energies; it tends to transform these groups from confessional unities into organizations for administration, offering a home to varying minds and energies. It is opposed to ecclesiastical spirit by its tolerance, its subjectivism and symbolism, its emphasis upon the ethical and religious inwardness of temper, its lack of stable norms and authorities.

Yet for all the truth here, as a description of American religion this statement is flawed. Troeltsch's other seminal institutional types—church and sect—do not fully conform to the American environment, and neither does mysticism. Seeing only the individualistic strands, it ignores the communal and group character of religion in this country that continues to find expression in that unique socioreligious form, the denomination. Moreover, it attracts attention away from some of the more crucial aspects of religious change in America over the past three decades, which should not go unnoticed in any mapping of the current religious scene.

Three observations about the current scene seem irrefutable:

1. Americans continue to identify with the historic religious traditions. The same polls that suggest the strength of religious individualism in this country also reveal that 90 percent of the population expresses a religious preference and two-thirds are members of a local church or synagogue. Even the unchurched and those only nominally involved in organized religion tend to a remarkable degree to profess loyalty to their religious tradition.

2. For Americans, religious groups continue to fulfill important quasi-ethnic functions providing millions with a sense of meaning and belonging. Even in a time when church religion may not be highly salient for many and connections between faith and life seem vague, such groups remain deeply embedded in American life as the major voluntary organizations. Like the family, the neighborhood, and other voluntary activities, religious groups are mediating structures, linking individuals and families to the larger social order; they are people-sized, face-to-face institutions where the things that matter most in personal and communal life can be dealt with.

3. Religious themes have taken on new significance in the public arena. A greater evangelical and fundamentalist religious presence plus the polarization along ideological lines have made Americans keenly aware of the differing religious traditions that make up the American religious mosaic. In a crystalized and very

forceful way, religious developments of the past decade have forced to the forefront the question of religious America—if, and in what way, the country can be conceived of as a sacred enterprise.

As organization, as heritage, and as community, denominational religion is still very much a part, even if in the background, of the changing patterns of religion and culture. Denominationalism has seen its character altered because it is so deeply embedded in the structures of American life; the story of its persistence and change since midcentury is in fact the story of the nation itself. What, then, can be said about the character of religious life in America from the standpoint of the existing collectivities that give it shape and flavor?

Expanding Pluralism

In the years since midcentury, the nation has become much more pluralistic in its religious life. Far from being the "triple melting-pot" of Protestants, Catholics, and Jews that Will Herberg envisioned in the 1950s, religious boundaries have developed in new and unanticipated ways. Denominational identities did not dissolve as some—including Herberg—expected they would in the course of assimilation; there have been denominational unions—mainly reunions—but institutional attachments are as strong and maybe stronger today than they were three decades ago. Beneath the gloss of popular religious labels—for example, "born-again," "evangelical," "charismatic"—Americans still identify with specific subcommunities: "I am a Protestant but more than that I'm a Baptist, and a born-again Southern Baptist at that," or "a post-Vatican II Catholic," or "a Jew and a member of the Lubavitcher movement," or maybe even "a Lake Wobegon Lutheran."

A broad profile of religious America currently is as follows: liberal Protestants—Congregationalists, Presbyterians, Episcopalians, and Unitarians—comprise 9 percent of the population; moderate Protestants—Methodists, Lutherans, American Baptists, Disciples, and Reformed—24 percent; conservative Protestants—Southern Baptists, Church of God, Pentecostals, Assemblies of God, and many others—15 percent; black Protestants, 9 percent; Catholics, 25 percent; Jews, 2 percent; other faiths, 8 percent; and non-affiliates, 7 percent. [These figures are based on a composite sample of over 17,000 Americans from the General Social Surveys, from 1972 to 1984. These surveys are conducted by the National Opinion Research Center and provide a representative sampling of the adult population. Unless otherwise indicated, data reported in this article are taken from these surveys.] Over the years there have been gradual but significant changes in the relative sizes of the three great religious communities, Protestant, Catholic, and Jewish.

Most notable is the steady decline of the Protestant majority. Since 1952 Protestant preferences have declined from 67 percent of the population to 56 percent, or a proportional loss of 16 percent. These losses continue a larger pattern of Protestant decline throughout this century. But more than a matter of numbers, the erosion of Protestant strength is a matter of ethos. Historians date the beginnings of the Protestant establishment's decline early in the twentieth century, but the age of the white Anglo-Saxon Protestant (WASP) did not really end in the minds of Americans until the 1960s. The nation elected a Roman Catholic president, and two Supreme Court decisions mandating one man, one vote, and rendering public school prayer unconstitutional profoundly undercut Protestantism's hold on the culture. Even more so now than when he wrote it, Herberg's comment is true: "Protestantism in America today presents the anomaly of a strong majority group with a growing minority consciousness."

In contrast, the Catholic community has steadily grown almost decade by decade. In the short space of 30 years Catholics increased from 22 percent to 26 percent of the population, or by 15 percent. Benefiting from a high birthrate and immigration, they have gained numbers in about the same proportion as Protestants have lost them. Of course, they have grown in social standing and cultural influence as well. In the postwar period, Catholics made spectacular gains in education, occupational status, and income, such that their overall status levels are now equal to those of Protestants. With upward mobility and assimilation, they have come to resemble Protestants in many respects: in social attitudes, political party affiliation, and in religious practices.

The Jewish population appears to have declined relative to the others. A low birthrate and high levels of intermarriage have worked to keep the size of this faith community relatively small. Because of the concentration of Jews in a few metropolitan areas, it is conceivable that their numbers are underestimated in the polls. Even so, they remain a distinctive and identifiable religious minority whose social standing and influence are disproportionate to their numbers.

All three religious communities are experiencing declines in religious participation. Throughout the period of public opinion polling, from the 1940s until the mid-1960s, roughly three-quarters of the American population consistently reported they were church or synagogue members. But polls in the 1970s and early 1980s began to show distinct declines, to a low 67 percent in 1982. Eighty percent of Catholics are church members, 73 percent of Protestants report the same, and 45 percent of Jews say they are members of a synagogue. Of course, many Americans who say they are church members are effectively unchurched because of lack of involvement in religious institutions. Using a more rigorous definition that includes active religious involvement, a major study in 1978 identified 41 percent of the adult population in the country as unchurched. The evidence suggests that the unchurched are overwhelmingly believers and quite religious in many respects, but choose to express their religiousness apart from churches and synagogues. Compared with the churched, they tend more to welcome social change, hold less to conventional values, and are less rooted in stable social networks in the communities in which they live. Although the cultural profiles for the two are not so distinct at present, should the downward trend in church membership continue, the differences quite possibly will become more pronounced in the years ahead.

The largest proportionate increase in religious preference has come in the categories of other religions or no religion. Now 4 percent of the population indicates a faith outside the three major traditions compared to about 1 percent in the early 1950s. Currently 9 percent identify as non-affiliates, which is 7 points higher than in the previous period. Of course, the percentage base for these categories is small, and hence the proportional changes should not be overdrawn. Still, the figures are striking. A heterogeneous grouping of non-Judeo-Christian faiths in this country now commands the loyalties of more Americans than Judaism does. This represents a sizable number of followers and practitioners falling outside the more conventional faiths. And the fact that almost 10 percent of Americans choose to identify as non-affiliates is revealing on several counts: it points to a growing non-affiliated sector and to the greater ease for Americans

now to reject a religious affiliation. It is interesting that the decline in religious membership since the early 1970s—7 or 8 percent—about equals the current percentage expressing no
religious preference. Their numbers suggest the possibility of a
widening secular constituency, perhaps more irreligious than
anti-religious, but in any case a force of growing cultural importance in a pluralistic society.

No one expected the rise of the so-called new religions and
the religious counterculture of the late 1960s. Many middle-class
youth dropped out of the churches and experimented with alternative religions that promised new modes of meaning and belonging. Beneath the superficial quality of much of the
counterculture, there was a deeply based spiritual ferment that
took the form of rejecting the establishment and of searching for
new realities. It was a time of turning inward and exploring the
self with new spiritual technologies, as expressed in the language
of "getting into" a range of experiential frames, from astrology
to Zen. Ironically, just at the time when Protestant, Catholic, and
Jewish mainliners had begun to blur boundaries, many others
were seeking them. The conventional, luke-warm religiosity of
the established churches paled in the face of newer, more esoteric
alternatives that seemed more capable of linking belief and behavior, or how one thinks and what one does.

Liberal Declines

The dislocations and tensions of the period were felt more
acutely in liberal Protestantism than in any other religious sector.
Beginning in about the mid-1960s, the historic mainline churches
began reporting significant membership losses. Protestant
churches with long-standing records of sustained growth and
prosperity, some dating to colonial times, experienced their first
major downturns. There had been a religious depression—
perhaps more accurately a recession—in the 1930s, but what was
later to come was of greater magnitude. To cite some examples,
the Episcopal church, the Presbyterian denominations, the United Methodist Church, the Christian Church (Disciples of Christ),
and the United Church of Christ, all of which had enjoyed considerable prosperity in the 1950s, experienced sizable losses in the
1960s and 1970s. The losses in the 1970–80 period were stagger-
ing: the United Presbyterian Church, down 19 percent; Disciples,

17 percent; the Episcopalians, 15 percent; United Church of Christ, 11 percent; and the United Methodist Church, more than 9 percent.

The declines were fairly abrupt, hitting all the churches at about the same time. Across the board, the liberal churches were suffering. In general, the losses resulted more from decreasing numbers of new members than increases in dropouts. Proportionately fewer persons were joining after the mid-1960s, and among those joining fewer were becoming active participants. Younger adults were conspicuously absent, raising speculation about a lost generation in these churches.

Trends in religious participation and support were the same. Institutional support was high in the 1950s, but attendance at services declined steadily during the 1960s and into the early 1970s. Among Protestants the declines were greatest for the moderate to liberal bodies—in particular for Methodists, Presbyterians, and Episcopalians. Religious giving—in relation to inflation—declined as well. Thus numerous institutional indicators pointed to a religious decline of considerable proportions.

To a lesser extent, Catholicism experienced some of the same reverberations. Membership continued to increase, but at a declining rate. Declines in religious participation were striking, from 74 percent of Catholics attending mass weekly in 1958 to 51 percent in 1982. The declines were most evident for young, upwardly mobile communicants. Rising socioeconomic levels and rapid assimilation into the culture in the years after World War II led Catholics to discard much of the old immigrant heritage. In addition, Vatican II brought about a new climate of lay involvement and voluntarism. As they joined the ranks of the mainline, they took on both the privileges and the burdens of the establishment.

Conservative Resurgence

Virtually all the churches that continued to grow after World War II were conservative—particularly Protestant evangelical and fundamentalist bodies—with membership increases often exceeding the nation's population growth rate. Among these bodies were the Seventh-Day Adventists, the Church of the Nazarene, Assemblies of God, the Salvation Army, and various small pentecostal and holiness groups. In both the 1960s and 1970s these churches grew at phenomenal rates, some as much as 60 to 70 percent each decade. The Southern Baptists also grew, becoming in 1967 the largest Protestant denomination. Indicators other than membership suggested an upswing in religious conservatism: church school enrollments, missionary support, book publishing, the founding of Christian schools. This marked growth in the conservative faiths along with the liberal declines indicated, as Martin Marty noted, a "seismic shift" in the nation's religious landscape.

Nor was the shift limited to conservative Protestantism. Within Catholicism there was reaction to the liturgical and modernizing trends set in motion by Vatican II. While some sought to adapt to new ways, others called for a return to traditional Catholic values and authority. Pope John Paul II's opposition to abandoning priestly celibacy and ordaining women confirmed for many that the church would remain a bedrock of stability and continuity, despite the changes underway. Within American Judaism there was a discernible shift in mood as well. Orthodox Judaism grew more rapidly than did either the Reform or Conservative branches in the 1970s. Rejecting what many regarded as the lax observance and permissiveness of the latter, growing numbers of Jews turned to the more traditional faith in search of a distinct religious identity and prescribed way of life. This turnabout in trends is noteworthy, considering that for years there had been a continual movement of Jews from Orthodoxy toward more liberal faith or non-affiliation.

In many sectors, then, conservative religious currents were flowing. A dominant secular culture provoked deep reactions—anti-pluralist and antimodern. In religion, as in other realms, a back-to-basics mood prevailed. Evangelical and fundamentalist faiths flourished as the cultural and religious center seemed to collapse. Rigid and demanding beliefs, traditional values, certainty, absolutist moral teachings—all seemed to fill the needs of the times. By drawing cognitive and behavioral boundaries and adhering generally to a non-accommodating stance toward modernity, they offered a clear alternative to secular and diffusely religious points of view.

A Moral Crusade

Nowhere was the rising tide of religious conservatism more visible than in the growing confrontation over moral issues. By the late 1970s, supporters of the conservative ideologies of the religious Right clashed on one issue after another with ideologies they unceasingly labeled "secular humanism." Views came to be most polarized around two basic social institutions: the family and the school. At the center of controversy were family and gender-role issues such as abortion, the Equal Rights Amendment, and gay rights. Pro-family leaders crusaded for a return to traditional roles for men and women and actively opposed equal legal protection for women and homosexuals. The polls show that evangelicals and fundamentalists are far more inclined than mainliners to favor a ban on abortion, to oppose the Equal Rights Amendment, and to be against the hiring of homosexuals as teachers in public schools; differences between evangelicals and non-evangelicals are often wider than those between Protestants and Catholics.

Like the family, public schools were viewed with great concern. Leaders in the pro-family movement accused the schools of eroding the morality of children by teaching evolution, by using humanist textbooks, and by not having mandatory school prayer. There is widespread support for a constitutional amendment permitting prayer in the schools, and the public seems to be about equally divided on whether evolution or creationism should be taught in the classroom.

The New Christian Right emerged as a visible force, partly as a result of the electronic church and its vast network of religious programming and popular television preachers. Using the most sophisticated of media technology, televangelists such as Jerry Falwell, Pat Robertson, and Jim Bakker are effective in mobilizing support for religious and moral causes. But the change is more than just an increase in media exposure: there is a new tone of political involvement. Long known for their more private faith and suspicion of involvement in politics, they have become more involved in voter registration; in speaking out on issues such as school prayer, abortion, pornography, and national defense; and in openly endorsing or denouncing candidates for public office on the basis of their voting records or positions on issues. President Reagan's landslide second-term victory reflects to some extent this new activism. The Moral Majority and Religious

Roundtable have thrust the religious Right into the public arena in an effort to reshape American public life, calling for traditional moral values and a return to Christian America. Focusing on moral, and not simply religious, concerns, evangelical and fundamentalist leaders have been able to forge an alliance with others also disturbed by these issues—religionists as diverse as Mormons, traditional Catholics, and some Jews.

The Changing Social and Demographic Profile

As the face of the religious establishment has changed, so has its underlying social and demographic basis. Three aspects of the changing social location of religion are especially important: the age structure, regional distribution, and class composition.

Poll data reveal striking age differentials among Protestant groups. The denominations that constitute the Protestant mainline have aging constituencies. With the losses of many youth in the 1960s, the average age is noticeably high in the liberal churches: 42 percent of Disciples of Christ, 41 percent of Methodists, and 43 percent of the United Church of Christ are age 55 or older. None of the conservative Protestant groups has as many as 40 percent over 55 years of age; indeed, fewer than one-third of the Jehovah's Witnesses, Pentecostals, and Assemblies of God constituencies are of this age.

Young adults, on the other hand, account for only 26 percent of the members in the Reformed Church, 21 percent of the United Church of Christ, and 28 percent of the Methodists. The significance of these figures becomes apparent when one considers that almost 40 percent of the nation's adult population belongs to the 18-to-34 age category. Young adults are far better represented in the conservative churches: more than 50 percent of Jehovah's Witnesses belong to this younger category. Compared with moderate and liberal churches, conservative Protestants are more successful in holding on to their young members.

Regional profiles for the mid-1920s and early 1980s suggest that most denominations have remained in their traditional areas of concentration: Catholics in the Northeast, liberal and moderate Protestants in the Northeast and Midwest; conservative Protestants in the South. But there have been changes. Episcopalians, Presbyterians, and the United Church of Christ—all branches of Anglo-Protestantism—are not as concentrated in the Northeast as they once were. Although the Northeast was at one time a stronghold of WASP power and influence, shifts to the Sun Belt have undercut the numerical base of those denominations in this region. Conservative Protestants are increasingly finding members outside their regions of strength. Southern Baptists are growing in all regions today but more in the Northeast and West than elsewhere. Now found in the West are 33 percent of Jehovah's Witnesses, 27 percent of Assembly of God members, and 30 percent of Adventists; 29 percent of all Mormons are found outside the West. Those without a religious preference are well represented in all the regions, but more so in the West.

Finally, there are the changes in class composition since midcentury. Jews and the old WASP establishment—Episcopalians, Presbyterians, United Church of Christ, and Unitarian—continue to hold their elite positions, yet there have been far-reaching changes in the status hierarchy. Status differences between many groups have declined, and some groups have noticeably moved upward in their standing. Catholics have moved upward: increases in their income levels lag somewhat behind gains in education and occupations, but they are now a solidly middle-class constituency. Evangelical Protestants in the 1960s and 1970s benefited from expanding education and job opportunities. Whereas in 1960 only 7 percent of members in evangelical and fundamentalist denominations had attended some college, by the mid-1970s that figure was 23 percent—a rate of increase that far exceeds the increase of any other group, including Catholics. These gains stand out against those of mainline Protestants, whose educational base hardly changed at all during this period. Increasingly represented in the lower-middle eschelons of American life, the conservative Protestant community has taken on a new style and presence as it accommodates the mainstream culture.

Profiles for non-affiliates have changed perhaps most of all. Once an uneducated, highly alienated, and marginal group, those fitting the secularist image today are young, single, urban, and highly professional. They are called yuppies and are much less alienated—in fact, they are firmly a part of the mainstream. In many respects, they are at the opposite end of the social and demographic spectrum from the evangelicals: more secure in their standing and more at the center of modernizing, secular trends. This more distinctly secular constituency is sometimes linked to

the rise of the so-called new class, a new stratum deriving its livelihood from the production and distribution of knowledge in modern society, distinguished from the old bourgeoisie, or
entrepreneurial class. Being more secular, more rational, and
more cosmopolitan, the knowledge class espouses values and an
outlook that differ sharply with bourgeois morality and life-styles;
indeed, abortion, the Equal Rights Amendment, gay rights, and
various environmental and consumer issues have taken on symbolic significance in a confrontation of class interests. Religion in
America—especially in the mainline churches that have solidly
middle-class constituencies and large bureaucratic staffs—is itself
caught up in this struggle between old and emerging classes.

The New Voluntarism

The traditional ascriptive loyalties that once shaped America's religious communities have lost much of their hold on the
contemporary setting. The lines of class, race, ethnicity, and region—the "social sources of denominationalism" identified by H.
Richard Niebuhr a half century ago—are not as clearly drawn today as they were in an earlier time. Niebuhr wrote of a time when
the country was in its formative stages and the religious communities were taking shape around the evolving caste and class cleav-
ages of the period. Since then social and demographic shifts have
significantly altered the social basis of religious life and have leveled many of the historical differences in doctrine and piety.
These trends, combined with the greater confrontation between
religious and secular forces, now place the denominational scene
in flux and are bringing about new relationships between religion
and culture.

Modernity creates a situation in which faith becomes a highly
individualized, privatized matter. In this respect Troeltsch is ab-
solutely correct. Less and less bound to an inherited faith, the
present-day believer is able to shop around in a consumer market
of religious alternatives and pick and choose among aspects of belief and practice. As Peter L. Berger points out, the modern
pluralistic world forces upon individuals a "heretical
imperative"—the necessity to choose among alternative interpretations and select those elements within a single heritage that are
illuminating from those that are not. That is to say, in the tradition of religious voluntarism, the individual is given a great deal

of autonomy as well as responsibility in arriving at a religious frame of reference. Religious pluralism of course encourages the privatization of faith, as it forces a denominational preference, and trends of the modern period have further accentuated this tendency. Greater opportunity to exercise choice on the part of the believer is simply the logical extension of religious voluntarism, or as [Talcott] Parsons says, "the individual is bound only by responsible personal commitment, not by any factor of ascription."

Trends toward religious privatism are evident in all the major faiths. Liberal Protestantism especially is vulnerable. Because the liberal churches have historically encouraged freedom of choice among their members, institutional loyalties often suffer. Consequently, some members in these churches can be thought of as believers but not belongers in the conventional sense. But even in the conservative churches, where group loyalties are stronger, there is great emphasis on individual salvation and personal responsibility. Evangelism thrives on individuals who make their own decisions; first comes the decision to believe, and then comes voluntary membership in the church. Perhaps the appeal of the electronic church to so many evangelical, fundamentalist Americans is that it particularizes and renders private religious experience and choice.

Even within the tradition with the greatest heritage of ecclesiastical authority—American Catholicism—there are ample signs of a growing religious individualism. Vatican II unleashed enormous energies in this direction. In this country especially, with its heritage of religious voluntarism, the relaxation of institutional standards led to what Andrew M. Greeley describes as selective Catholicism—with emphasis on participation as a matter of individual conscience and on drawing on the tradition as one chooses. Over the past decade many young Catholics have opted for religious styles that allow for greater individuality in matters of belief and practice, and with this choice has come less respect for the authority of the church, especially in matters of sexual morality and personal life-style.

Yet it would be easy to overstate the case for a growing religious individualism. With the possible exception of liberal Protestants, group-based institutional attachments remain fairly strong for conservative Protestants, blacks, Jews, and many Catholics. Quasi-ethnic communal ties are not diminishing in any significant way. The declines in church attendance appear to have bottomed out in the late 1970s, which may portend a more stable period of institutional religious attachments for the future. And even those who are highly privatized in their faith tend not to lose their religious identities. For example, many who have drifted away from regular mass still think of themselves as Catholics. Today there are growing numbers of communal Catholics—that is, young well-educated persons not so much involved in the institutional church yet self-consciously, and at times even militantly, Catholic in outlook. Even liberal Protestants have their alumni associations; such Protestants are no longer very active but on occasion they rise to defend their religion's causes.

Patterns of Religious Switching

The new voluntarism is apparent in patterns of switching among the faiths. Switching from one faith to another is common in the United States: one-third of all Americans no longer belong with the tradition in which they were born; fully 40 percent of today's Protestants have changed affiliation at one time or another in their lives.

Switching from conservative to liberal Protestant churches has long been observed as accompanying upward mobility. As people's socioeconomic status has improved, they often have changed religious affiliations. Theologically liberal and higher-status churches are deemed to be in keeping with advances in educational and occupational attainment. Over the years the liberal churches have benefited from this movement. In the past Episcopalians especially, but also Presbyterians and Congregationalists, enjoyed net gains from switching at the expense of moderate and conservative religious bodies. Today there is still some shifting of this kind but to a lesser extent. Since the 1960s switching has become more diverse and has taken on symbolic qualities peculiar to the cultural climate of the times.

Today there are three distinct streams of religious movement. Two amount to a circulation of the saints among Protestant churches, and a third involves a secular drift out of organized religion.

The liberal movement is one of the streams. Those shifting into liberal churches are older, more educated, and have high-level occupations; they are less active religiously than those they leave behind in other churches; they tend to be liberal on moral issues. The liberal churches enjoy net gains in the switching process, almost wholly accounted for by older switchers. Many of these in-switchers are only nominally religious as church members.

The second stream is the conservative movement. Those switching to the conservative churches tend to be somewhat younger and have lower status levels. They are more active in the churches, and they are more conservative on issues such as abortion, the Equal Rights Amendment, and civil liberties.

Liberal churches enjoy somewhat larger net gains from switching, but conservative churches pick up better converts in the sense of institutional belonging and commitment. Those switching have characteristics similar to the traditions to which they switch, and thereby contribute to the maintenance of existing life-style and institutional differences among the faiths. The big losers in the switching directions are the large moderate denominations—Methodists, Lutherans, American Baptists, and Disciples of Christ.

The third stream, qualitatively different, is the switching to no religious preference, or the growth of the secular constituency. In all the sifting and sorting in the recent period, this group has become the main beneficiary. For every person raised without religion who adopts a church, over three people forsake the churches for no organized religion. All religious groups lose people to this category, but losses are greatest among liberal and moderate Protestants, Catholics, and Jews. Those becoming nonaffiliates are young, predominantly male, well educated, committed to the new morality, and oriented generally to an ethic of personal fulfillment.

Greater diversity in switching patterns, however, does not mean that institutional religious attachments are crumbling. The opposite may actually be the case. A new religious order appears to be in the making in which life-style choice and moral values play a bigger part in selecting a religious affiliation. With the erosion of traditional group loyalties, individually based choices can now operate more freely; people can affiliate on the basis of genuine religious preference. Individuals sharing a common outlook or behavioral style are likely to cluster around those institutions identified, officially or unofficially, with a preferred constellation of beliefs and moral values. To the extent that this happens, the religious communities could take on clearer social and religious identities as they become ideologically more homogeneous.

The Future

It would be risky, of course, to predict the religious future on the basis of current patterns of switching. Trends such as these change, and often rather abruptly and in unanticipated directions. Of greater long-term importance in shaping the religious composition of the country are the demographics: declining birthrates, migration, and birth-cohort changes over time. These factors virtually assure that trends now set in motion will continue throughout this century and into the next.

The Catholic population is growing, and will continue to do so, because of its birthrates and immigration. In the post–Vatican II era, American Catholicism suffers from being pulled in conflicting directions—toward greater personal religious freedom, on the one hand, but also toward traditional stands in matters of faith and morality, on the other. Last year's presidential election brought these tensions to the fore in exchanges between vice-presidential nominee Geraldine Ferraro and Archbishop John J. O'Connor over abortion. The growing activism of the bishops on matters such as nuclear warfare and the economy signal a dramatic shift toward greater public involvement. American Catholicism is at a crucial moment in its cultural and institutional alignments and is now in a position to exercise considerable influence in shaping public life. Much depends on the vision that is articulated and on the church's success in resolving issues of personal faith and morality without alienating large sectors of its constituency.

Already we observed age discrepancies for Protestant groups, which translate, of course, into fertility differentials. Conservative Protestants have far higher birthrates than liberal and moderate Protestants. Rates are highest for Nazarenes, Pentecostals, Mormons, Church of God members, and black Southern Baptists. For younger women in liberal and moderate churches, the average number of children is well below the replacement level. Not only are there fewer young women, but even those that remain have fewer children. The birthrates are partly due to class patterns of fertility, but the demographics today also reflect the heavy losses of young adults from the liberal churches in the 1960s. Even the net gains that the liberal churches enjoy from switching are not sufficient to offset this lack of natural growth.

Even more telling are the figures pertaining to birth cohorts. Throughout this century there has been a gradual erosion of the liberal Protestant community. Most of the moderate to liberal groups have lost ground, almost decade by decade; defectors include those born in the post–World War II period in particular. Methodists, for example—often cited as the most representative American religious group—made up 16 percent of all Americans born around the turn of the century but only 7.7 percent of those born between 1958 and 1965. Similar declines are observed for Lutherans, Presbyterians, Episcopalians, Jews, the United Church of Christ, and Unitarians. Overall the evidence is unmistakably clear: the liberal sector of Protestantism as well as of the total religious community in this country is shrinking and will continue to do so for the foreseeable future.

Gradually, and at times almost imperceptibly, numbers have increased over the decades at the extremes of the religious distribution—for conservative Protestants as well as for non-affiliates. In the aftermath of the Scopes trial fundamentalists lost ground, but actually their numbers have grown in the years since World War I. They made up 11.8 percent of the generation born at the turn of the century, dropped to 7.8 percent for the 1907–23 cohort, but have risen ever since, reaching a record high of 12 percent for the 1958–65 cohort. This pattern, extending over three-quarters of the century, combined with the shrinkage in the liberal camp, suggests that the size of the conservative Protestant community will be proportionately larger at the end of the century than it was in 1900. Whatever their power or influence in the culture in the future, the numbers favor the conservative side.

The non-affiliates have also increased, especially in the baby-boom years following World War II. They accounted for about 3 percent of those born around the turn of the century; about 11 percent of those born between 1941 and 1957; and 13 percent of the 1958–65 birth cohort. The number of Americans growing up outside the religious traditions is increasing. The fact that this growing sector differs from the religious conservatives on so many issues—civil liberties, life-styles, child rearing, and family values—portends the possibility of diverging separate cultures and ever-sharper confrontation over issues of great public significance. As older cohorts die and the more recent cohorts come to make up a larger share of the population, there is a good chance of heightened conflict between the two sectors. Quite possibly, religiously grounded values will be at the center of much debate for the future, maybe even the basis for struggles over the public posture of American life and who will exercise decisive influence over it.

But even this scenario is a tentative one, for much depends on what happens in the religious middle. Despite the plight of the liberal Protestant mainline currently, the moderate Protestant faiths may recover a new middle ground. By virtue of their size and heritage, moderate to liberal groups are in a position and have the resources to forge a broadly based synthesis of belief and culture. These groups are at the center religiously at a time when there is no center. The temptation is to move either to the left or to the right—or fluctuate in one direction or the other depending on the issue—but neither extreme is really natural for these groups. Yet to remain in the middle requires creating a new vital synthesis, a prospect that at present is not apparent but may yet evolve. If this happens it will likely occur by engaging other groups—most notably, conservative Protestants and Catholics—in debate and compromise on specific issues bearing upon public faith, and by generating a social vision capable of broadly encompassing middle America.

Today the lack of a public religious presence is lamented. Richard Neuhaus speaks of the "naked public square" and observes that various groups are now contending to become culture-defining forces in American life. It is noteworthy that the religious voices now attempting to articulate a public vision—Catholics, conservative Protestants, and, to a lesser extent, black Protestants—all have and draw upon a strong group or ethnic experience. Those faiths most capable of galvanizing a new cultural center are those deeply rooted in the life of the people. In the debate over religion and its role in public life that will certainly continue, no doubt new religious and cultural configurations will yet emerge, but it is hardly imaginable that this will happen without the historic religious traditions as major players.

RELIGION IN POST-PROTESTANT AMERICA[2]

In June 1985 the U.S. Supreme Court overruled an Alabama statute authorizing public schools in that state to observe a one-minute silence "for meditation or voluntary prayer." The reasoning behind the decision was that the statute represented an establishment of religion and thereby violated the First Amendment to the United States Constitution, which states that "Congress shall make no law respecting an establishment of religion, or prohibiting the free exercise thereof."

I was abroad a few weeks after this decision and was put in the position of trying to explain it to a group of by no means unfriendly Europeans. It was not an easy task. Their first puzzlement—how is it that an act of a state legislature can be overruled on the basis of an amendment specifically referring to acts of Congress?—was relatively easy to dispel. I explained that the Fourteenth Amendment had "nationalized" all the rights spelled out in the first ten amendments to the federal Constitution. Fortunately, no one asked me to explain just what the Fourteenth Amendment was in the first place, or I would have had to discourse at length on the way in which an act intended to outlaw slavery came to bear such a grave additional burden. But there was no way I could deal with their second puzzlement: how a minute of silence in a classroom of noisy schoolchildren could possibly endanger the religious liberty of Americans. We are not an easy people to understand.

Sidney Mead, the eminent American church historian, has described the United States as "a nation with the soul of a church." The phrase is apt and serves well to illuminate various aspects of the American national character, such as its deep-rooted sense of historic mission and its inveterate moralism.

If the nation is churchlike, then surely the Supreme Court is its most obviously ecclesiastical institution, endlessly engaged in interpreting and reinterpreting the sacred text on which the nation-church is supposed to be based. As Muslims call Jews and Christians people of the Book, the United States may be called

[2]Reprint of a magazine article by Peter L. Berger, University Professor at Boston University. *Commentary.* 80:41–5. My. '86. Copyright © 1986 by The American Jewish Committee. Reprinted from *Commentary*, May 1986, by permission; all rights reserved.

a polity of the Book. No wonder we have more lawyers, both in absolute numbers and per capita, than any other country on earth. And at the pinnacle of this hierarchy of clerks are those whose business is constitutional exegesis in the federal courts, a business with striking similarities to the scholasticisms spawned by those religious traditions (notably Judaism, Christianity, and Islam) that derive from a revelation in a holy book.

Scholastic interpretations evolve from generation to generation; after a while, it becomes a little difficult to relate the latest exegetical exercise to the original meaning of the texts at issue. Some look altogether askance at the effort; these are the judicial activists, who, like Roman Catholic theorists of the Church, put their faith less in the original texts than in the institutional process by which they are transmitted. Others, our strict constructionists, recapitulate the classical Protestant effort to get back to the texts—though this often involves them in rather complicated intellectual acrobatics, for no amount of determination can change the fact that present-day America is a very different place from the America in which the Constitution was written.

As several recent books make clear, the men who drafted the First Amendment not only did not have in mind what later exegetes have imputed to them, but different ones among them had quite different things in mind. In view of the historical evidence, for example, it is hard to sustain the later interpretation that the two clauses of the First Amendment, the "establishment" clause and the "free-exercise" clause, implied a balanced theory of church-state relations. In any case, the main concern of those who drafted the amendment was not to formulate a positive statement about the rights of religion but rather to make sure that the new national institutions (some members of Congress balked at the very word "national") would not usurp rights and powers won in the several states. What is more, the present wording was arrived at fairly quickly after bargaining over several discarded alternatives, as Congress was anxious to get on to other matters.

This is how Thomas Curry puts it in *The First Freedoms: Church and State in America to the Passage of the First Amendment:*

The passage of the First Amendment constituted a symbolic act, a declaration for the future, an assurance to those nervous about the federal government that it was not going to reverse any of the guarantees for religious liberty won by the revolutionary states. . . . Congress approached the subject in a somewhat hasty and absentminded manner. To examine the two clauses of the amendment as a carefully worded analysis of church-state relations would be to overburden them.

That is a historian's judgment. It goes without saying that lawyers
and constitutional theorists are not likely to be much restrained
by it: overburdening texts is their vocation.

From Curry, and from William Lee Miller and A. James
Reichley as well, we get a vivid picture of the bewildering variety
of the colonies in the matter of religious arrangements (as indeed
in everything else). There was New England, dominated by the
powerful Puritan presence—although with a sharp divergence
between theocratic Massachusetts and latitudinarian Rhode Island. There was Virginia with its Anglican establishment, which
was latitudinarian in its own way, permitting the sort of mellow
deism that characterized most of the great Virginians of the period, notably Thomas Jefferson, James Madison, and, last but not
least, George Washington. Maryland and Pennsylvania were two
different experiments in religious liberty, the first a rather short-
lived attempt at Catholic libertarianism, the second, rooted in
Quaker ideology, leading to what was surely the most motley collection of religious eccentrics in 18th-century Western civilization. And New York, with its tradition of Dutch mercantilism,
demonstrated that religious liberty could be the fruit as much of
commercial pragmatism as of lofty ideas.

It is one of the miracles of American history that the representatives of these discrepant political entities could agree on anything; possibly the First Amendment was one of their less
miraculous agreements, since no one desired to see the new nation institutionalize church-state relations along the lines of the
English establishment. In this, as is not unusual for a revolutionary coalition, they were mainly united in what they were against.

Miller devotes a large part of his book [*The First Liberty: Religion and the American Public*] to two representative if wildly divergent individuals, James Madison and Roger Williams. He makes
a good case for seeing these men as prototypes of the two principal traditions of religious liberty in the American republic. Madison, of course, was one of the great Virginians—a gentleman of
ample means, a friend of Jefferson, a relaxed deist comfortable
in the Anglican church, an advocate of "republican virtue" in the
spirit of the American Enlightenment. Williams, born amid the
murderous fanaticisms of English Protestant dissent, was a can-
tankerous Puritan, no less so for eventually concluding that religious liberty was a desideratum in this world. Williams arrived at

this conclusion not out of any Enlightenment ideas about the nobility of man's quest for truth but out of his deeply Calvinistic conviction that, all existing churches being hopelessly corrupt, none must be given the power to coerce.

Out of these twin roots, Miller writes, grew a set of peculiar political and ecclesiastical attitudes. Enlightenment skepticism brought the idea that since no certainties were available in the area of religion, tolerance was the only reasonable position. Protestant sectarianism contributed a strong sense of theological certitude which, however, included the conviction that, since the state and any state-established church would always misuse its power, the church that was faithful to the truth of the gospel must be fiercely independent.

These discrepant ideas combined, at a particular juncture of history, to create a unique fabric of church-state relations. To be sure, circumstances helped a great deal: even in the absence of these ideas, it would have been difficult to replicate on American soil any of the religious establishments of Europe. There were simply too many different groups, too many religio-political interests, for any one to establish dominance. Willy-nilly, they had to learn to live with one another. But whether the ideas were conveniently at hand to legitimate pressing pragmatic concerns, or whether the ideas had history-changing efficacy of their own (or whether, more likely, both things were true), the arrangement so created is with us today. And so, indeed, are the two traditions out of which it grew. Thus, regularly, lawyers for the American Civil Liberties Union with nary a religious certitude in their bones find themselves on the same side on church-state issues— i.e., the side of strict separation—with born-again Baptists who, if one is to believe them, have never doubted their orthodox faith by one iota.

Another thing made clear by these authors is that within the institutional framework of liberty brought about by this paradoxical conspiracy of skeptics and believers, there has been an unending intrusion of religiously based values into the public life of the nation. The Constitution, as it came to be interpreted, might well have set up a wall of separation between church and state, but it most certainly did not set up a wall between religion and politics. Reichley [*Religion in American Public Life*] traces such interventions right through the 1984 presidential election, and he clearly expects them to continue, possibly with renewed force, in the coming years.

Indeed, the "nation with the soul of a church" has always had a deeply religious tendency to turn political campaigns into great crusades. Two high-points were the anti-slavery and the temperance campaigns. The first achieved permanent victory (though at the price of a bloody civil war), the latter only a brief and Pyrrhic victory. Both demonstrated the enormous capacity of churches and church-related groups to mobilize Americans for a political campaign defined as a struggle between virtue and vice. The format of these two classical crusades continues to reproduce itself in this country whenever political agendas are infused with high religious pathos. There is the same unwillingness to compromise or to weigh costs against benefits (prophets do not calculate), the same tendency to diabolize the opposition, and the same curious alliance of clergy and activist women that in other contexts the historian Ann Douglas has dubbed the "feminization of American culture."

In recent decades we have seen three such religio-political eruptions, each characterized by this now-typical format: the civil-rights movement, the anti-war movement with its various Left-leaning offshoots, and, most recently, the powerful phenomenon that Richard John Neuhaus has aptly called the "bourgeois insurgency," once again generating miscellaneous offshoots but with the anti-abortion movement at its core.

These movements have mobilized different strata of the American population and the last two are in sharp antagonism to each other. Yet all three stand in "apostolic succession" to all the earlier crusades of moral fervor sustained by religious certitude. Perhaps a final irony is that, today, each movement defines its opponent as an illegitimate intrusion of religion into politics. Thus the Reverend Jesse Jackson and the Reverend Jerry Falwell accuse each other of misusing their religious status for political ends, and the followers of each believe (sincerely, one may stipulate) that any increase in the power of the opposing movement will lead to an age of inquisitorial intolerance and oppression.

To be sure, religious liberty is not an American monopoly. It is a common feature of all democracies and one of the important legitimations of the democratic form of government. Yet the United States can validly claim to have most successfully institutionalized religious liberty. Given the heterogeneity of the American population, this has been a remarkable achievement, all the more so when one compares the civic peace that has characterized relations among religious groups here with the record of many other societies. In this achievement, as speakers on many patriotic occasions regularly and correctly point out, present-day America demonstrates the wisdom of the generation that produced the Constitution. Here, too, we see a remarkable continuity between past and present.

But it is just as obvious that the social environment of religion in America has changed profoundly since the time of the First Amendment. The most important change can be stated quite simply: the Protestant social and cultural establishment has ended. Indeed, with just a little license one can speak of a post-Protestant America.

The term "Protestant establishment" may at first sound grating. Nevertheless, although the Constitution effectively prevented the legal establishment of Protestantism, first in the new nation and then in the states, it did not and could not change the fact that American society was crucially shaped by Protestantism. Its social order, its ethos, even its manners bore an unmistakably Protestant cast, readily recognized as such especially by observers who were not themselves Protestant (Alexis de Tocqueville, for example).

Although to some extent this remains the case today, the social and cultural domination of the country by a cohesive Protestant elite has been severely weakened. Other groups have successfully made their way, different elites have been formed, and both society and culture have become vastly more pluralistic than could have been imagined even at the turn of this century. The Protestant character of American civilization has become more of an echo, a nuanced survival of what used to be a robust socio-cultural reality. John Murray Cuddihy has aptly described this as a change from a Protestant ethic to a Protestant etiquette: the fervid moral intensity of the earlier period has become a mood, a morally neutral civility—that "Protestant smile," now widely diffused among Americans from every conceivable ethnic and religious background, which continues to impress newcomers to these shores as either heartwarming ("Americans are so friendly") or hypocritical ("they don't really mean it").

The major reason for the change has been the pattern of immigration, bringing masses of non-Protestant people, especially Catholics and Jews, into society. Today, the influx of Latin Amer-

icans continues the gradual "Catholicization" of American society
(though one should note that Latin American Catholicism differs
in important ways from that of Southern and Eastern Europe, not
to mention the very particular Catholicism of the Irish). A new
and potentially significant factor is the large immigration from
Asia. Although religious statistics in the United States are not
models of exactitude, it has been reasonably claimed that Hawaii
is the first state of the union in which Christians are a minority.
Anyone driving out of Honolulu on the Pali Highway, past edi-
fices and shrines of Asian cults of every description, can easily vi-
sualize an America far more pluralistic than the one described in
1955 by Will Herberg in his perceptive book, *Protestant-
Catholic-Jew.* (Public-service advertisements on Honolulu buses:
"Attend the church, synagogue, or shrine of your choice!")

There may be another, more subtle reason for the demise of
the Protestant establishment. Those at its core came to lose their
own belief in it. There were cultural as well as political failures
of nerve. E. Digby Baltzell, the only American sociologist who has
studied the Protestant upper class with care and without destructive intent, has traced this socio-cultural decline in several excellent books; the recent history of the Episcopal church, once the
elite denomination *par excellence,* offers the best insight into it.
One glance at the weekly program of the Cathedral of St. John
the Divine in New York City provides wondrous examples of the
Protestant transformation from self-confidence to a nervous and
guilt-prone search for some way, any way, of socio-cultural survival.

As long as the Protestant establishment was a reality, it provided a reliable symbolic center despite (perhaps even because of)
the legal disestablishment of religion. Its inner decline, combined
with the increasingly rigorous interpretation by the courts of
church-state separation, has led to the situation characterized by
Richard John Neuhaus as the "naked public square": that is, a
public life increasingly swept clean of the religious symbols that
used to legitimate it and make it plausible.

This is a problem in and of itself. Society, deprived of plausible legitimating symbols, increasingly becomes a merely contrac-
tual arrangement. Although this may be fine as long as there are
no serious problems confronting a society, when such problems
do arise it becomes more and more difficult to motivate people
to make sacrifices for any collective purpose. Emile Durkheim, in

his last great work, *The Elementary Forms of the Religious Life,* argued that a society will not survive unless people are prepared, if necessary, to die for it. Human beings are not prepared to die for a contract based on the pragmatic accommodation of interests. When, a few years ago, the Carter administration reintroduced draft registration (not the draft itself, just registration for a possible draft), a picture that appeared in many newspapers showed a demonstration of Princeton students, one of whom carried a poster with the inscription, "Nothing is worth dying for." To say that this is a problem is an understatement at a moment when American democracy faces the greatest military threat ever to its survival.

But there is more to the matter. As Neuhaus has observed, the public square will not remain "naked": other contents inevitably come to fill it. In our case today, the contents are those of "secular humanism." The phrase is used pejoratively by, for example, the followers of Jerry Falwell, but in fact it quite aptly catches the gist of the values, antiseptically free of religious referents and emphatically humanistic, that have been elevated to the status of a largely tacit and unacknowledged new cultural establishment. It is precisely such an ethos of "secular humanism" that is embodied, for example, in Lawrence Kohlberg's program of "moral education" and in the various pedagogic systems based on "values clarification." It is the ethos of a new, post-Protestant establishment (many if not most of whose members are themselves of elite Protestant ancestry).

A key problem of our time is the relation between this new elite and the rest of the American people. In recent years there has been an impressive accumulation of new data about American religion (as in the survey on American values undertaken by the Connecticut Mutual Life Insurance Company, or the superb *All Faithful People,* by Theodore Caplow *et al.*). These data show that the majority of Americans are as furiously religious as ever—and very probably *more* religious than they were when Tocqueville marveled at this quality of American life.

The most dramatic expression of American religious turbulence today has been the upsurge of evangelicalism in its various forms. At least since the mid-1970s—Jimmy Carter's campaign for the Presidency can be taken as a convenient marker—traditional religious and moral beliefs, which had been assumed to survive, if at all, in the hinterlands of society, suddenly erupted into the center of public life. Even those safely located within the cultural enclaves of "secular humanism" have been forced to take notice of this veritable explosion of religious fervor, first in bewilderment, then (especially as significant elements of the evangelical world became mobilized in the service of Right-of-Center political causes) with growing alarm.

The evangelical renascence, though, is only the most spectacular expression of the perduring religiosity of most of the American people. With the exception of the so-called "mainline" Protestant denominations (a misnomer if ever there was one, as these denominations are increasingly marginal to the nation's religious life), it has manifested itself elsewhere as well. Spurred on by Rome, especially under the present papacy, powerful neotraditionalist impulses have made themselves felt in the Catholic community. There has occurred an increasingly robust religious revival within all three denominations of American Judaism. Least noticed but of great potential importance have been the increasing vitality and "Americanization" of Eastern Orthodox Christianity, now no longer an ethnic enclave. There has been the spectacular increase of the Mormons. Whatever else most Americans are, they are *not* "secular humanists."

These developments have created serious intellectual difficulties for those (like myself) who thought that modernization and secularization were inexorably linked phenomena. To say the least, the United States appears to be an exception to this linkage. Indeed, if one compares sociological data on religion worldwide, America sticks out as a remarkable exception. The most modernized societies, notably in Western Europe and in Japan, are in fact high on any secularization scale, be it subjective (recording what people say they believe) or objective (recording what people actually do in terms of religious practice). The prototypes of secular modernity are the Scandinavian countries, with Sweden in the unchallenged lead. At the other end of the list would be societies like India.

When one looks at the United States as a whole, in terms of the subjective and objective indicators of religiosity, one sees a remarkable resemblance to India (the content, needless to say, being different). Yet if one moves around in the cultural centers of America, one breathes a remarkably Scandinavian air. (Could this be why there are so many Volvos on Ivy League campuses?)

And thereby hangs a tale of great significance: when it comes to religion, America is an India, with a little Sweden superimposed.

In more conventional social-scientific language we might say that secularization in America today tends to be class-specific. It is most diffused in the college-educated upper middle class—or, more pointedly, in those strata that Irving Kristol and others have called the New Class, people who derive their livelihood from the production and distribution of symbolic knowledge. It is least diffused in the old middle class, the lower middle class, and the "respectable" working class. This means that the general drama of secularization and counter-secularization has been drawn into a major conflict between classes. In America today and very likely in other Western democracies as well, the New Class is increasingly resented by other strata in society, and not the least factor in this resentment is the hegemony exercised by the New Class over the institutions of elite culture, including large segments of the educational system and the media.

The evangelical upsurge may at least in part be understood as a rebellion of other groups against the culture of the secularized New Class, and especially against the coercive imposition of that culture on children in the public schools. Thus it makes sense that education has been one of the major battlefields in this conflict. The "Indians" are rising against the "Swedes," and neotraditionalist religious symbols are weapons in this uprising. (To say this, of course, in no way negates the sincerely religious motives of those engaged in the various evangelical campaigns.)

There is also a specifically religious dynamic here, in which counter-secularization takes a more or less fundamentalist form. This dynamic can be observed in many parts of the world, not least in the Muslim societies. In the United States the ironic fact is that an overall social climate of tolerance and relativism has kept on being disturbed by seemingly irrational eruptions of unbridled fanaticism. The various "revolutions" and "liberations" of the last two decades provide a number of secular analogues. How can it be that all these nice people, many of them long-time smilers of the Protestant smile, have suddenly come out of the closet with their various agendas of absolute claims, non-negotiable demands, and the determination to pursue their purposes by any means necessary? How can Protestant niceness be so quickly replaced by rage?

This alternation becomes more understandable if one reflects on the psychic costs of pluralistic relativism. The latter is experienced by many as a great liberation, affording the opportunity to emerge from one's own narrow subculture into a broad milieu of cosmopolitanism, and in addition freeing one from all sorts of taboos and "repressions." But the price of liberation is the loss, or at least the weakening, of all certitude—social, moral, religious. Pan-tolerant individuals are thus peculiarly conversion-prone, and conversions can be sudden and violent. The same individuals may quite frequently come to experience as oppressive that which was once liberating; their rage is a reaction to the intuition that they have been had. In this light, the emergence of various movements with claims to absolute certitude is no longer surprising, although the choice an individual makes among the movements available in the ideological marketplace will remain a matter of biographical chance or social location.

But to return to the church-state issues with which we began: Reichley gives a helpful overview of the different positions in play today. The two most important are held by those who advocate a strict separation and by those who would somehow accommodate the religious character of the American people. Both positions (there are, of course, many gradations in each) face serious difficulties.

The doctrine of strict separation flies in the face of a social reality that remains persistently, stubbornly religious. The unending turmoil engendered by the Supreme Court decision on prayer in the public schools is the best example of this collision: whatever may have been the careful legal reasoning behind the decision, the fact remains that millions of Americans have perceived it as a solemn declaration that, their most dearly held beliefs and values having been disavowed by the highest authority of the Republic, their country has become officially godless. The political difficulties this has led to are evident.

But there is a deeper difficulty. As I have already noted, every society, and a democratically governed society more than others, requires legitimation. It requires the belief that it is morally justified. And in the nature of the case, such legitimation cannot be invented *ex nihilo,* it must be credible in terms of beliefs and values that people actually hold. When a people is as religious as the American people, it is going to be very difficult to purge the official legitimations of society of all religious symbols and still have them remain credible. The doctrine of strict separation (not just between the state and specific denominations, but between the state and religion as such) has thus contributed to a crisis of legitimation.

The accommodationist position, however, faces serious difficulties as well. These are all grounded in the equally stubborn reality of American pluralism. Just *which* religious symbols are to be accommodated in the "public square"? The answer to this question has usually been rendered in terms of the so-called Judeo-Christian tradition. One may leave aside for the moment how this answer will sit with Hawaiian Buddhists and with agnostics (not all of them members of the New Class) who have experienced their emancipation from various Christian or Jewish subcultures as a personal liberation; taken together these groups still constitute a minority of the American population, and perhaps they, or most of them, might settle for a few Judeo-Christian symbols as an acceptable price for civic peace. But there is the more intractable fact that those who do identify with that great tradition, in its various denominational forms, are themselves deeply divided as to its moral meaning.

America has been very successful in dealing with its religious pluralism. The *moral* pluralism that has now emerged will be much more difficult to deal with. Currently the most dramatic expression of this is the abortion issue. What symbolic accommodation can be struck between two groups, each containing roughly 50 percent of the American people, one of whom perceives abortion as involving the fundamental right of a woman over her own body and the other as being an act of homicide? How can such an accommodation be struck when each side makes use of religious symbols and religious language to legitimate its position?

On the other hand, American society has long experience with settling irreconcilable positions. And the American polity has developed a genius for institutionalizing such settlements. Barring national disasters of catastrophic scope, it is not unreasonable to expect that new formulas can be found to institutionalize new balances, new compromises. Religious institutions will certainly have a major role to play in such a new settlement. But they will be in a better position to play that role if they draw back from their respective positions of partisan advocacy (most of it very class-specific indeed) and return to what has been their most creative function, that of mediation. Churches as mediating institutions are more likely to contribute to the solution of these problems than churches as partisan armies.

IN THE NAME OF GOD[3]

[The University of Pennsylvania's] academic year begins with an invocation to God. The appeal, made each fall by the chaplain of the University at the Freshman Convocation, asks God's blessing on all who teach and learn here. The academic year ends with the benediction the chaplain offers at Commencement. Unobtrusively, not calling attention to itself, religion frames campus life.

A significant number of Penn students commit time and energy to the ritual, intellectual, and humanitarian aspects of religion. Their actions suggest what they confess only hesitantly to others, that a system of spiritual belief is an important part of the structure of their lives.

The cynicism toward organized religion so widespread on American campuses a generation ago seems to have been supplanted, here and elsewhere, by a cautious hope on the part of a growing number of students that the institutional church or synagogue can provide them with guidance in their struggle with problems of identity and meaning.

Weekly, they gather for worship, about 275 at *Shabbat* services at the Hillel Foundation, nearly 1,600 at Newman Center Masses and those celebrated next door at the Church of St. Agatha and St. James, perhaps 125 at Sunday services in the four Protestant churches located on or near the campus. Some 300 undergraduate and graduate students are enrolled in courses offered by the Department of Religious Studies. Community service programs, which include work in soup kitchens and shelters for the homeless, visits to the elderly, and tutoring poor youth and prisoners, attract 250 student volunteers from campus religious organizations each term.

[3]Reprint of a magazine article by Mary Ann Meyers, secretary of the University of Pennsylvania. *The Pennsylvania Gazette.* 85:14–21. D. '86. Copyright © 1986 by *The Pennsylvania Gazette.*

Such good deeds would doubtless have found favor with Benjamin Franklin, Penn's putative founder, who honored virtue over orthodoxy. Alone among the colleges established before the Revolution, the College of Philadelphia, as Penn was once known, was intended to be nonsectarian. Still, three-fourths of the University's original trustees were affiliated with the Church of England, and the functions of the early College were carried out in a framework of Anglicanism. The first head of the institution, Provost William Smith, was an Anglican priest. His immediate successor, John Ewing, was a Presbyterian minister, and a succession of five ordained Anglicans headed the University for all but 15 years between 1802 and 1868, the last year the chief administrator was a clergyman.

Students were required to attend daily chapel services until 1910, when Room 200 College Hall, which had been designed for religious services (what with its stained glass windows and chestnut pews), was converted into an architectural drafting room.

Doubtlessly, the abandonment of compulsory chapel, 24 years after Harvard University abandoned its compulsory chapel but 54 years before Princeton University abandoned its, suited students very well. They even undertook a campaign to increase participation in the voluntary services that were held each morning in Houston Hall Auditorium, lest poor attendance trigger the reinstatement of a required service. The average turnout seems to have been about 100 through the early 1920s. But the distractions of the Jazz Age took their toll, and by March of 1932, Provost Josiah H. Penniman would write to President Thomas S. Gates that, "since chapel is attended by only a half dozen students and often not so many," it must "either be discontinued or put on a wholly different plane."

The president's response was to establish the Office of the University Chaplain. Independent religious foundations for Protestant, Catholic, and Jewish students, under the direction of ordained professionals, already existed on the campus, but there was a feeling among at least some alumni that Penn had an institutional responsibility for the spiritual welfare of students—an obligation it had neglected since discontinuing compulsory chapel. After consulting with student leaders, as well as members of the faculty, President Gates came to share this view. In June of 1932, he made a personal gift to the trustees of $600,000 to pay the salary and living expenses of a chaplain. The incumbent also was to have an endowed lectureship in Christian ethics and a house on campus.

There is no evidence of a debate over what denominational background would be best for Penn's chaplain. The president turned to the clergy of his own church, wooed a bishop, and ended up selecting a young graduate of the University of Virginia and Alexandria Seminary, the Rev. W. Brook Stabler, who was a member of the staff of the National Council of the Protestant Episcopal Church. He first took up residence at 4328 Spruce Street, then, a year later, seeking to be nearer the hub of student activity, moved to 3805 Locust Street, which is the house of the present chaplain.

Stabler's seven-minute sermons seemed to have had no greater drawing power than the talks given previously at daily chapel by the provost, members of the faculty, and obliging local clergymen. On his recommendation, the services in Houston Hall were discontinued in 1933, at the same time that the administration doubled from four to eight the number of all-University chapel services, which were held in Irvine Auditorium; for such occasions, all undergraduate classes were suspended. University choral groups performed at these events, and (voluntary) attendance initially averaged about 1,000 students. But in the years following World War II, it fell off.

By the early Sixties, Penn's interfaith services were being criticized as "trivial" on the one hand and as "offensively presumptuous" on the other. The faculty was reluctant to dismiss classes, and the chaplain himself argued that the religious needs of an increasingly residential student population could be better served by a Sunday morning service in the Protestant tradition to complement those at Newman Hall and the Hillel Foundation.

The present chaplain of the University, the Rev. Stanley E. Johnson, announced the discontinuation of interdenominational chapel shortly after taking office 25 years ago. But there has been no institutionally sponsored substitute. "I came to the conclusion that I should try to revive traditions that already existed on campus rather than risk drawing students away from them by creating a Sabbath rival," he says. "Furthermore, we lacked an appropriate place to hold a University worship service. Another reason was my concern that, if I officiated at a regular Sunday liturgy, I would be identified as Penn's Protestant chaplain. I saw my role more broadly."

Chaplain Johnson's blond hair has faded to white over the past quarter century. The 57-year-old clergyman describes himself simply as "pastor to the campus." The four children that he and his wife, Sally, an assistant director of alumni relations, raised in Penn's parsonage are all launched on careers of their own. Although still partial to the tweed sports coats he favored when he came north from Vanderbilt University in 1961, he seldom wears a clerical collar now, preferring, instead, to present himself as an "ecumenical minister." Only on Thursdays does he regularly don alb and stole to celebrate the noon Eucharist at St. Mary's Church on Locust Walk.

Johnson, who earned his bachelor's degree from Princeton University in 1950, studied philosophy at Penn for a year, then went on to earn his collar from the Philadelphia Divinity School in 1954. Nowadays, he spends his weekdays visiting sick members of the campus community at University hospital and counseling students, faculty, staff, administrators, and, on occasion, trustees about personal and family problems. A close observer notes that people treasure his nonjudgmental nature and his absolute respect for the confidentiality of any exchange. He is admired as well for his sure sense of when he should refer those who have come to him for help to other professionals.

The chaplain maintains an office in Memorial Towers at the entrance to the Quadrangle dormitories, where, as he puts it, he has an "opportunity to talk to people in a quiet, unhurried fashion." And the peripatetic pastor regularly tours the campus, seeking out "his parishioners" at lectures, receptions, concerts, and athletic events (Johnson sometimes travels with the varsity football and basketball teams). Currently serving as president of the Faculty Club, he was director of admissions from 1974 to 1977.

During the early Sixties, the chaplain officiated at some 25 weddings a year. The number plummeted to about five a year during the mid-Seventies and now averages about 15. He also conducts 20 to 25 memorial services annually—occasionally, and especially sadly, for students. The most wrenching part of his job, by far, is having to inform parents of a child's death.

Chaplain Johnson is the de facto chief of Penn's Campus Ministry Council. It presently includes: Rabbi Morton Levine, director of the Hillel Foundation; Rabbi Bonnie Goldberg, program coordinator for Hillel; Rebecca Glass, Hillel's director of student affairs; Father William F. McGowan, chaplain of the Newman Center; Newman's associate director, Sister Catherine Pisarczyk; Alan Moore-Beitler, campus minister for the Newman Center; the Rev. Walter H. Schenck, executive director of the Christian Association; and Rev. Florence Gelo, assistant director of the Christian Association. It also includes the five ministers affiliated with the Christian Association: the Rev. John M. Scott, rector of St. Mary's Church, and his assistant, the Rev. Elizabeth Eisenstadt; the Rev. Jeffrey Merkel, pastor of University Lutheran Church; the Rev. James McDonald, a Presbyterian minister who is pastor of Tabernacle Church, which serves both Presbyterians and those affiliated with the United Church of Christ; and the Rev. Dean Snyder, pastor of Asbury Methodist Church.

The council meets periodically throughout the academic year and, occasionally, with Dr. Sheldon Hackney, president of the University. Its discussions focus on such matters as campus morale, educational initiatives, and cooperative community-service ventures. As Chaplain Johnson observes, "it is hard to detect any rivalry." The chaplains share a mutual interest in bearing witness to ethical concerns in University life. Ironically, Protestant clergy outnumber others on the council, as they have since its establishment in 1935, but Protestants are today a minority of the student body. John Scott, who has served as the campus Episcopal chaplain since 1962, estimates that nearly half of Penn's students are Jewish, a quarter Roman Catholic, and somewhat fewer Protestant. "There are probably as many observant Muslims," he says, "as active members of mainstream churches." (The University maintains no official figures on the religious preferences of its students at present, but other religious leaders on campus tend to agree with Scott's estimates.)

Fifty years ago, before most college-bound children from Irish, Italian, or Polish families were likely to consider secular institutions, a campus religious census indicated that 54 per cent of the University's undergraduates described themselves as Protestant, 32 per cent as Jewish, and 13 per cent as Roman Catholic.

Changes in the religious composition of the student body have had a greater impact on the Christian Association than on any other organization. Once a vital force in undergraduate life, it is now struggling to rebuild a constituency. Not only has the absolute number of students it could hope to involve shrunk, but a refocusing of student interests away from distant global issues to more immediate personal concerns left an organization with a historic connection to Protestants engaged in social and political causes in something of a time warp. "The C.A.," in Chaplain Johnson's view, "is going through an identity crisis."

The oldest University religious foundation traces its origin to the Y.M.C.A. established on the campus in 1892. It was incorporated in 1901 and, using funds subscribed by 4,000 students and members of the faculty and 5,000 alumni and friends, erected its present, handsome building in 1928, at 36th and Locust Streets. The C.A.'s budget that year was $175,000, just $25,000 less than this year's, and it had a paid professional staff of 14, compared to the present staff of four.

In its heyday during the 1920s, '30s, and '40s, the C.A. owned and operated three settlement houses in Philadelphia and two summer camps for children outside the city. It maintained an International Students House on campus and sponsored several medical missionaries in foreign lands (among them, the Olympic gold-medalist Dr. Josiah C. McCracken, '01M). The C.A.'s denominational representatives conducted study sessions and discussion groups and sought to involve students in the activities of nearby churches. Their labor toward common ends under one roof was known as the "Pennsylvania Plan"; it was a model of ministry built on an acceptance of religious heterogeneity.

Walter Schenck, the present executive director of the C.A., came to Penn last spring from the "God Box," an office building at 470 Riverside Drive in Manhattan where many Protestant denominations have their American headquarters. He was on the staff of the general board of global ministries of the United Methodist Church before accepting the C.A. position formerly held by the Rev. Ralph M. Moore, Jr., who is now the rector of an English-speaking church in Nicaragua.

Brought into the world by the physician/poet William Carlos Williams, '06 M, '52 Hon, Schenck was graduated from North Carolina's High Point College in 1962 and from Boston University School of Theology in 1965. An ordained Methodist, the mustachioed clergyman describes his new job as a "rebuilding and refocusing effort." He inherited a large building in need of repairs and what he describes as "an organizational commitment to social justice in the context of Christian faith and witness."

Schenck reports to a 19-member board of directors. Half his program budget comes from renting space. One tenant is the

University; another is the Gold Standard, a restaurant group that operates the upscale Palladium in the building's former west lounge and a basement cafeteria, both of which serve food outdoors in good weather. Other operating funds are derived from appeals and from income on a $500,000 endowment. Once heavily invested in the stocks of companies that do business in South Africa, the Christian Association has been quietly divesting that stock for four years. "We didn't want to parade the issue because we had no wish to put pressure on the University unfairly," says board vice president Thomas T. Winant, '69 G, assistant to Penn's vice president for development and University relations.

The Christian Association provides space and moral support for the Penn Anti-Apartheid Coalition, the Central American Solidarity Alliance, and the Penn Campaign for the University of El Salvador. For 11 years, it has also nurtured and sheltered the campus Gay and Lesbian Peer Counseling Program. Schenck has no intention of abandoning these groups. Nevertheless, his mandate from the board is to reach out to a broader community of faith.

A Sunday night supper at the C.A., which draws about a dozen students, is a new initiative. The executive director also is developing short midweek study programs. Although the C.A. has no student organization, it does have two student representatives on its board of directors.

An interest in helping with program development was the primary reason Lynn Clowes accepted appointment to the board of the Christian Association. A College junior from Waldoboro, Maine, where her mother is the pastor of the United Church of Christ (Congregational), the history major says she "occasionally attends St. Mary's," since she had considered herself an Episcopalian until her mother's ordination in 1979. Clowes's principal extracurricular interest is the Central American Solidarity Alliance. "We raised $750 on Locust Walk for victims of the El Salvador earthquake," she declares with pride, adding that students associated with the organization also have solicited funds for political refugees from El Salvador who have been given sanctuary in Tabernacle Church. A member of the Penn Anti-Apartheid Coalition, Clowes is contemplating a career in Third World development.

The graduate representative on the C.A. board is Marc Ostfield, '86 C, a candidate for a master's degree in the human sexuality program at the Graduate School of Education. A Quaker who grew up in an agnostic family in Pittsburgh, majored in women's studies, and wrote his senior thesis on gay male pornography, he spends three hours a week working as a peer counselor for lesbian and gay students.

Ostfield attends meeting for worship several times a month at the Philadelphia Friends Meeting House in Center City as there is no Quaker meeting on campus. Once a member of the Palestinian Awareness Association, he says his politics are based on his religious beliefs. "Religion," this grandson of Austrian Jews declares, "involves finding the little of God that is in me and that of Him in others."

Eloisa Hidalgo is a senior from Miami who is thinking about joining the Peace Corps, then attending law school in preparation for a career in public policy. She says that religion provides her "a framework for struggling with difficult questions." The fact that she is a Roman Catholic on a secular campus is not an obstacle for her—rather, she asserts, it is "freeing." Hidalgo, who attended parochial schools all the way from kindergarten through 12th grade, was "always headed for Georgetown or Notre Dame" but ended up never even applying to the two well-regarded Catholic universities because she sought "a more integrated, diverse experience. I wanted my religion to have to be a conscious choice, not part of the ethos of the place."

Hidalgo is president of Penn's Newman Council. Composed of 16 students, the group meets weekly to plan liturgies and arrange educational, sports, and social programs. Hidalgo first became involved in Newman affairs after attending a weekend retreat at which the topic of discussion was the integration of spiritual and academic life. An English major who is a member of the Philomathean Society and Kite and Key, she has helped put together a Newman-sponsored program on the tension between ethical imperatives and career goals and another on sexual values.

"My own opinion on a whole range of religious issues is still evolving," she says. "I read and listen and watch how certain choices are working out in the lives of friends and family members." She mentions an aunt who is a nun and teaches in Peru, another who has nine children who are under 11 years old, a third who is the mother of four and a social worker, and a fourth who is an unmarried child psychologist. "I've seen a lot of feminist awakening among Catholic women," Hidalgo says: "Students express a desire to control their lives in terms of career options and the size of their families. They are concerned about the effect of delayed marriage on sexuality, and they're interested in the subject of female ordination because they're not convinced that only males willing to practice celibacy are called to the priesthood."

The priest who serves as director of the Newman Center at 3720 Chestnut Street is the youthful Bill McGowan. The campus ministry to which he was assigned in 1984 by the Cardinal Archbishop of Philadelphia was organized at Penn in 1893. It was the first organization to serve the needs of Roman Catholic students ever established at a private secular university and provided a model for Newman clubs throughout the nation. The Mass has always been at the center of Newman activities, and it is presently celebrated in the Newman Chapel three times a day during the week, on Saturday evening, and twice on Sunday. A dorm Mass and a Communion service outside of Mass are held weekly in student residence halls.

Father McGowan initiated the *extra ecclesia* services when he came to Penn from a teaching post at Philadelphia's Cardinal Dougherty High School. A casual dresser, given to corduroys and colorful crewneck sweaters, he studied for the priesthood at St. Charles Seminary and was ordained in 1976. His principal associate on Newman's pastoral staff, Sister Catherine Pisarczyk, has been a member of the Sisters of St. Joseph for the past 30 years. She is a 1970 graduate of Chestnut Hill College and holds two master's degrees—one in music, which she received from Temple University in 1976, and another in spirituality, which she received from the University of San Francisco in 1981. An outgoing, energetic woman who typically wears simple skirts, striped shirts, and pastel cardigans, she has done additional graduate work in liturgy at both Catholic University and Notre Dame University.

Her special task at the Newman Center is to coordinate liturgies. She also runs two off-campus retreats a year for graduate students and, with McGowan and a team of six married couples from the University community, conducts "pre-Cana" conferences for young people planning to marry in the Catholic Church. Another program in which she shares teaching responsibilities with the Newman director, as well as with the pastoral

staff of St. Agatha and St. James and the Newman staff at Drexel
University, is the Rite of Christian Initiation of Adults. Designed
for people interested in joining the Catholic Church or in renew-
ing their faith, it typically attracts about a dozen members of the
two university communities.

During the academic year, the Newman director has, on the
average, about 12 appointments a week with students seeking
guidance on personal matters. "Often they come questioning
their self-worth," he muses, "and I try to say that, quite apart
from any failures or accomplishments, they are valuable because
they are the children of a God Who sees sparrows fall, has num-
bered the hairs on their heads, and sent His Son to die for them."
Sister Catherine observes that she, too, sees a "distressing amount
of low self-esteem among exceptionally gifted students." Her approach to the problem is to try to develop their leadership abili-
ties.

The Newman Center offers opportunities for both men and
women to provide music, read Scriptural lessons, and distribute
Communion at Mass, as well as to conduct Communion services
in the dormitories. Other Newman activities involve the more or
less traditional Sunday night suppers, brunches, dances, picnics,
casino and movie nights, and intramural sports, along with rather
exceptional educational programs, such as a conference on values
and the economy that brought Archbishop Rembert G. Weakland to the campus from Milwaukee. (Weakland served as head
of the American Catholic bishops' committee that drafted the recently issued pastoral letter on Catholic social teaching and the
economy.)

Since 1983, the Newman Center has challenged its campus
constituency to express solidarity with the powerless through a
special program. Funded from the center's $120,000 annual op-
erating budget and coordinated by a member of the Newman
Council, the student-run, city-wide effort now draws nearly half
its volunteers from outside the campus Roman Catholic community. In particular, students active in the Hillel Foundation have
joined in trips to places like Holy Family Home, where the young
men and women visit with the elderly and infirm residents; St.
Francis Inn, where they serve food to the homeless; Ryan School
for the Deaf, where they tutor children; and Holmesburg Prison,
where they teach illiterate adults to read. Some of the volunteers
are testing career interests, but most are drawn to the program

for humanitarian reasons. "The world is so complicated in terms of poverty and suffering," Ellie Hidalgo says with a sigh, "you wonder how it will be possible to make even a little dent in the sum total of human misery." By reaching out to the least of their brothers and sisters, she and her fellow students have found a way.

"I believe one act by one person can tip the scale of the universe," declares Deanna Kaplan softly. A senior who is majoring in both marketing and international relations, she has made the Penn Jewish community "the very center" of her present life. "I've only scratched the surface of my religion," she says, "but the more I learn about Judaism, the greater obligation I feel to relate to others in for what is, to me, a new and different way." She cites, as an example, a Talmudic imperative never to walk past slowly moving persons lest you make them conscious of infirmity or age. "Judaism is really a life style," the Reading, Pa., native says. "In my high-school graduating class, there were five Jews out of 717 seniors, so coming to Penn was like going to Mecca for me."

Penn's first center for Jewish students, a house in the 3400 block of Walnut Street, was opened in 1920. University Provost Edgar Fahs Smith had called the need for such a facility to the attention of the Philadelphia Jewish community the previous year, and funds for it had been raised by sisterhoods associated with the United Synagogue of America. A second, larger house in the 3600 block of Locust Street was dedicated in 1926. A local rabbi acted as an adviser to Jewish undergraduates until the position of a resident chaplain was established in 1934. Three years later, the student organization adopted the name Louis Marshall Society to honor the memory of a leader of the national Jewish community who had been an early spokesman for civil rights. The present building, adjacent to the Christian Association, was purchased in 1945, and an addition was completed in 1985. Made possible by a gift from Bernard J. Korman, '52 W, '55 L, and the generosity of other friends, it provided a 150-seat auditorium, a second kitchen, and expanded dining facilities.

Hillel strives to create *haymesh* (a "homey" atmosphere) under its new roof. Seth Brody, a doctoral student in Penn's religious studies department who acts as a rabbinical assistant to Hillel director Morton Levine, describes the expanded building as already "bursting at the seams." Hillel is intended to be a somewhat pluralistic organization, that is, one that attempts to facilitate life for members of the University Jewish community whether they choose to identify themselves with the Orthodox, Conservative, or Reform branches of Judaism—or with none of them. "There is a strong emphasis on having fun," Rabbi Brody says. "Students come to Hillel to explore all aspects of Jewish cultural life. A core community has been created through public worship, but sacred time is all-pervasive."

There is a daily orthodox *minyan* in the Frederic R. Mann Chapel, which brings together a minimum of 10, but usually about 15, students for prayer. The largest Sabbath service, attracting some 140 worshippers, is the Friday evening Conservative gathering. Another Conservative service is held on Saturday morning. Orthodox services, at which men and women are seated separately and only men take leadership roles, are held on both Friday and Saturday, and there is also a Reform service every Friday evening and one Saturday a month. Several times each semester, a *Shabbaton*, a retreat lasting from Friday evening to Saturday night, draws students to Hillel to listen to a visiting rabbi and reflect together upon a particular theme.

On the High Holy Days, Rosh Hashanah and Yom Kippur, both Penn's 2,000-seat Irvine Auditorium and Harrison Auditorium, an 800-seat facility in the University Museum, are filled with worshippers. At the larger (Conservative) services, well-dressed students, the men wearing white shawls, known as *tallithim*, and *yarmulkes* of various colors, sway slightly as they chant their prayers in Hebrew—some haltingly, others with a felicity that reflects years of study.

Rabbi Levine leads the Irvine worshippers, while this year visiting alumna Amy Schwartzman, '84 C, a rabbinical student at Hebrew Union College, conducted the smaller (Reform) services. Orthodox services are held in Lubavitch House, a center of Hasidic Judaism at 40th and Spruce Streets, which exists to foster stricter observance of a traditional Jewish way of life among area college students. But Levine points out that "most Orthodox undergraduates go home for the holidays," and he notes that University policy prohibits the scheduling of examinations on these dates.

The Hillel director came to Penn in 1983 from the University of Arizona, where he held a similar post for 10 years. A native of Cleveland, he was graduated from Case Western Reserve in 1966 and from the Jewish Theological Seminary in 1970. During three years as a chaplain in the United States Air Force, he was the chief and only rabbi of Thailand. Levine wears a small brown *yarmulke* and large glasses; his broad, pleasant face can be seen on the back cover of a novel called *The Congregation*, on which he collaborated with free-lance writer Hal Kantor.

Dismissing the book with a grin and a shrug, he speaks of his chaplaincy with satisfaction. He explains that Hillel's operations budget of about $180,000 a year is provided by the city-wide Jewish Campus Activities Board, which receives its funding primarily from the Jewish Community Federation, an organization supported by the Allied Jewish Appeal and B'nai B'rith. Hillel also has a food budget. Its dining room operates on a nonprofit basis, providing kosher meals, prepared in conformity with Jewish dietary laws, at lunch and dinner, Monday through Friday. Approximately 160 students are served in the dining room weekly.

The University's chief rabbi describes the foundation he directs as "a place where kids can escape academic pressures" but goes on to note that Jewish students are "far less likely to feel the need for Hillel on the Penn campus than at institutions where they are a distinct minority. The vast majority know we are here," he says, "and they know they can come by if they need help." The issues that bring them for counseling are often "about relationships—with their parents (how do you tell them you don't want to be a doctor?) or with a girlfriend or boyfriend, especially if the person with whom they're involved isn't Jewish."

Many of the young people who can be found more or less regularly at Hillel are enrolled in noncredit evening classes. Among the course offerings are Torah and Talmud study, Hebrew, and an examination of the theology and tactics of Christian missionaries who aggressively seek to convert Jews. "We attract a lot of professional students," Seth Brody says, jokingly. But Jewish interest groups, which have their headquarters in the building, also act as a magnet.

There is the Penn-Israel Alliance, the political Penn-Israel Action Committee, Jewish Students Against Apartheid, the Holocaust Memorial Committee, the consciousness-raising Struggle for Soviet Jewry, and the United Jewish Appeal, which traditionally has raised more money at Penn than on any other campus. Children of Holocaust Survivors is a group of some 20 students who meet once a month to share experiences, seek understanding, and affirm the enduring nature of the Jewish people. The Jewish center also draws those who want to learn Israeli dances and to sing with Philadelphia's choir for young Jewish adults, Arbel, at least half of which is made up of Penn students; it uses the Hillel lounge for practice sessions.

Zalman Suldan is a basso in the chorus. A sophomore from Pittsburgh who collects tapes of modern Jewish music, he eats lunch and dinner at Hillel four days a week. On weekends, he usually prepares kosher meals for friends in his third-floor suite in High-Rise North, a living area known as the *shtetl* because the first four floors of the dormitory are favored by observant Jews who will not use electrically powered devices, such as elevators, on the Sabbath. Suldan identifies himself as Orthodox. Each morning upon rising, he wraps a leather strap attached to a small square leather box seven times around his left arm and another box secured by a strap around his forehead. Known as phylacteries, the boxes contain slips of parchment inscribed with scriptural passages, and he wears them as he recites 20 to 25 minutes of prescribed prayers.

Suldan, who mentions that his "best friend is a Presbyterian," says he discusses intermarriage frequently with his Orthodox roommates. "My religion means a lot to me," he observes, "and I don't think I would marry outside of my faith, although there is a lot of intermarriage in my extended family." Christian missionaries, "like the Campus Crusaders who handed out their literature in English House last year," anger and upset him. "I object to aggressive proselytizing," he says.

Religious fundamentalism, once more noticeable on campuses in the South and Midwest, has been growing at Northeastern schools since the early 1980s. "We don't beat people over the head," says David R. Barndt, a senior majoring in computer science in the School of Engineering and Applied Sciences, "but we think it's important to share our beliefs. I feel God will be pleased if we do what He told us to do, that is, spread the Good News about Jesus."

Barndt, a native of Newton, Mass., is the president of Intervarsity Christian Fellowship, an interdenominational student-run organization, which shares with the Campus Crusade for Christ and the Navigators a core of fundamentalist beliefs centered upon the verbal inerrancy of the Bible and a personal acceptance of Jesus Christ as Lord and Savior. "Intervarsity is the most important nonacademic part of my life," Barndt says. "We have 50 active members, and the number is steadily rising. Our primary aim is to help students achieve maturity as Christians. I guess you could say we're less militant than Campus Crusade, and, unlike the Navigators, we don't stress memorization of Biblical texts. But all three groups cooperate on outreach projects we call friendship evangelism.

"Penn upperclassmen lead the Bible study sessions Intervarsity holds each week in the undergraduate dorms," he adds, noting, "We're reading the Acts of the Apostles this fall, and we've had some good discussions about the meaning of the Church's earliest missions for our own lives." Intervarsity holds large group meetings for worship on Friday evenings and, like both Campus Crusade and the Navigators, sponsors an off-campus retreat each term.

On Sundays, Barndt attends the conservative Tenth Presbyterian Church in center-city Philadelphia. His three roommates in High-Rise South share his fundamentalist convictions. "Christians need to be involved with other Christians," he says, but he also suggests that, at Penn, they have a special opportunity "to minister to Jewish students and students from abroad." His career goal is to share American technology and his religious beliefs with the people of developing nations.

The largest society of international students on the campus is the Muslim Student Association. Founded in 1963, it facilitates the practice of Islam for between 300 and 400 members of the University community from more than 30 countries. Maged El Gammal, a graduate student in city planning, is from Egypt. Married and the father of a young daughter, he holds a bachelor's degree in architecture from Cairo's Ain Shams University, where he taught for five years before coming to the United States to pursue further studies, first at Kansas State University and then in Penn's Graduate School of Fine Arts. A devout Muslim, he describes his religion as "a life-organizing faith." He neither drinks alcoholic beverages nor smokes tobacco, and each year he gives a fixed percentage of his capital to the poor.

Wherever he is, El Gammal prays five times a day. On Fridays, he is one of some 125 Muslims, about a quarter of them black, who gather at midday for public prayer in the easternmost room on the second floor of Houston Hall. They roll out rugs and, removing their shoes, stand (the half-dozen women separated from the men) to recite prayers facing *Ka'bah*, the house they believe

Abraham built in Mecca. They sit to listen to a sermon delivered by an *imam*, a learned member of the community, then chant in unison, occasionally bending to touch their foreheads to the floor. "During the month of *Ramadan* [the ninth month of the Islamic calendar], Muslim students must fast from dawn to sunset and attend prayer services each evening," El Gammal notes, adding, "It is then that I feel closest to God." Seminars on Islamic social teachings and weekly social gatherings are also part of the campus program for Muslims.

Islam, the newest to the world's great monotheistic religions, honors Moses, as well as Jesus, among its prophets, and during the past several years, Muslim students have sought closer relationships with other campus congregations. Seth Brody believes that there is an ecumenical spirit on campus that is rooted in "respect for religious traditions other than one's own and recognition of their legitimacy as valid ways of coming into the presence of God. A great deal of work remains to be done," says Brody, who studied at Columbia and Jewish Theological Seminary before being ordained in 1984. "But I am certain that the possibilities for cooperation are enormous."

Ecumenism has been manifested on campus in public witness, educational programs, meetings for worship, and collaborative work projects. During the first week of classes this term, Jewish students reciting the *kaddish* on the College Hall green for the 21 Jews killed in a terrorist attack in a synagogue in Istanbul were joined in the mourners' prayer by Catholics, Protestants, and Muslims.

For the past two years, students have conducted an ecumenical Thanksgiving service in the Chapel of Reconciliation on the third floor of the Christian Association. A prayer service with the ecumenical songs of Taizé is held every Wednesday evening in the chapel under the combined sponsorship of the Newman Center, the C.A., and associated churches. During Lent, Roman Catholic, Episcopalian, Methodist, and Lutheran students join one another weekly for spiritual study sessions at University Lutheran Church. Last spring, about 30 Roman Catholic students affiliated with the Newman Center attended a joyful Passover Seder at the Hillel Foundation as guests of the Reform Jews of Penn.

A historic moment in the relations between campus religious groups occurred last spring on the Feast of the Ascension when

Chaplain Scott read the Gospel and delivered the homily at a Mass in the Newman Center. In the fall, Father McGowan preached at a liturgy at St. Mary's on the eve of All Saints' Day.

Scott says that the present spirit of cooperation among campus religious organizations was kindled by a tragedy to which students responded with compassion. In January of 1983, a homeless man, who lived on steam vents around the University, was found dead on one. Students took up a collection to bury him. Scott conducted a memorial service in the C.A. chapel. In the course of meetings over several months, members of the campus religious communities wrestled with the possible meaning of the ragged vagrant's death. Joseph F. Kollackey, '85 W, a Newman activist who had worked at St. Francis Inn, eventually organized the University City Hospitality Coalition as a living memorial.

The coalition, which involves volunteers from Penn, Drexel, and local parishes, began by serving one meal a week to the hungry and homeless at St. Mary's Church. It now provides dinners to between 75 and 120 people a night, five nights a week, at four other locations: the Newman Center, University Lutheran Church, the Church of the Saviour, and Woodland Presbyterian Church. The University Dining Service and campus restaurants donate food; staples are purchased with contributions. "It is not just a matter of the rich feeding the poor," says Father McGowan. "Our guests work with us, cooking, serving, and washing up."

Over spaghetti or chili, bag ladies, gentlemen of the grate, and Ivy League undergraduates discuss politics and the weather. The atmosphere is one of acceptance and fellowship. Students who become involved in the Hospitality Coalition "have a tremendous sense of joy," Chaplain Johnson says, noting, "You see it in their eyes and hear it in their voices."

Those involved in campus religious organizations do not necessarily pursue religion as a subject of classroom study, although, of course, some religious activists are enrolled in formal religion courses. According to the department's undergraduate chairman, Dr. Stephen N. Dunning, religious studies attracts many students who "are simply curious about why people are religious." He says the students "tend to come from overwhelmingly secular backgrounds, and they find it hard to understand a tradition of self-denial. Many are raised to believe that self-interest is the only motivating factor in life. The idea of overcoming self through an identification with a higher self is initially a very alien notion.

Some students arrive at the University without any awareness of ways of seeing the world that involve transcendence."

Established in 1949, the Department of Religious Studies has always avoided courses that involve exploration of the validity of certain kinds of theological thought. "We study theology as part of the history of religion or the biography of religious people," Dr. Dunning observes. His popular course on contemporary religious cults in America is something of a departure for him and an anomaly in a department that stresses textual analysis from cultural, historical, linguistic, and structural perspectives. The faculty's intention is to acquaint students with major theories and methods of interpretation of religious phenomena and enable them to gain a relatively sophisticated appreciation of the major religious traditions.

As a small department with only five fully affiliated professors, religious studies draws on the faculty of a dozen other departments. While the religious studies faculty itself offers about a dozen courses each term, half of the 162 courses the department lists in the academic bulletin either are taught by faculty with secondary appointments in religious studies or originate in other departments. Deanna Kaplan explored Biblical interpretations of abortion in a Jewish law course offered in Oriental studies. The paper Ellie Hidalgo is writing on feminist spirituality in Roman Catholicism is for a course in women's studies.

Dunning describes Penn students as more likely to be "skill-seekers than truth-seekers." He finds, however, abundant "curiosity about why people are religious." Other members of the faculty note a serious interest in ethics and an eagerness to discuss religiously resonant issues. By applying the analytical techniques they acquire in their classes to an examination of their personal beliefs, students can learn to probe their assumptions. In the process, many undoubtedly arrive at a more mature understanding of faith, even as they struggle with the tension between reverence and skepticism intrinsic to an academic environment. "When I was a freshman," Hidalgo says, "I never questioned the Church. I've come to see, however, that it is run by very human beings, that it is imperfect and evolving—and that, in my life, it still has value and meaning."

II. TRADITIONS IN CONTRAST

EDITOR'S INTRODUCTION

The 1987 *Yearbook of American and Canadian Churches* lists no fewer than 224 religious groups, some of which can be further subdivided along sectarian lines. Added to these are numerous undocumented or independent groups.

The characteristics of these religions vary widely, as the articles in the second section show. Many people are familiar with only a single form of religious life—for instance, the customs of mainline Protestant churches, with congregations of families participating in orderly worship services led by ordained ministers. Each of the following articles presents a form of religious life that stands in distinct contrast to this stereotype. They include communal, monastic, familial, and individualist models; groups organized on authoritarian lines and others that stress personal freedom; groups whose members live apart from society and others that maintain varying degrees of integration.

The German-speaking pacifists known as Hutterites, the subject of an article from *Natural History* that forms the first selection, live in the United States and Canada in agricultural communes where conformity and obedience are stressed. The Roman Catholic nuns described in the second article, reprinted from *New York Times Magazine,* while equally concerned with obedience, have isolated themselves from the world in order to spend their lives in constant prayer. The forms of Christianity practiced by these two groups contrast strongly with each other and even more so with the variant practiced by the subjects of an article from *Science '83,* the Holy Ghost People, pentecostals who twice a week risk death to make a public trial of their faith.

The next pair of articles, reprinted from *New York* and *Ms.* magazines, deals with efforts by two groups to come to terms with ancient religions within the context of American pluralism and modernity. The "New Orthodox" of Manhattan's Upper West Side are part of a general return among American Jews to a spiritual tradition that has flourished for more than three thousand years. A segment of the American feminist community is engaged in a revitalization of the matriarchal, Goddess-centered religions that are thought to have preceded social reorganization under patriarchy.

Since World War II, and especially in the 1960s, Asian religions have gained an increasing following in the United States. The article from *Christian Century* that concludes this section describes how the Japanese nature religion Shinto has taken root in Hawaii.

CHILDREN OF THE HUTTERITES[1]

All of us have by nature a tendency toward evil and to have pleasure in sin. . . . Children, however, know neither good nor evil.
                              Account of Our Religion, Doctrine and Faith
                              Given by Peter Rideman, 1565

In 1963, when I embarked on a series of field studies in a Hutterite colony in Canada, I did not realize how very different the child-rearing practices of this communal Christian sect would be from those taken for granted in the New England college community in which we had been living. Otherwise, my husband and I might not have been so sanguine about taking our three children to an isolated, German-speaking community in which they would be immersed in a socialization process so thorough that it has maintained the Hutterite culture through some 450 years of persecution and protection, hardship and affluence.

My mother, a child psychologist and elementary-school teacher, came with us to the colony. The children had had little preparation other than time spent on Amish farms—and the family-centered culture of the Amish proved to be no preparation for the communal childhood they were about to experience. The Hutterite culture is rigidly age graded; not even as a child had I so often been asked, "How old are you?" Our three-generational family had a member in every age category except adolescence, but our fifth-grade daughter, because of her wider experience, was admitted to the edge of the adolescent's private world. As the

[1]Reprint of a magazine article by anthropologist Gertrude Enders Huntington. *Natural History.* 90:34+. F. '81. With permission from *Natural History,* Vol. 90, No. 1. Copyright the American Museum of Natural History, 1981.

oldest person in the colony, my mother was called grandmother by everyone. She was identified with the three grandparent couples. My husband and I were in the middle generation. Each of our children was in a different category: Abigail, nine, was a "German school" child; Daniel, who had his fifth birthday in the colony, was a kindergarten child; and Caleb, two, was a house child. Thus it was natural for us to participate in the various socially defined age grades and to experience personally the socialization process.

We were assigned a two-room house about forty feet from the nearest family (with whom we shared an outhouse) and about sixty feet from the nearest "long house," consisting of apartments for four families. The center of the colony had the feeling of a medieval village. It was bounded on one end by the communal kitchen, which housed the dining room, bakehouse, washhouse and bathhouse, and at the other end and slightly to one side was the public-school building, which was also used for German school and the daily church services. All buildings related to home and family were painted white with blue trim; those that served an economic function were usually painted red. All living buildings were built true to the compass, running due north and south or due east and west; the floor plan of the living houses has changed little since the sixteenth century.

The uniformity of the color and architecture, the physical proximity of the buildings, the grassy commons, the flowers around the houses, and the neat walks proclaim visually the orderly existence of the inhabitants. Time is measured out as discretely as space, and there is a proper activity for each moment of the day, each day of the week, each season of the year, and each stage of one's life. An individual's dress establishes sex, age, activity, and obedience to the rules of the colony. When it became evident that we were not simply visitors but participants, we were urged to take off our "ugly" clothes and put on Hutterite attire. The dress signified our willingness to accept our age- and sex-determined position in the colony and to abide by the rules. We became a part, first, of the visual environment, then of the behavioral environment, next the emotional environment, and finally, we almost became a part of the intellectual environment, usually understanding but never quite internalizing the Hutterite world view.

This failure at the last step did not prove an insurmountable problem both because we were not permanent members of the community and because the Hutterites stress correct behavior over correct thinking. Their catechism asks, "What is inner shame?" The reply is, "When a man has sinful thoughts, which he should dispose of." It asks, "What is sin?" The answer is, "The transgression of the law." In a communal society, wrong thinking is bad, but if kept to oneself, is not disruptive; wrong behavior, no matter what the motive, is sin. And as participants, we were not to sin. We were helped to be good, for as the minister gently assured us, "You are fortunate to be living in the colony, for there are always one hundred eyes watching you."

The Hutterites, or Hutterian Brethren, live in discrete colonies on the plains of the United States and Canada. They migrated to the United States from Russia in 1874, having, it is claimed, been assured by President Grant that their absolute pacifism would not cause any trouble because "America would never fight in another war." Of the eight hundred Hutterites who came, about half took advantage of the Homestead Act and finally settled in dispersed family units; the other three to four hundred settled in three colonies in South Dakota. Through biological increase and by an orderly process of establishing daughter colonies, the population has grown to about 24,000, and the original three colonies have become 230. Today, colonies are located in Alberta, Saskatchewan, Manitoba, North and South Dakota, Montana, Washington, and Minnesota. Theologically, the Hutterites are Anabaptists, practicing adult baptism, total nonresistance, and apostolic communism. They trace their origin to a moment in the spring of 1528 when a cloak was spread before a group of religious refugees fleeing through Moravia, and each member of the group laid upon it his money and other worldly possessions. Thus, occasioned by necessity and sanctioned by religion, the practice of "all things in common" (Acts 2:44) was adopted as the Hutterite way of life. They called themselves Brothers, but were named Hutterians or Hutterites by outsiders after an early leader, Jacob Hutter, who was burned at the stake in Innsbruck in 1536. A minister's translation from the *Geschichts-Buch,* a history book kept by the Hutterite leaders through the centuries, describes Hutter's ordeal:

After they had him captured, they tied a club in his mouth and transferred him to Innsbruck. They punished him and tortured him but he would not recant. . . . They proceeded to put him in ice cold water until he could not move. From there they put him in a warm room and lashed him unmercifully. They cut wounds into his body and poured alcohol into the wounds, lit it, and let it burn. But still he would not recant. After much suffering and torture, he was sentenced and burned at the stake alive.

The persecution of the Hutterites did not subside until 1551. By 1592, there were approximately ninety colonies in Moravia with an estimated population of twenty to thirty thousand. But by 1767 renewed persecution, war, and the Counter-Reformation had reduced their number to nineteen. This hand-ful, joined by fifty-six Lutherans from Austria, fled to Russia, where they settled in 1770. When denied exemption from mili-tary service and the right to maintain their own schools in 1874, they emigrated to the United States. There conditions were fa-vorable until the outbreak of World War I, when the Hutterites were harassed by their neighbors and Hutterite draftees were subjected to barbaric treatment. After months in solitary confine-ment, two North Dakota Hutterites who had refused to wear army uniforms died of physical mistreatment, malnutrition, and pneumonia. When the wife of one of the men asked to see his body, she was shown it—dressed in the military uniform he had so steadfastly refused to don. As a result of this episode, most Hutterites moved to Canada, where the majority still live. The men who died in prison during the First World War are remem-bered as martyrs to their faith.

Hutterites do not stress historical dates or even historical se-quences, but stories of the martyrs and times of tribulation are copied by children in German school and are retold at informal gatherings where the children learn, and the adults remember, that it is better to "die the bitterest death, yea ten deaths, than to forsake the truth." Retelling their history reinforces their be-lief in the sinful and corrupt ways of "the world," their belief that this life is difficult and arbitrary and the true Christian must ex-pect to suffer for his faith. The Hutterites have never believed their life to be utopian, viewing it instead as an exacting religious regimen that demands denial of self and of private property and absolute obedience to God and the community. A Hutterite work describes "a way of life that not even we who live it, always like, according to the flesh; but we know it is . . . the way the God of love wants his children to live on this earth. . . . "

The goal of child rearing among the Hutterites is the young adult's voluntary decision to submit himself to the church community. The Hutterites have been remarkably successful in achieving this goal by guiding their children through a series of socially defined age grades, each characterized by specific behavior and teaching.

During the first three years of life, the Hutterite child is known as a baby, or a house child, because it is fed at home and is primarily under the care of its parents. This is a privileged period in the individual's life and a time of intense socialization. Although little attention is paid to pregnancy, other than to maintain that the harder a woman works, the healthier her baby will be, and the role of the mother in the birth is de-emphasized (babies are viewed as a gift from God), the neonatal period is a very special time for both mother and child. The new mother is relieved of all colony responsibilities and given the full-time help of a mature woman. Typically, the woman's own mother comes from her home colony to care for and mother her daughter, who, in turn, cares for and mothers her new baby. The caretaker-nurse feeds and cares for the mother and her house children, does all her family work, and even sleeps with her at night, helping her twenty-four hours a day. Colony members and relatives from neighboring colonies come to visit the mother and to see the new baby.

Hutterites consider the neonatal child demanding and vulnerable but at the same time a great joy and a pleasure to care for. The mother is confident of her ability to supply her baby's needs and enjoys nurturing the completely dependent child. The baby wears a cap on its head, is swaddled with a blanket wrapped over its clothes, and is tied into a firm, straight bundle with a narrow cord woven just for this purpose. Swaddling is said to make the baby easier to handle and play with (that is, less easily injured and more enjoyable). A red ribbon or cord is tied onto the baby to protect it from the evil eye, from being fussy, from having colic. Its widespread use indicates the vulnerability attributed to small babies. When the child is four weeks old, the mother's caretaker leaves and the father takes over the nighttime care of the baby. For two more weeks the mother is relieved of colony work, then she is gradually reintegrated until, when the baby is thirteen weeks old, she resumes cooking for the colony and once again becomes a full participant. For the next three years, the colony schedule determines the time the baby will be fed, the time it will be played with, the time it will be left alone, and the time it should sleep.

Everyone in a Hutterite colony loves a baby. Children of both sexes will crowd around a baby to play with it. A child as young as two will be rewarded by being allowed to hold an infant. When the adults, especially the men, are not working, the babies are always held, and everyone who passes a very young child—adult Hutterites, colony members, and visitors—gives it cheerful attention. The baby is spoken to, picked up, tickled, played with. However, when it is time for church or the adult meal, the baby is promptly placed in its crib and the parents walk out. After seven weeks of age, a baby is always either in a socially stimulating environment or alone in its crib.

A child is believed to be completely innocent until it is observed to strike back or to pick up a comb and try to comb its hair. Either of these activities is believed to indicate that the child's level of comprehension is sufficiently high to understand discipline. The child is displaying self-will and understanding. If house children quarrel over an object, the object is removed; if they are quarreling for another reason, they are often told to kiss one another. Very young children will hit each other and then immediately hug and kiss, avoiding adult displeasure by quickly making up. An older house child may be strapped for refusing to go to someone other than its parents, for refusing to share food, or for being noisy and disturbing adults. Immediately after punishment, the crying child is comforted.

Hutterite women almost never take their house children with them when they are doing colony work. If the mothers are busy, the older toddlers, especially the boys, accompany their fathers and play near the place where the men are working, usually in the company of the youngest schoolboys. There is a united effort on the part of the colony, in which the parents cooperate, to wean the house children away from their parents and into the group. Most of the activities that are considered especially pleasurable, such as riding in a wagon or on the back of a truck, can be enjoyed only if the toddlers will leave their parents to join in the fun. When the little ones are in a group of children, however, they often become the butt of aggressive teasing.

House children are socialized to like people and to respond positively to every person (or at least every Hutterite) who comes within sight or earshot. They are taught to be aware of, and to respond quickly to, the wishes of others, but they are also taught not to initiate contact or disturb them. It is difficult to know what factors influence a child's development, but certainly Caleb, the house child we brought to the colony, has turned into an adaptable person who is comfortable with people and intuitively responsive to those around him. When we returned to New England and he began nursery school, he never spoke above a whisper in front of strange adults, but played happily with the children. He was a master at avoiding quarrels. By the time he was in kindergarten, he still rarely initiated contact, but college student observers reported he was the most sought-out child in the group. Caleb, who was at a socially favorable age stage, responded most positively to the Hutterites. For months, he asked daily when we would go back to live in the colony, and he has enjoyed each return visit, stepping naturally into the proper age- and sex-determined niche.

"Our kindergarten school is from three to six years. Here they learn to obey, sing, sleep, memorize, and pray together," explained a Hutterite minister. "We need the kindergarten," remarked a Hutterite kindergarten mother (teacher). "It helps the children and their mothers to realize that everyone should know his or her place." The status of the kindergartener is low. The child has plummeted from a relatively desirable position to the very lowest. Kindergarteners are considered willful and useless: "They can't do anything but memorize." The willfulness is somewhat threatening to a rigidly controlled people, and because the uselessness is no longer combined with complete dependency, it cannot be enjoyed by succoring caretakers. Verbal threats are used on children of this age for they are old enough to experience fear, yet not old enough to realize that the threats are empty. Most threats fall into one of two categories: those that teach that exclusion from the group is unpleasant; and those that teach that beyond the boundary lurks danger. Thus, a child may be warned that he will be locked in a hole under the house or given to a non-Hutterite visitor. If he opens a door, a bee in the closet will sting him, the dog in the (off-limits) barn will bite him, or a bear "outside" will eat him up. When it thunders, children are told that God is telling them they must be obedient.

Children pass the whole day in kindergarten, arriving before breakfast and, depending upon the convenience of the colony, leaving after an afternoon snack or after dinner. They learn to recite their prayers and hymns kneeling by the long benches, hands folded under their chins, the girls at one bench, boys at another. Rocking rhythmically, they recite very rapidly, the older ones doing so quite loudly. (This is the only occasion on which a kindergarten child may raise his voice.) No effort is made to explain the meaning of what is memorized. Children of this age are not permitted to touch any dangerous object. Until the age of six, they use only a spoon for eating and are not allowed to handle scissors, a knife, or a pencil. Several kindergarten children were strapped for playing with our five-year-old son's hammer and saw.

To the Hutterites, it is obvious that children have stubborn wills that must be broken; kindergarten helps teach the children not to be stubborn or willful. As one kindergarten mother explained when she swatted a child who was licking his boot, "He's only three years old and still very young. He'll need many *britschen* before his will is broken." Children must obey the person in charge; they may not leave the kindergarten yard; they must share; they are not allowed to fight, quarrel, or hit; they are not to call one another names or use "bad words." In a *Gemeindordnungen* ("colony rules") of 1812, the members are reminded that "it is very sinful and rude" to call each other such insulting and contemptuous names as "pig" or "dirty dog." Yet the first Hutterite words our five-year-old used spontaneously were those for "you pig" and "you dirty dog."

The kindergarten mothers use encouragement, praise, and rewards with the children. The little boys are told to "eat up! eat up! so you can drive a Massey [tractor]." A child who has been helpful may have the privilege of going with the kindergarten mother to bring the food from the kitchen. A child who has behaved very well may be the first to be dismissed in the afternoon. A small child may be comforted with a little candy from the kindergarten mother's pocket, or a group of children may be promised a walk if they are good. Punishment includes scolding, switching, and threats. Some kindergarten mothers feel that a leather strap is too cruel for children and makes them tough without correcting them; a willow switch is better. The children are given only a couple of switches, and those older than four rarely cry. When a three-year-old was crying after being punished, one of the five-year-olds remarked, "We're already tough, we don't

cry anymore, only Michael does." (Michael had just begun kindergarten.) The children are not punished in anger or vindictively.
Their kindergarten mother, who as the name implies, regards
them almost as her own children, is confident that she is helping
the children grow into worthy Christians.

Kindergarten introduces children to their peer group and
teaches them how to function in it. "They learn to obey, sing,
sleep, memorize, and pray together." At an age when the child
in North American society is developing individuality and a concept of self, the Hutterite child is placed in a setting that mini-
mizes self-assertion and self-esteem and maximizes identity as a
member of a group. Of all the age groups within the colony, the
kindergarteners experience the most restricted, most regiment-
ed, and least varied program. Physically, the children spend virtually the whole day in one little building and small enclosed yard;
they are cared for throughout the day by only one adult. There
are no vacations during the school year except for half-day sessions on weekends and church holidays. The children learn to tol-
erate a restricted environment. They are rewarded for
cooperative, docile, passive responses to correction or frustration. After entering kindergarten, the child's parents and the
adult colony members no longer will accept the varied range of
behavior permitted the child who is still considered to be a baby.
The child must now be quiet around adults, even cry quietly. Visitors from other colonies do not greet kindergarten children or
German-school children. Adults rarely play with them and no one
wants them around. As a Hutterite mother said of her kindergar-
ten-age son, "I'd certainly like Danny less if I had to see any more
of him." The children can easily interpret these changes as rejec-
tions. But even though they have fallen from the "garden of
Eden" status of house children, they have started the steady, re-
warding ascent that leads to full, responsible membership in the
colony.

Our kindergarten child, Daniel, vigorously protested his low
status in the colony, did not identify with his Hutterite peer
group, and saw no reward or purpose in the long climb to colony
membership. He did not even want to drive a tractor, then or
when he grew up. We protected him somewhat from full colony
participation by not sending him to kindergarten regularly and
by discouraging other adults from administering physical punishment, but we could do little to protect him from the older

children. By Hutterite standards, he had not been sufficiently weaned from his mother and grandmother for he spent more time with the women in the family than is typical for Hutterite boys. The colony tried to integrate Daniel into the group, but his stubborn will had not been broken; he did not passively accept punishment at the hands of the older boys. He responded to teasing with anger; if an older boy called him a bad name, he responded in kind. The crueler the children were to him, the harder he fought back and the louder he yelled his objections—a response that is totally unexpected (and altogether unacceptable) in a Hutterite child of his age. The colonists considered him a woeful example of a child whose will was not broken at the proper time. His situation improved after his father arrived and he could go around the colony with the school-age boys who spent part of the time working with their fathers or brothers. Nonetheless, today he deplores the Hutterite way of life. Since we left the colony he has returned only for very short, uncomfortable visits. On the other hand, it may have been in the colony that he learned to minimize physical discomfort. He still ignores public pressure. He knows that if one is willing to pay the price, one can go against convention and probably survive; the group does not have to determine one's values or behavior.

"Just as iron tends to rust and as the soil will nourish weeds, unless . . . kept clean by continuous care, so have the children of man a strong inclination towards injustices, desires and lusts," wrote a Hutterite leader in 1652. And today the German-school teacher reminds his charges, "Good children are obedient, peace-loving, and God-fearing." Hutterites believe that children are inclined by nature to misbehave, but this belief does not mean the misbehavior should be tolerated. Rather, the responsibility for the children's behavior is placed on the adults, whose duty it is to watch over the children. Although these adults customarily use physical punishment to elicit good behavior, there are no battered or neglected children among the Hutterites. As children do not know the difference between right and wrong, it is determined for them; they are taught "rules," not "ethics."

On his sixth birthday, the kindergarten child is taken by the kindergarten mother and handed over to the German-school teacher. Until his fifteenth birthday, the child will be under the care of this adult, eating all meals with the peer group, attending German and English school with them, and doing colony work assigned by the German teacher. The children are taught table manners and work roles. They learn to read German and to write in the Gothic German script. They learn to count, to be proficient with weights and measures, and they memorize innumerable biblical passages and hymns, as well as episodes from Hutterite history. German school is ungraded, and the children sit by age and sex. Material must be covered in a certain order and learned thoroughly, but children work at their own speed. Slow learners are praised as frequently as fast learners. Diligence, not aptitude, is demanded, and only a certain kind of questioning is considered acceptable. For instance, six-year-old Susanna received three slaps on her hand from the German teacher when she asked, "Why should I?" It would have been all right if she had asked "when" she should do a task, "how" she should do it, and "if" she should do it, but if told to do something, she must be obedient and not question why.

Children are not pushed to grow up either intellectually or morally. They are not taught self-discipline for it is not their prerogative to decide what is right; they are to do what they are told and those in authority will watch over them and punish and protect them. Similarly, children are not made to feel guilty; it is only natural for a child to sin and therefore it is not "his fault" that he misbehaves. Our school-age daughter angrily complained how unfair it was for us to expect "good" behavior when she was out of sight—none of the other children had to behave when they were not being watched.

Punishment by the German teacher is administered uniformly and fairly. Everyone receives the same punishment for the same offense. When several of the boys were late to German school because they were catching polywogs, the consensus was that the three straps they received were well worth the fun. They had known they would be late and what the punishment would be. The children were not lectured about their behavior, which Hutterites consider typical for boys, who naturally prefer polywogs to memorizing. The punishment was payment for the misbehavior, wiping the slate clean. Everyone knew that when the boys were older, they would be less interested in polywogs than in their colony responsibility. No one moralized, no one worried, no one was offended. A young child angry about being punished may tattle on other children, who will then be strapped as well, and they in turn may tell something on the first child, who will receive a second strapping. When the children are alone, they will pick on the original tattler, however, and so by the time the children are seven or eight, they rarely tell on one another. The peer group can punish more severely than adults, but it can also protect. When the children present a united front to authority, they can often avoid punishment.

The sisters in each family have their own playhouse and there are ever changing cliques determining who can play in which house. Social fickleness teaches the girls the unpleasantness of being excluded. The cliques quickly coalesce, however, to present a united front before the boys or the adults. The children's play reflects the community's de-emphasis of physical pain and complaining. They play games such as "whistle when it hurts" and invent spontaneous games of physical stress and daring. Their play is characteristically vigorous and often entails a great deal of roughhousing. Boys don't play with girls, except in group situations where conflict and competition between the sexes is the typical pattern.

When our house child, Caleb, returned to the colony as a schoolchild, he reported that German school was better than English school; the German teacher was kinder and more impartial than the English teacher. Caleb was more comfortable being swatted by the German teacher for playing with polywogs than being praised by the English teacher for a good recitation. He was comfortable and happy in the vigorous boys' groups, working hard and playing hard, knowing that breaking the rules meant punishment, but experiencing a kind of pack freedom where undue demands are not made on the growing child.

During our first summer in the colony, our schoolchild, Abigail, quickly internalized the rules of dress and conduct and instructed us accordingly. She identified closely with her peer group and participated fully in German school and Sunday school (except that she did not answer questions on the sermons), did all the colony work expected of children her age, and regularly waxed the floors for a woman with a large family but no school-age daughter. Abigail learned to act shy in front of adults and to show no other emotion unless she was alone with the children, joining in their rough and boisterous play. Wholly submerged in colony life, she found it difficult to distance herself sufficiently to comment on her activities. However, the energy it took to "become" Hutterite was indicated by a request she made the only time our family was together outside the colony: "Drive slowly, it is so easy to breathe out here."

Perhaps because of her experience in the colony, today in almost every situation, Abigail picks up behavioral cues and notices how people are relating to one another. While she was living in the colony, Abigail did not want to differ from her peers. She passively accepted the "pruning" given all the "young, tender plants" as she learned the rituals that insure the smooth social functioning of the group. But because she was an outsider, she knew it was her choice to accept the pruning passively. It never occurred to her peers to exercise their choice, and she realized that they were unaware they had a choice. Having lived with people socialized not to recognize their individual freedom has made her sensitive to the lack of awareness of the freedom of choice exhibited by many individuals in our own culture. As she learned to see with Hutterite eyes, she realized how differently the world can be viewed and how from the same set of facts different conclusions can be drawn.

The most important birthday for a Hutterite is the fifteenth, for on that day the schoolchild becomes an adult, moving from the children's dining room to the adult dining room, from the children's group into the adult work force. Even the word used to identify the child changes: the *mandel*, "little man," becomes a *buah*, "boy"; the *dindla* becomes a *die-en*. As this is a change involving a single individual, it is not celebrated by the colony. There is no party, no formal recognition, only orderly progress to the next step. The colony does not administer physical punishment to those older than fifteen, and so the other children teasingly tell their schoolmates that they will get a final whipping on their birthday. Instead the German teacher gives the fifteen-year-olds several religious books, discusses their future roles as adults, and emphasizes the importance of giving cheerful obedience to those who are above them. Gradually, at the colony's convenience, new adults are given various gifts that reflect their altered status and are needed in their new roles. Both boys and girls are given a locked wooden chest in which to keep personal belongings. The boy receives new cloth for good suits and shirts, the girl material for dresses. Boys are handed work tools, which they are responsible for keeping in good working condition; a spade, a pitchfork, a hammer, a saw, and in some colonies, a spoon with the individual's name inscribed on it. The girls receive equipment that they will care for and use for colony work: a scrub pail, a paintbrush, a hoe, kitchen knives, a broom, knitting needles, and in some colonies, a rolling pin. For the next two years the young adult occupies an apprentice position before being assigned specific responsibilities, such as taking charge of a small tractor or doing the colony baking. These boys and girls constitute a mobile labor force that can be deployed throughout the colony as needed (in jobs considered suitable to their sex) and may be sent to other colonies to help during a time of need. The boys in this group do most of their colony's hard labor and enjoy the opportunity to demonstrate their strength and stamina.

Hutterite young people are in transition between childhood and adulthood. The colony recognizes both aspects of their identity. Physically, the young people are adults who can work responsibly with other adults. Religiously, they are children who must attend Sunday school and memorize and recite weekly verses. Emotionally, they vacillate. Appropriately, this period is sometimes called "the in-between years." Certain limited disregard of colony mores is expected, but moodiness or poor work performance is not tolerated. A good young person is "always obedient and never talks back."

The in-between years are a time for exploring the boundaries, for flirting with the world and learning about that which will later be rejected. Most young people occasionally watch TV, have photographs taken (Hutterites believe no one should make a graven image), and even own cheap cameras. From hidden transistor radios, they memorize popular songs. Quite a few of the boys own wristwatches and occasionally a boy will smoke secretly. To earn extra money, some boys trap during the winter and sell the furs or moonlight on neighboring farms. The girls have colored nail polish and may use it to paint their toenails, which are hidden under heavy, black-laced shoes. They have perfume and dime-store jewelry, fancy underwear and perhaps a pair of slacks—all of which are forbidden in the Hutterite community. The in-between years are a period of limited self-realization. A young man may even leave the colony for a few weeks, several months, or sometimes for a couple of years. In most cases, however, he is a "tourist" in the outside world who plans to return to marry and raise his family within the disciplined community.

There is a tendency, especially pronounced among the girls, to create a secret world during this time. As long as the make-believe does not interfere with their work and is not flaunted, adults tacitly accept it and, remembering their own youth, are indulgent. Sometimes the secret world is confined to a locked wooden chest; sometimes a corner of the attic is made into a personal microcosm. Here are stored bits of the temporal world—photographs, sheet music, suntan lotion, souvenirs. These artifacts represent, however meagerly, what the individual has the freedom to pursue or the freedom to renounce. They represent the world outside the colony, the self in its indulgent, vanity-pleasing aspects. As individuals mature and measure these trinkets and conceits against the full life around them, they generally find that the satisfactions received from active participation in the colony far outweigh those of self-indulgence. The Hutterite self-image requires colony identification.

During the last year or so of their status as young people, adolescents are expected to show by their proven works—in other words, by their daily behavior—that they can adhere to the rules of the colony. When they have displayed by their actions and know with their heart and mind that they cannot continue as irresponsible children, they willingly and humbly request baptism, so that they may become true members of the colony. The goal of the Hutterite system of child rearing is achieved.

Throughout the centuries, Hutterites have developed subtle ways to elicit social conformity. Not only our children were exposed to intensive socialization—so were we. The first step was our dressing Hutterite. Accepting the symbols of the culture reinforced acceptable behavior. My husband had his hair cut and his beard trimmed by a colony member, indicating not only that he was a married man but that he accepted the rules of the community. My mother and I wore long, dark dresses with high necks and long sleeves, and even when we were working in the ninety-degree temperature we kept our heads covered with a cap, which buttoned under the chin, and a closely woven, double-layered, black polka-dot scarf. The minister quoted to us, "By their fruits ye shall know them," which was interpreted to mean that by dressing correctly, we indicated our acceptance of our proper place in the universe. When my mother commented that she did not see why we could not just wear the cap and take off the head scarf when the weather was so hot, she was told, "We can't expect to be comfortable here and there both." (If you are comfortable in this life, you should not expect to be comfortable in the hereafter.) When she found many of the small regulations pertaining to the lower status of women irksome, members of the colony implied that perhaps she was forgetful of them because of her advanced age. This was an effective means of soliciting conformity from a professional competent child psychologist. With me, they implied that perhaps the colony work was too demanding. As status is closely tied to one's ability to work hard, long, and fast, I shaped up and conformed. Because by Hutterite standards my husband (an art historian) was low on skills, he worked with the older adolescent boys, as well as with the married men. When they felt he was not paying enough attention to his job, they would call out the number of strokes it took him to sink a nail.

The pressure on us to conform could not be resented because it grew out of the Hutterites' deep conviction of the rightness of their way of life and out of their acceptance of us. Patiently they instructed us and helped us. I learned to pluck live geese and was helped to create a spotless, flower-accented house to welcome my husband to the colony. We were reminded that being a nice person had nothing to do with where we would spend eternity; we were either "in the ark" or we were "not in the ark." The depth of their concern and generosity was evident when they offered to come any time to start a community with us. Although they do not go out as missionaries, the Hutterites were willing to send their centuries-old sermons with us. Twentieth-century individualists, we were privileged to share the details of everyday life with people who have all surrendered their own will and given themselves with singleness of heart to God and church.

THE CLOISTERED LIFE[2]

When Carolyn O'Hara received her master's degree in philosophy at age 24, she did something she had secretly been planning ever since her freshman year at Boston College. She entered a Carmelite cloister and became a member of a community of nuns who spend their days in silent prayer. "My mother thought

[2]Reprint of an article by Julia Lieblich, a writer for the Teletext information service. *New York Times Magazine.* p12+. Jl. 10, '83. Copyright © 1983 by The New York Times Company. Reprinted by permission.

she'd failed in some terrible way," the now 41-year-old Sister Carolyn recently recalled at the order's cloister in Beacon, N.Y. "She was sure there was something deeply wrong with me. My friends also thought I was crazy. A few could understand a religious vocation, but not a call to the cloister."

Sister Rachel Lauzé, who at 33 looks more like a college student than a nun, spent five years working as a Maryknoll nurse in Indonesia before deciding to enter her order's Maryknoll, N.Y., cloister. Her family, she says, "thought I was going through a masochistic phase."

Sisters Carolyn and Rachel are among the more than 3,800 Roman Catholic nuns in the United States who have removed themselves from the distractions of a worldly life to the cloister, devoting their lives to the search for God through prayer. It is not a self-centered meditation. They believe that their union with God contributes to the salvation of all people, and that their prayers for humanity touch the lives of the suffering everywhere. In an earlier century, they might have been respected by families and friends as women with an exceptional calling. Today, they are often viewed as rebels by a secular society that values action over contemplation. Their special way of life sets them apart in a world where even many Catholics dismiss the cloister as an archaic institution and the nuns inside as people with an unhealthy attraction to solitude—weak women who are not carrying their weight in the world.

Sister Marjorie Robinson, 35, a former teacher from Philadelphia and now a Carmelite at the Beacon cloister, recognizes that "to our society, it's almost like we're marginal people, a countersign to a lot of what our society goes after—the practical and the material." What she and her sisters are saying, however, she points out, is that "there are deeper realities—something beyond the everyday illusions and distractions." As a symbol of her permanent commitment to God, she, like many sisters, wears a plain gold ring inscribed with the word "Jesus," which she received at her final vows ceremony.

The timeworn image of cloistered nuns as escapists, spurned lovers or naive waifs has little basis in reality today. It takes more than a botched-up love affair to lure educated women in their 20's and 30's to the cloister in the 1960's. For many, choosing to leave behind family and friends, the possibility of marriage and children and worldly careers that offer tangible rewards is a long, difficult and frequently painful decision. And opting to stay in the cloister after all romantic notions about the life have been stripped away is tougher still.

Yet at a time when almost three times as many nuns are leaving than entering active teaching, nursing and missionary orders each year, the number of cloistered nuns in the United States is slowly increasing. Some still elect to enter highly traditional orders as "brides of Christ," to live behind grilles, to walk barefoot and to practice penances, such as self-flagellation, that date back to the Middle Ages. A few seek even greater solitude in hermitages. But most of those who choose the contemplative life today gravitate toward orders whose broad interpretation of the guidelines set out by the Second Vatican Council have freed their members from the hairshirt habits and the almost total silence of the past.

The wrong reason to enter any kind of cloister, says Sister Carolyn, "is to escape. It takes a certain amount of psychic strength to face yourself and your reactions to the same people in a cloister 365 days a year. You go to the convent to find solitude, and you find God, and you find yourself."

The majority of the more than 200 Catholic cloisters in the United States today are offshoots of convents founded in Europe during the Middle Ages. The largest order—about 850 sisters in 65 convents—is the Discalced (shoeless) Carmelites, founded by St. Teresa of Avila in Spain in 1562 and brought to the United States in 1790. There are at least a dozen other major American cloistered orders, including the Poor Clares, the Sister Adorers of the Precious Blood, the Sacramentines, the Passionists, the Cistercians, the Redemptoristines and branches of the Dominicans, the Visitation Nuns and the Benedictines. While other Christian religions also have cloistered communities, their numbers are far fewer.

In all but two of the six American Catholic cloisters and the community of hermit nuns visited over a recent period of four months, it was possible to speak to the sisters without any physical barrier separating us. At one, conversations had to be conducted through a grille; at another, from behind the wooden turn used to pass items in and out of the convent. It was also possible to talk to some sisters on the telephone, although at times only after a call back from a message left on an answering machine, which in one order notifies callers that "The sisters are at prayer . . . re-

membering your intentions." More open discussions took place
at a two-day meeting last September of the Metropolitan Association of Contemplative Nuns in Yonkers, N.Y. And during a visit
this spring to Israel and France, several cloistered nuns of Mount
Carmel and in Paris spoke of their concerns, the former, through
a grille, the latter, face-to-face.

That the special role of the contemplatives has continuing rel-
evance was emphasized by Pope John Paul II last November when
he praised cloistered nuns in Spain for their devotion to absolute
principle in a world that, he said, "exalts relative values."

Between A.D. 500 and 1200, all nuns were cloistered. Because a large dowry was generally required for entry, most of the
sisters were daughters of the aristocracy. For centuries, a religious life was considered the respectable alternative to marriage.
In many cases, it also offered women a more independent and intellectually stimulating life—in northern France and Germany,
several orders were renowned for the academic level of the all-
girl schools they operated.

During the late Middle Ages, the public began to view the
cloister less as a holy institution and more as a dumping ground
for the nobility's rebellious daughters, discarded mistresses and
the widows of enemies. Some of these unwilling recruits were notorious for their neglect of religious duties and their general disregard for the vows of poverty, obedience and chastity. Although
several Catholic reformers, notably St. Teresa of Avila, restored
strict monastic order to dissolute convents, nuns never quite re-
gained their exalted stature.

In the last century, a few former sisters have reinforced the
negative image of nuns through highly publicized, sometimes fac-
tually suspect, accounts of cruel penitential practices in some
North American convents. While some overly zealous convent
heads may have stretched the concept of penance to extremes in
the belief that intense physical pain and humiliation led to holiness, they were certainly exceptions. Film makers further colored
the public's perception by sometimes portraying nuns as inane
schoolgirls, ethereal creatures or despotic spinsters. Rarely have
contemplatives been presented as mature women with a vocation
as challenging as any other "career."

Before turning to cloistered life, Baltimore Carmelite Sister
Barbara Jean LaRochester had spent 17 years as an active nun in

Philadelphia. During the week, she worked as an X-ray technologist in a Catholic hospital and on weekends as a volunteer teacher's aide in an inner-city school. As a board member of the National Black Sisters Conference in 1968, she was active in the civil rights movement during the height of the race riots. But in 1972, she decided her real call was to contemplation.

"As a physical presence out in the world I could only be one person with two hands and two feet," says the now 50-year-old nun. "But through prayer, I felt I could reach more of my brothers and sisters. The spiritual dimension is limitless."

For Carmelite Sister Annamae Dannes, the decision came 15 years ago, when she was 26 years old and well-launched on a career as a teacher in a northern Ohio public school. "When I was in school, I felt that if I dated the right person I'd be happy," she says. "After college, I thought that if I traveled in Europe I'd be satisfied. Then I got the idea that moving to New York City and going to Columbia Teachers College would be grand. Later, it was getting the right job. But, somehow, it was never enough."

"I delighted in teaching, but I was beginning to question the meaning of my life. I have a friend who used to pray with the nuns at the Cleveland Carmelite and one day I joined her. I felt right at home here from the start. I just knew that was where I belonged."

Cloistered nuns believe that their vocation is to witness the primacy of prayer in the Church, to serve as a reminder of the contemplative dimension in all lives, and to intervene for others before God. "If people are aware that I'm praying for them," says Sister Michaelene Devine, prioress at the Beacon Carmelite, "it's a real source of comfort. Even if they're not aware, I feel that our intercessory prayers help them to be more open to the influence of God." Desert Mother Mary of Jesus, who heads the Carmel of the Immaculate Heart of Mary, a hermitage in Chester, N.J., expresses the effect in terms of secular linkages. "People are conscious of radio, TV and the telephone," she says, "but they're not always conscious of this spiritual network of communication through prayer." Contemplatives do not, however, says Sister Annamae Dannes, feel that their prayers have more weight than those of anyone else.

If the sisters come to the cloister to pray for the world, they stay because of the relationship they develop with God. Contemplation may be deep and mysterious, but it is not abstract.

"It's not a psychological mind-game we're playing," says Sister Rachel. "When we pray, we meet a real person—God. It's like a regular relationship with anyone. On some days, it's ecstatic. On others, I wonder how I ended up here."

"For prayer, you need silence and you need solitude," declares Sister Michaelene. "In community, we provide this for one another."

But just how cloistered a convent must be to facilitate prayer is a matter of debate among contemplatives. In affirming the role of the cloister in 1965, Vatican II stated that "it should be modified according to conditions of time and place, and outdated customs done away with." It did not, however, decree specific changes. Individual orders consequently reached different conclusions.

Until the 1960s, the inner-sanctums of almost all cloistered convents were cut off from the world by heavy iron or wooden grilles, some with sharp spikes pointing outward to discourage persistent lovers or distraught fathers. Nuns rarely left the convent grounds. Extern sisters, who were not part of the cloister, greeted visitors, answered the telephone, shopped for food and supplies and conducted other worldly business.

All contemplatives then wore heavy wool habits, whatever the weather. Some went barefoot, even in winter. Rules of silence were rarely broken, and then only after saying a prayer and kissing the floor. In some convents, nuns communicated much of the time in writing or through sign language.

The Mother Superior was the unquestioned leader of the community. The sisters had to ask her for permission for everything from getting supplies to staying up an extra hour. Mortification was considered an essential part of most cloistered life, and common penances included frequent fasting, kneeling during meals and praying for extended periods of time with arms outstretched.

After Vatican II, many communities decided it was time for a change. Some began with the convent building itself. One morning in 1969, the Yonkers Sacramentines voted to remove the grille in their front parlor, and by noon it was down, thanks to a sister who knew how to use an electric saw. "I was so happy," recalls Sacramentine Sister Mary of the Eucharist. "When my mother visited, I could hug her for the first time in years."

In all but the most traditional cloisters, the rules have been relaxed considerably. A sister may now leave the grounds alone to go to a doctor, to visit a sick parent, to shop or to vote. The emphasis is less on conformity and more on the intellectual, emotional and artistic development of each sister. A few nuns have even attended college classes.

Many traditional vows are differently interpreted today. Poverty does not mean going without nutritious meals or forgoing an occasional treat. According to Sister Michaelene, "It means respect and enjoyment of material things without being attached to them." Obedience no longer means asking the Mother Superior for "permissions." Rather, says Sister Helen Werner, the 63-year-old coordinator of the Maryknoll cloister, "it means being accountable to God and the rest of the community." And the rule of silence is no longer "enforced." Instead, Sister Helen says, it is "looked upon as a value, but so is sharing in relationships."

For many nuns, sharing means communicating with other orders. In the past, one community had virtually no contact with another, even when their convents were within walking distance of each other. In 1969, 130 sisters from all over the United States gathered in Woodstock, Md., to form the Association of Contemplative Sisters. Today, the A.C.S., which meets every two years, has 400 members who pool their financial resources to sponsor workshops and lectures on theology, psychology and the role of the contemplative in the modern world.

"Getting together as a group of women with common needs," says Sister Annamae Dannes, president of the A.C.S., gave the nuns "the strength to stand up for themselves," in a male-dominated church.

Sisters are also communicating more with their lay neighbors. Some of them, says Sister Annamae, "hold prayer groups and act as spiritual counselors for people who want to talk about prayer or their lives in general." And in many cloisters, the chapel is open to the public during daylight hours and invited visitors may attend mass.

But the nuns say they try not to let these involvements disrupt their lives of prayer. "We want to stay in touch with the world and be available to people, but we can't get overly active," says Sister Mary Devereux, of the Blessed Sacrament cloister in Yonkers, N.Y., an order of perpetual adoration whose nuns keep a constant vigil of prayer in their chapel. "It's a constant struggle. We're living in the world, but we're not of it."

Perhaps no contemplative community is more aware of the world outside its walls than the Maryknoll cloister. The 12 nuns in the tan brick convent on the grounds of the Maryknoll Sisters' headquarters are all former missionaries who have spent at least two years in active service, a prerequisite for entering the order's cloisters. Their special calling is to focus their prayers on the more than 1,900 Maryknoll priests, brothers, sisters and lay-workers in their "loneliness and struggles on the mission." In December 1982, two Maryknoll sisters were murdered in El Salvador.

In the mid-1960's, the role of the cloister was questioned by many within the Maryknoll community, as it was throughout the Catholic Church. Now, many Maryknoll missionary nuns on home leave go to the cloister to make a retreat. "When you're out on the mission," says Sister Muriel Vollmer, "you see your own helplessness. Very often the missionaries can't even work because they're so curtailed by governments. Many come home because they're on hit lists. You can't survive in these times without prayer."

The prayers begin before dawn at the Carmelite's Beacon cloister, a modern, red-brick building overlooking a large pond on 30 secluded acres in the Hudson River Valley of New York. The 12 nuns in the community range in age from 35 to 84. A few of the older sisters still wear long, veiled brown habits. The rest dress in brown knee-length dresses or skirts and blouses. The routine at Beacon is similar to that at most cloisters. Before the first light of day, each sister rises to pray privately in her cell—a small cement-block room, simply furnished with a desk, chair and bed, above which hangs a large wooden cross—or in the chapel, a modern octagonal building.

At 7:15 A.M., the whole community gathers in the chapel to sanctify the day with the morning portion of the Divine Office, or Liturgy of the Hours, arranged so that the entire day is made holy by the praise of God. The office concludes with intercessory prayers, with each sister rising in turn to pray aloud for a particular person or group.

A local priest arrives at 8 A.M. to say mass. The nuns gather in the chapel again at noon, in the late afternoon and early evening for communal prayers. During the afternoon, another hour is spent in private contemplation. The nuns also pray silently as they work. Some clean and maintain the convent. Others earn money for the community sewing clerical vestments or by doing keypunching for the archdiocese. For the rest of their financial needs, they rely on donations. While their annual operating costs were not available, another cloister of similar size estimates its at about $60,000, which includes medical insurance and building maintenance.

The sisters at Beacon take turns preparing dinner, the one communal meal of the day, taken at 6 P.M. For an hour afterward, they may walk around the grounds, or, when the weather is warm, take a rowboat out on the pond. This is one of the few times during the day when they break their silence to share their thoughts.

In dramatic contrast to more open cloisters like Beacon are those that have left things much as they were in the Middle Ages. Tucked between rundown buildings in Brooklyn's Crown Heights section is a large white brick Carmelite convent enclosed by a 10-foot-high cement wall, the outside of which has been irreverently covered from top to bottom with graffiti. Amid the jagged colored glass scattered on top of the fortress-like wall stand two larger-than-life-sized statues of Jesus Christ and the Virgin Mary.

The rare visitor who is buzzed into the front parlor of the convent—the security system is a concession to the realities of 20th century urban life—will never actually see the 15 nuns who make up the community. He or she must talk to the sisters through the wooden turn in the parlor wall. A 4- by 2-foot revolving cupboard, the turn is employed to receive food and other necessities and to send such items as prayer cards out of the convent.

The nuns, many of whom are young, believe they are living the life of prayer the way it is meant to be lived, and they feel no need to explain further. "No matter what you write, no one will understand," one of them said through the turn.

Less extreme and more accessible are traditional communities such as the Discalced Carmelites in Morristown, N.J. Inside this convent, however, the metal grille remains. "To some people it looks like we live in a prison," says Sister Agnes, "but the grille is not to keep people away. It is a symbol for the spirit of solitude." The 13 cloistered sisters and three postulants who make up the community leave the grounds only to visit a doctor or dentist. Local benefactors and an extern, Sister Eliane, buy their food and perform such worldly chores as banking.

Modernization at the Morristown cloister has been more subtle than in progressive cloisters. The vows, for example, are still interpreted literally. "For me, as a subject, obedience means I do whatever my prioress tells me to do," says Sister Agnes. "It's just to be humble. We see in our Mother God's representative."

As at most cloisters, the Mother Superior, prioress or abbess, is elected for a three-year term. When she steps down, she must ask for permissions from her successor.

Although penances are no longer practiced in many convents—"We don't feel the need to invent difficulty in our life," says Sister Michaelene—more traditional communities still believe mortification is an integral part of contemplative life. The 38 Poor Clare Nuns of the Monastery of Our Lady of Guadalupe, who live in an enlarged old farmhouse in Roswell, N.M., continue to go barefoot throughout the year, fast regularly and nightly interrupt their sleep for an hour and a half of prayer. But perhaps the penance strangest to outsiders is "the discipline"—three times a week, the Roswell nuns whip themselves on their backs with scourges of knotted cord.

"There's a lot of misunderstanding about the discipline," says Sister Chiara, who came to the cloister in 1968. "We do penances to unite ourselves to the passion of Christ," she explains. "It's a way of seeking reparation for our sins and the sins of the world."

The Roswell Poor Clares, who do not use surnames, have also retained the traditional clothing ceremony during which a second-year nun receives the formal habit of her order. On the morning of her clothing, the novice attends mass attired in a long white gown and veil. After the liturgy, the nun walks in procession with her sisters to the community meeting room. There, in an act symbolic of divesting herself of worldly beauty, her hair is cut short by the Mother Abbess, who then dresses the new sister in the order's heavy habit of rough brown cloth, which had earlier been blessed by a priest. The high point of the ceremony comes when the abbess gives the sister a new name suitable for her new life of chastity, poverty and obedience.

To explain their retention of a ceremony many cloistered sisters have abandoned, the nuns at Roswell refer to a section of a paper they and nine other communities published in 1978: "The vow [of chastity] is the nun's human and public response to a divine call uttered in the depths of her own being to show forth the brideship of the Church in her total surrender directly to God. This blessed vow is our personal bridal covenant with God."

One step beyond the cloister is the hermitage. If the call to the cloister is exceptional, the call to hermit life is rare, indeed. Sometimes a sister who desires more solitude is given a few rooms in a convent for her exclusive use. There she eats, sleeps, works and prays alone. Others, such as the Carmelite hermits in Chester, N.J., live in separate, small communities. Because the movement toward hermitages is still relatively new in the United States, statistics are difficult to come by, but it is known that the Handmaids of the Most Holy Trinity have established a hermitage at South Bend, Ind., and the Hermit Sisters of Christ in Solitude have one in Sebastopol, Calif.

The four hermit sisters in Chester live on 10 acres of land. Each nun has her own sparsely furnished 16- by 12-foot knotty-pine hermitage, built with the aid of local residents and other benefactors. A nun's only contact with the other three is during Divine Office, at Mass, during daily spiritual counselings with the Desert Mother and an hour of communal recreation, the only time when they indulge in private conversations. The hermitage nuns eat only one full meal a day, and they never know from where it will come. "God will provide" is the prevailing attitude, and they haven't gone hungry yet. Townfolk and visitors bring food and supplies on a sporadic basis. To augment such gifts, the hermits also do calligraphy and make spiritual cassette tapes.

Desert Mother Mary of Jesus, whose title reflects an ancient monastic tradition, founded the small community in 1976 after spending 26 years in the Schenectady, N.Y. Carmelite cloister, because she wanted "a life of total abandon to God without the support of a lot of human security." But not everyone who comes to the hermitage can adjust to the severe regimen. Since its founding, half a dozen nuns have left the Chester hermitage, after what Desert Mother Mary calls "a period of discernment."

Cloistered nuns everywhere struggle with the question of what their particular role should be in today's fast-changing world. High above the Israeli port of Haifa, an international community of 17 nuns practice their life of prayer on Mount Carmel, closely associated in biblical times with the lives of the prophets Elijah and Elisha. Speaking through an interpreter in a mixture of Italian and French, Mother Maria Giuseppina explained that her convent has chosen to take a middle course with the changes offered by Vatican II. "But we were not meant to remain like the nuns in Brooklyn," she said, referring to the ultra traditionalists in Crown Heights. "We are evolving toward a new equilibrium."

As they do, she said, "We will try to hold onto the purpose of this kind of order. Because Christians pray less now, there is a greater need for our work. We are intercessors between men and God—not just with our mouths, with our lives."

Sister Angela explained the particular direction of the community's prayers. "After we read Vatican II, we interpreted a new spirit," she said. "We decided to pray for all people to pray as they believe. Our main purpose is to pray for the Jewish people to be faithful to their own religion. If they are faithful, splendid things can happen. The Jews give us something in return, by letting us have this convent in Israel."

In Paris, Poor Clare Sister Ghislane, a former abbess of the community of 23 nuns which has provided temporary lodging for Vietnamese refugees outside the convent's enclosed area since 1978, was concerned about the decline in religious vocations. She feels various orders, her own included, must accept a certain responsibility for having lost touch with a fast, changing world. Nevertheless, she believes that "people understand we have found something true, solid and real. They are envious," she said in her halting English. "To live our life you must be a strong, reliable person—someone who is not overly concerned with herself. I pray, and I don't mind what God does with my prayers."

The always rigid cloister entry requirements have never been more difficult. Contemplative orders are looking for evidence of a genuine calling from God—not an easy thing to discern. Most orders today require psychological testing and interviews with several members of the clergy before a candidate is accepted. Two years of college, or work experience, is preferred.

"We want women, not girls," says Sister Michaelene. "You can't make choices about your life until you know what your options are."

A nun must live in the cloister for five to seven years before she makes her final vows. The sisters say that's how long it takes to determine if a vocation is real and if a woman has what it takes to live an often stark life devoid of everyday distractions.

Between 1977 and 1979, the most recent years for which comparable statistics have been compiled, 288 women entered, and 267 women left American cloisters. By contrast, 1,887 women entered active orders and 5,694 left during that same period. For those who stay in the cloister, it is a life of extreme faith. If an active nun occasionally sees the sick healed or the poor fed, the cloistered nun has no such visible satisfaction. "It's not easy," says Sister Michaelene. "We don't see the hostilities in Lebanon ceasing because of our prayers."

The lack of concrete evidence inevitably leads to periods of near devastating doubt. "One day you come to your hour of prayer and you feel nothing," says Sister Annamae. "You begin to think, 'Am I making this all up?' Sometimes a spiritual counselor or a friend who's been through it can comfort you," she says. "But essentially you go through it alone. Once you get beyond the doubt, you're purified. You can give yourself completely to God—not in a servile sense, but as a free person."

Dealing with loneliness and the pull toward an active life is an ongoing challenge. Most communities are now quite open about discussing sexuality and the psychological implications of a celibate life, and Mother Superiors, priests and Catholic psychologists, who no longer view psychology and theology as contradictory sciences, provide sympathetic counseling.

For Sister Annamae, "The hardest thing is not to be loved exclusively by one person. We go through the gamut of emotions as much as anyone," she says, "maybe more, because we lead such a reflective life."

"I'm a red-blooded American woman," says Maryknoll Sister Rachel. "I love kids. I love men, too. I think it would be nice to have a husband. I face it. I admit it has an appeal, but I feel the pull toward religious life is stronger."

Sister Helen Werner points out that living in a cloister today does not rule out the possibility of deep platonic relationships with the men and women who visit, and with the sisters in the convent. In the past, close or "particular friendships," from the French, *amitiés particulières*, were forbidden. In some convents, two nuns were not allowed to be together without the presence of a third. Some sisters said the intent was to discourage exclusiveness or platonic friendships that would interfere with the primary relationship with God. Others say the unspoken reason was to prevent lesbian relationships from developing. Today, many nuns discuss the once-taboo subject quite matter-of-factly.

"We've talked about lesbianism," says Sister Michaelene. "I'm sure it happens, but it's not something we've experienced. If we did have a problem, we'd deal with it openly and sensitively. Anything that involves people living together in a small community you have to treat gently."

As to what the future holds for cloisters, Sister Michaelene thinks the contemplative life "may not be lived exactly the same way, but I think the life of prayer will continue. It's so much a part of human nature."

Despite the loneliness and doubts, most of the sisters interviewed say they are at peace in the cloister. "Like any life, if it's not for you, it can be a living hell," says Sister Marjorie. "But if the cloister is where you truly belong, it can be a beautiful life, a life of pain and sorrow balanced with peace and joy."

Many veteran nuns say their families and friends still have a hard time understanding a contemplative vocation. Sister Mary Devereux, who has been in a cloister for a quarter of a century, says her mother recently asked her, "Why do you have to get up so early when you have nothing to do all day?"

Occasionally, there are surprises. "My opinion of a cloistered vocation has changed drastically," says Helen O'Hara, who first thought "What a waste," when her daughter, now Sister Carolyn, told her she was entering a Carmelite cloister. But after reading everything she could get her hands on about the order and its founder, Mrs. O'Hara says she began to understand the contemplative life "as much as a lay person can. My husband and I began to respect Carolyn's choice. She was always quiet and strong. Now I notice an inner peace in her. It's been a gift. I feel we have a powerhouse of prayer in Beacon."

THE HOLY GHOST PEOPLE[3]

For the Holy Ghost people of Appalachia, it is a fragile fabric that separates this world from the next.

They are serpent handlers.

They take up poisonous snakes in church—timber rattlers, copperheads, even cobras—and they drink strychnine. They handle fire, using coal oil torches or blow torches. And they speak

[3]Reprint of a magazine article by writer Michael Watterlond. Reprinted by permission from the May issue of SCIENCE '83. 4:50-7. My. '83. Copyright © 1983 by American Association for the Advancement of Science.

"with new tongues." They lay hands on the sick, trusting that—
God willing—the sick shall recover. And when necessary, they
cast out devils in Jesus' name.

"We live in the world, but we are not of the world," they say
repeatedly during their twice-weekly church services, as though
this were the statement that most distinctly defines them from us.

That these people are of another plane is unquestionable.
They exist wholly in the thin, almost dimensionless region of
"hard doctrine," of "getting right with Jesus" and most important-
ly of what they offhandedly call "this thing" or "this."

"This" is the featureless article of language they use to encompass the fiery, dramatic, even deadly practices that set their religion, their lives, and their select social grouping apart from most
of Christian culture.

They belong to a variety of independent, fundamentalist sects
called loosely Jesus Only. And they belong specifically to churches that subscribe to a doctrine based on what they call "the signs"
or "the signs following."

The basis for these doctrines is a stone-hard reading of the
last few verses of the Gospel according to Mark and other passages in the New and Old Testaments as presented in the King
James version of the Bible, an English translation published in
1611.

In the pertinent section of Mark, Jesus has already risen from
the tomb and appeared to several characters, including his disciples. As he is about to ascend, he issues these final pronounce-
ments:

Mark 16:17 "And these signs shall follow them that believe;
In my name shall they cast out devils; they shall speak with new
tongues;

Mark 16:18 "they shall take up serpents; and if they drink any
deadly thing, it shall not hurt them; they shall lay hands on the
sick, and they shall recover."

The Book of Daniel, in which Shadrach, Meshach, and Abed-
nego are cast into the fiery furnace, is the basis for fire handling.

The fundamentalist serpent handlers take these passages as
absolute. That these verses in Mark do not appear in the earliest
extant texts is of no importance to them at all. Only the King
James Bible counts. It acts as a major initiator of personal action,
behavior, and decision making in their lives. It defines them.

Mary Lee Daugherty, formerly a professor of religion at the University of Charleston, estimates that there are now about 1,000 members of serpent-handling sects in West Virginia. She says numbers have dwindled recently because high unemployment has forced many members to migrate to urban areas. Since no organization links these congregations, a total member count would be guesswork.

Though there are local laws against handling dangerous animals in public in many states where serpent-handling churches exist, the laws aren't always strictly enforced. There are congregations in most areas of Appalachia, stretching from West Virginia south through Kentucky, Tennessee, the Carolinas, and into Georgia. Migrations from hill country into some of the urban areas of the Midwest have led to serpent-handling churches in nonrural areas such as Columbus, Cleveland, Flint, Indianapolis, and Detroit. The Full Gospel Jesus Church of Columbus, under the leadership of Willie Sizemore, has purchased and renovated a building in one of the city's industrial areas.

George Hensley, who began the practice of snake handling in rural Tennessee around 1909, could not have predicted its spread to urban environments. Hensley, a Holiness circuit preacher, died of a snake bite near Atha, Florida, in 1955. He is not revered by these people and is not considered to have been a prophet of any sort. His death, however, does illustrate a point one frequently hears in Jesus-Only congregations: The Bible says to take up serpents; it doesn't say they won't bite.

"Make sure it's God," a deacon warns. He holds the microphone close to his lips like an entertainer. His hefty coal miner's shoulders straighten as he whips the mike cord away from his feet. "Only God can do it. Not me. Not you."

The loud, mechanical sounding buzz from the white pine serpent box makes his point unmistakable. The box this afternoon contains four timber rattlers and a rosy, velvet-textured copperhead.

"Death is in there," he says. "Don't go in the box unless it's with you."

By "it," the deacon means "the anointing"—the protection and spiritual direction of God that is manifest in what believers report as physical and emotional sensations.

"It's different for everyone," according to Sizemore. "Some people get a cold feeling in their hands or in their stomachs. Some don't."

Investigators in the past have reported that members say the anointing has a different and, for them, recognizably distinct sensation for each sign. The anointing to handle serpents may appear as a tingling, chilled feeling in the hands. An anointing to drink strychnine may appear as a trembling in the gut. The reports vary just as the sensations vary.

The deacon's warning about acting on the signs only if the anointing is present is a typical part of services, and the saints, as the members call each other, enthusiastically applaud. As he turns from the pulpit, the underlying rhythmic drum beat that has throbbed subliminally in the background becomes distinct and powerful. It is joined by electric organ, electric guitar, tambourine, and a room full of the clapping hands, stomping feet, and hearty, frantic voices of 40 saints.

As the service gets underway, the saints stand, clapping with the music, and walk slowly toward the open area between the pulpit and the first row of pews. The movement forward and together is called a "press." There is some feeling that the spiritual power of the group is concentrated by this gathering together. Should a member be bitten by a snake or "get down on strychnine," the gathering of saints around the victim is also called a press. Members refer to this communal praying and support of the stricken person as a "good press."

The services themselves have an informal structure that begins with loud, insistent singing. Most songs are belted out in four-four time, and each lasts as long as 20 to 30 minutes. After a few songs there will be requests for prayers or healings and testament. The prayer requests may be for "sinner children" or for members of the church who are sick or injured. There will be more songs before the sermon. Services last from two to five hours depending on the time of year and work schedules in the mines.

The signs may show themselves at any time during the service but are most apt to be manifest in association with the driving rhythms of the music. The enthusiasm may verge on violence. One woman slumps to the floor, "slain in the spirit," they say. As she trembles in front of the pulpit, other saints close in on her screaming, "JESUS! JESUS! JESUS!" in her ears.

"I saw one man get up and run around the inside of the church more than 50 times," says sociologist Michael Carter of Warner Southern College in Lake Wales, Florida, an experienced observer of the sect.

Members wail and shake and lapse into the unintelligible, ecstatic "new tongues" of glossolalia. Each member has his or her own style of speaking. As one saint sails into a new oration of tongues, another clamps his hands to her head and speaks in tongues himself; the ecstasy spreads like contagion. "He's translating," Carter observes.

There are two camps of psychological explanation and description of such services. Some researchers theorize that the wild activities are attempts to transcend reality, while others believe the point is self-actualization. Possibly both are right. It takes only a brief conversation with participants to learn that their daily life is one ongoing seance. They see God's movement and directives in every action, object, or thought.

Jerking as though his head were being battered by some unseen opponent, one brother moves across the floor toward the canister of coal oil next to the pulpit. He lights it quickly and thrusts his hands into the fire as though he were washing himself in flame. Next to him a young woman has been dervish-like for several minutes. She continues spinning under the tent of her long brown hair for nearly half an hour. In the back, the children play tic-tac-toe, practice spelling exercises, or sleep, unconnected to the proceedings.

Investigation into psychological and sociological aspects of fire and serpent handling has been conducted sporadically since the 1940s. A paper presented last year by Carter and sociologist Kenneth Ambrose of Marshall University in Huntington, West Virginia, at the Fifth Annual Appalachian Studies Conference, attempted to determine the satisfaction church members derive from such activities. They interviewed members of an urban congregation to compare the rewards of church versus non-church activity.

Results of the study indicate that taking part in the signs gives these people personal reward equalled in no other aspect of their lives. Participation in "signs of the spirit" were statistically evaluated by Ambrose and Carter to reveal the highest level of satisfaction for members when they spoke in tongues. Handling serpents and handling fire were also rated highly, while drinking strychnine—clearly the most deadly sign—provided more shallow levels of satisfaction.

"When you drink strychnine," members say, "you're already bit"—your fate has been decided. Strychnine, commonly a white or colorless powder, causes a warm feeling in the gut, tingling sensations, and muscle spasms. In poisonous doses—15 to 30 milligrams for a human—the spasms can be severe enough, as the serpent handlers say, to "snap muscles right off the bone" and stop the heart. However, it is possible to ingest a considerable amount of strychnine and not exhibit the symptoms of poisoning. The drug does not accumulate in the body because it is rapidly oxidized in the liver and excreted in urine. The likelihood of developing a tolerance to it is remote.

While members of serpent handling churches—as well as most Jesus Only churches—forego worldly diversions such as films, television, and politics, they do hold down jobs. Sizemore, for example, is a factory worker. But they consider mingling with the world on the job part of their earthly burden.

Since most members have had to face stern criticism and even ostracism by friends and relatives—including husbands and wives at times—they are even more strongly pushed into this cluster of supportive friends at church, where they speak of themselves as the chosen people. The social and psychological bonds are reinforced more or less constantly by hugging, touching, kissing. This creates a rich, meaningful world for them—a sense of being special.

Also, the pastor rides herd spiritually on the congregation. During service he will approach a member he suspects (or "discerns," as they would say) is backsliding, or going to other churches. He will preach to that member eye-to-eye, only the microphone between them, and talk in generalities about worldliness, sin, or traipsing around.

"I don't hold with people going from one church to another," says Brother Sizemore.

It is sometimes a strenuous task for the outsider to pry himself loose from all this music and high spirits and remind himself that these people take poisonous reptiles out of the countryside, bring them into their churches and drape them over their bodies, wear them in bundles on their heads. While the churchgoers are enthusiastic and emotional and committed, they do not appear to be disturbed and certainly not suicidal.

"I'm just as afraid of serpents as anybody," one 22-year-old West Virginia man says. He has attended these churches since childhood and has left the church his mother attends in recent years because that congregation has stopped handling serpents.

"I'm afraid when I am in the flesh," he explains, "but when it is the spirit, there's nothing. I'm just not afraid."

He pulls up his sleeve to illustrate the critical point he wants to make: that these serpents are real and that their venom is real.

"It bit me here," he says, pointing to his wrist. "And it swelled up so much that the skin just pulled apart up here."

"When Richard died," one member says, "his whole arm split open from the shoulder down to the elbow."

Richard was Richard Williams. He died in 1974 after being viciously bitten by a huge eastern diamondback. Like most members who suffer bites, Williams refused medical aid and waited for fate to reveal itself.

The people of this church still talk about Richard Williams' anointing and about the serpent-handling feats he performed. Pictures on the walls of the church show him with his face in a mound of snakes; lying with his head resting on them like pillows, stuffing them into his shirt next to his skin. In a photo of Williams and the snake that killed him, it appears as if he is holding the felled limb of a tree rather than a snake.

"What really killed him was that the serpent got his vein when it hit the second time," one member says.

"You just can't tell," Willie Sizemore says, "you just have to make sure you have the anointing."

The folk myth that individuals who suffer repeated snake-bites develop an immunity to the venom is viewed skeptically by Sherman A. Minton, Indiana University School of Medicine microbiologist and toxicologist. Minton says that such immunity is developed rarely and only when regular, gradually increased doses of the venom are administered. He points out that many people have allergies to venom, making successive bites more painful and causing greater swelling, asthma, and other symptoms.

As one snake expert puts it, however, the chances of dying by snakebite in the United States are comparable to the probability of being struck by lightning. One 10-year study showed that 8,000 venomous bites occur each year resulting in an average of only 14 deaths.

There are many theories about why snakes strike the saints infrequently. It is possible that given many warm-bodied targets pressing closely around it, a snake lapses into a sort of negative panic, a hysteria that makes it unable to single out one target.

Some observers have reported that church members' hands feel cold to the touch after handling fire or snakes. "I have felt their hands after serpent handling or fire handling," says Ambrose, who has observed these services for 15 years. "Their hands are definitely cold, even after handling fire." This would correspond with research in trance states involved in other religious cultures. It would also account for the vagueness of memory, almost sensory amnesia, that researchers have reported in serpent handlers as well as fire handlers. In his doctoral dissertation at Princeton University in 1974, Steven Kane reported that in North Carolina serpent handling congregations, young women were known to embrace hot stovepipes without injury or memory of the event. It has also been suggested by some observers that cold hands on the body of the snake would camouflage the touch and prevent it from feeling the handler.

Retired sociologist Nathan Gerrard, formerly of the University of Charleston, observed serpent handlers for seven years in the 1960s. By administering portions of a psychological test to measure deviate personalities, Gerrard concluded that serpent handlers had healthier attitudes about death, suffered less from pessimistic hypochondria, and generally seemed better adjusted in certain ways than "conventional" churchgoers he used as a control group.

However, one of Gerrard's conclusions at the time was also that serpent handling represented a sop to desperation. He called them the "stationary working class" and attributed their stern doctrine to highland ignorance and poverty—a fatalistic creed that offered death and salvation as the only way out of West Virginia. Since that time, however, Jesus Only churches have spread out of Appalachia as economic hardships pushed followers into urban centers perched on the edge of the Midwest.

Also, the members of the Full Gospel Jesus Church of Micco, a creek-bank town about 10 miles from Logan, West Virginia, are distinctly not the archetypal mountain folks. They come to church in well-polished, late model automobiles and dress like middle-class people in most parts of the country.

While it may be difficult for outsiders to say that it is simply common faith that keeps these groups together, that would be the first thing they would say themselves. And this is a self-definition that has been immensely important to Western civilization.

"You can clearly see early Christianity as having very strong sectarian overtones," says Robert Bellah, a sociologist at the University of California, Berkeley. "Without that at the beginning, there would not have been any Christian church."

"Sect religions," Bellah says, "are most apt to occur in relatively low-status groups, relatively low-educated groups where a combination of intense religious experience and rather high group discipline create a kind of separate world in which the people in the sect live.

"They largely reject the surrounding culture," Bellah explains, "rejecting many of the prevailing cultural forms. In other words, the whole round of life tends to be bound up in the sect itself. Social contact is limited by the sect, and the meaning of most things that one does derives from the sect."

Bellah makes the distinction that churches involve a structure which attempts to encompass the whole of society. They include a range of social classes and do not oppose the dominant social power but view themselves as having influence on how that power is exercised.

"The church accepts the culture while working within it," Bellah says. "A sect is exclusive."

It is the current public concern about total-commitment sects that has many people wondering about what have come to be called cults these days.

"'Cult' is really not a sociological category," Bellah explains. "It is a pejorative, popular term that we use for groups that are unfamiliar to our culture." Generally, the word is used to describe groups that are non-American in origin or are aberrantly individualistic—"in that they have been created by some 'kook,'" Bellah says. "Like Jim Jones."

"We are not a cult," Sizemore says forcefully. "If Jim Jones had been right with Jesus, those people wouldn't have died."

And still, outsiders want to know why anyone handles serpents.

"Because it is written," says Bishop Kelly Williams of the Jesus Only Church of Micco, West Virginia. "The main purpose in our doing this is to obey the Word of God." He points out that it really does not matter that the snakes symbolize Satan.

"Now, we don't think that everyone has to take up serpents," Williams says. "It doesn't say that all signs will follow all believers.

"You," he says to a visitor. "You might only speak in tongues. It depends on how God moves.

"Everyone knows that it is the nature of those serpents to bite you," he nods toward the buzzing pine box of copperheads and rattlers. "But you saw last night that God gave us a victory over those serpents. They were new serpents. They'd never been handled."

In fact, in a quiet evening before, Williams had gone to the box, lifted out a rattler and held it close to his body. He stared down at the serpent in his palms, smiled calmly for about three minutes, and set the snake back down in the box.

"You've seen that there is not one way to handle serpents," he says. "You've been around enough to know that. There's no trick."

The styles of serpent handling are as various as the vocabulary of new tongues. On one Sunday afternoon, several men lift up the box, shake it hard and dump a mass of rattlers and copperheads onto the wooden floor without much caution. One man reaches into the tangle of scales and rattles and pulls up a timber rattler about four feet long. The other snakes, as well as a microphone cord, are tangled up with it, so he just shakes the whole mess until the excess snakes drop off. They coil stunned on the floor, as if paralyzed by the bad manners of it all.

The serpents are passed between hands. Loose copperheads wander around the box, uncertain of any particular route of escape. The heavy beat of gospel music picks up and the floor vibrates, the congregation claps and wails and sings.

In the back row of pews a girl about 11 turns back over her shoulder to talk to the visitor. She is playing hairdresser with another girl and holds an unfinished braid in her hands. She smiles halfheartedly and rolls her eyes heavenward as though her patience were limitless and unconditional.

"Boring," she says, "isn't it?"

THE NEW ORTHODOX: A JEWISH REVIVAL
ON THE UPPER WEST SIDE[4]

Three years ago, Ellen and Mark Goldstein (as we'll call them)
were no different from a lot of other people on the West Side.
He was a Wall Street lawyer. She was a writer. They had each other and a $250,000 co-op on West End Avenue. They figured they
should be satisfied.

They weren't. Somehow, the prospect of a summer house or
a new car seemed hollow. "We'd grown up believing that we
could have anything, do anything, be anything," says Ellen Goldstein. "We were overwhelmed by the constant pressure to buy
things, to go places, to know everything that was new. It didn't
make us feel good. To us, it felt empty."

Neither of the Goldsteins had grown up in a highly religious
environment. Their families' identification with Judaism was
purely cultural. Like many American Jews, they went to synagogue three times a year, on the High Holidays. Their relation
to their religion, though, was ambivalent. Ellen's mother kept a
kosher home, but when the family went out to dinner, they ate
shrimp. Mark's family made sure that he had a bar mitzvah. After
that, they let him play ball or go hiking on Saturdays.

From their front window on Saturday mornings, the couple
saw a stream of well-dressed people, the men in yarmulkes, on the
sidewalks of West End Avenue. One day, the Goldsteins followed
them to Lincoln Square Synagogue; they were astonished to find
that it was an Orthodox *shul*. When they'd think of Orthodoxy,
they'd think of the diamond district, of 47th Street Photo. Where
were the long black coats and black hats? The crowd that gathered in front of the synagogue on Saturday morning was affluent
and attractive. These people seemed to be having a wonderful
time. The Goldsteins signed up for a course called Basic Judaism.

During the next two years, they took the road to becoming
observant Orthodox Jews. It was a slow process. "We stepped into
the waters very gingerly, evaluating every move," says Ellen. For
the first months, their observance was erratic. They would go to

[4]Reprint of a magazine article by Cathryn Jakobson, a journalist specializing in sociology. *New York*. 19:52–60.
N. 17, '86. Copyright © 1986 by Cathryn Jakobson.

synagogue on Saturday and then, instead of heading home for a traditional Shabbat lunch and quiet, contemplative afternoon, they would go shopping.

In time, they gave up trips to Zabar's and trips to Vermont. They began eating kosher. Ellen swore off shrimp. Because of the prohibition against using fire—or, in modern terms, electricity—on the Sabbath, Mark gave up watching football and even the World Series. They made their kitchen kosher. That meant taking the oven apart, scrubbing each piece, and then turning the heat up all the way. It meant giving away all of Ellen's carefully collected flea-market crockery. What was left they boiled thoroughly and took to the *mikvah*—the ritual bath—on West 78th Street, to be dunked and sanctified.

Mark began to say *Shacharit*, the morning prayer, as often as he could, though it meant rising an hour earlier. Sometimes he'd put on the tefillin (leather straps and leather boxes containing biblical passages on parchment). It was a start. They didn't try to be perfect. There were areas of observance where they fell short, but they took heart in their rabbi's words: How much they did wasn't what was important. What mattered was that they were trying. The weekend after they finished making their kitchen kosher, they conceived their first child. "We thought that was a nice touch, a present," says Ellen. They named their daughter Sarah, and Ellen stopped working to stay at home with her.

Why would people who could have all the sensory pleasures of the Upper West Side choose to adopt a restrictive way of life? Why, in an age of technological ease, would they choose to forsake some of the things that the rest of us take for granted?

The people making this sweeping change in their life grew up in a secular world. They went to good colleges and got excellent jobs. They didn't become Orthodox because they were afraid, or because they needed a militaristic set of commands for living their lives. They chose Orthodoxy because it satisfied their need for intellectual stimulation and emotional security.

For the Goldsteins, Orthodoxy has brought a calmness and a certainty. "It is the antithesis of yuppie-ism," says Ellen. "You learn immediately that you aren't the most important person in the world. There's a higher authority—there's God, and he says no. I like the feeling that there are limits."

Forty years ago, the Upper West Side was home to several thousand Orthodox Jews. The numbers dropped sharply in the 1950s, as nearly everyone who could afford to fled the declining neighborhood. Now Orthodox Jews are coming back. At the center of the revival is Lincoln Square Synagogue, at Amsterdam and 69th Street, but many of the Orthodox synagogues in the neighborhood—the Jewish Center, on 86th Street; Ohab Zedek, on 95th Street; West Side Institutional, on 76th Street; Congregation Kehilath Jacob, on 79th Street; and Young Israel of the West Side, on 91st Street—are also showing distinct signs of renewed life. Even the *shitblach*—closet-size synagogues that were moribund for years—are once again busy. There are some apartment buildings on West End Avenue populated almost entirely by Orthodox families.

That Orthodox Judaism is so attractive to so many younger people is reflective of a national trend toward tradition, family values, and conservative thinking. The trend is evident in other faiths as well, even in Manhattan, where a few years ago, organized religion appeared to be on its way to extinction. Riverside Church has 3,300 members, 60 percent of whom are under 45. In just a few years, the congregation of St. Michael's Church, on West 99th Street, has grown from 30 people to between 200 and 300. For Christians and Jews alike, fundamentalism seems to draw crowds. All Angels' Episcopal Church, on West 80th Street, scraped by with 50 members until seven years ago, when a new woman minister with a decided evangelical bent put 400 new faces, many of them young, in the pews.

The number of Orthodox Jews is increasing in pockets all over the country. There are more than 1,800 Orthodox synagogues in North America, and about half a million Orthodox Jews in the United States—double the number fifteen years ago. Conservative Judaism is also attracting a new crowd, mostly people who want ritual and tradition but are not prepared to accept some of the more rigid precepts of Orthodoxy, particularly those concerning the status of women. (Orthodox women cannot become rabbis. The sexes are separated in the synagogue, and women are not allowed to read the Torah scrolls during services in synagogue.) Ansche Chesed, a Conservative synagogue on West 100th Street, has in the past five years drawn a large group of intellectuals, many of whom are women.

Unlike their Reform and Conservative brethren, modern Orthodox Jews don't want to become absorbed into secular society. Their goal is to make it in the secular world without diminishing their observance of the Halakah, the commandments that make up the code of Jewish law.

Modern Orthodox Jews are lawyers, doctors, investment bankers, advertising executives, professors, computer experts, artists, writers, and teachers. They are also clerks and secretaries. Many of them are *"baalei teshuva,"* people who grew up with little religious training. The term means "those who have returned," but among the *baalei teshuva* on the West Side, there are more than a few who never practiced their Judaism or who grew up in another religion.

In a matter of months, people who have never had a Shabbat, who have eaten bacon all their lives, not to mention veal with cream sauce, who have never heard of the Halakah, undergo a most amazing transformation.

Like Ellen and Mark Goldstein, many of the newcomers get their start at Lincoln Square. It's a big, bustling synagogue, with over 3,000 members and five Sabbath services. Most of the *baalei teshuva* first go to the beginners' service. On Saturday morning, the room is packed: 50 people seated, another 10 standing, and a half-dozen in the hall. They come because of Rabbi Ephraim Buchwald, a man possessed of zeal, patience, and an abundance of charm. His efforts—and the efforts of those before him, particularly the synagogue's founding rabbi, Shlomo Riskin—have made Lincoln Square well known. Before Buchwald got started as educational director at the synagogue, in 1972, Jewish outreach was virtually unknown, except among the Lubavitcher Hasidim. There are now dozens of programs similar to Buchwald's in synagogues across the country. Buchwald wants more: He's planning to raise money for a national advertising campaign. "Don't fool yourself," he says. "I've got a terrific product. The Torah sells itself. I just market it and package it in a very palatable way."

Most of the members of the beginners' service are young, professional, and single. David Feld, 32, a product-liability lawyer for the Wall Street firm of Fuchsberg & Fushsberg, plays tennis every morning after he finishes davening (praying). His bachelor kitchen is entirely kosher. He first went to Lincoln Square a year and a half ago.

Feld, an only child, grew up in Kew Gardens Hills, in a family that was aware of its cultural Jewish roots but was not observant. "We did very little," he says. "We had the standard screw-in-the-light-bulb menorah. I went to religious school for a while before my bar mitzvah. I learned how to walk on stilts there, and I learned to play poker, but I can't say I learned anything about Judaism." After his bar mitzvah, he did not set foot in a synagogue for about ten years, until a friend invited him to his son's bar mitzvah. "There was all this getting up and sitting down," he says. "It was bizarre. To me, it looked like mass insanity. It was almost terrifying."

Feld got a job doing litigation in New York. One of the firm's clients was an Orthodox rabbi. "He and his wife were both very nice and very well educated," he says. They keep in touch. One day, the rabbi's 25-year-old daughter had an accident on a bicycle. The rabbi called the young lawyer immediately, and Feld found himself with an Orthodox girlfriend. "I was so ignorant of what her life was like that it was laughable," he says. One night, he suggested that they order in Chinese food. "I told her I knew this place that made the best shrimp." Eventually, he and the woman split up.

When Feld's father died, it seemed like a good time to re-evaluate his life. "I wasn't particularly happy," he says. "It seemed to me that there had to be more. Once you've played all the tennis you can play, what then?"

He wanted to find out. Still, it wasn't until a year and a half later that he said to himself, Let's see why all those people are getting up and sitting down. Maybe there is something to it. He talked it over with a friend at the office. "He was like me, a regular New York Jew, who thinks bagels and lox are religion," he says. "But he'd heard about this Rabbi Buchwald at Lincoln Square who had a service for beginners." They agreed to give it a try. "I started going," says Feld, "and I never stopped."

The beginners' service at Lincoln Square starts at 9:15 A.M., but only a few have arrived by then. Rabbi Buchwald is davening, carefully enunciating every syllable of the morning prayer in Hebrew so neophytes can get the pronunciation and cadence. Dozens of people rush into the classroom and seat themselves on either side of the mechitzah—the partition that divides men from women.

The atmosphere in Buchwald's classroom is intimate and casual. Much of the service is conducted in English. What is in Hebrew is always translated. People continue to walk into the room for the first hour, some carrying gym bags or pocketbooks. They don't know yet that Orthodox Jews don't carry objects on the Sabbath—not even their wallets. Rabbi Buchwald strides around the room, insisting that everyone join in. The D'var Torah is next: Somebody who volunteered the week before will explain what is being studied that day, often with personal reflection on what it means to be a *baal teshuva*. These speeches are thoughtful. They have not been scrawled over morning coffee. Buchwald encourages. "Very impressive," he says to a young lawyer. "When are you going to give up the law and join the rabbinate?"

Beginners are always testing. Buchwald takes on all comers, and although he's answered these questions a hundred times before, there is nothing pat about his answers. "Why can't a woman be a rabbi?" "Why can't a woman wear pants?" "Why can't you play tennis on Shabbes if you find it relaxing?" "How do you reconcile the story of creation with the theory of evolution?" "How could God, who cares, allow 6 million Jews to perish?" "What's the matter with a cheeseburger?" "My goal," says Buchwald, "is to give every adult Jew an opportunity to choose. If they opt out of Judaism, I don't want it to be because they are ignorant of it."

At the end of the service, Rabbi Buchwald says the kiddush (a Sabbath prayer) over wine or grape juice and cookies. That's the start of a very sociable half-hour—an opportunity to talk with people you haven't seen all week and perhaps be introduced to some new members. (In the past two years, 90 marriages have come out of Rabbi Buchwald's beginners' service, a record he's proud of.) Then, for the beginner, it's off to lunch at the home of a family with more experience. Buchwald makes sure that no one goes home alone. Often, the hosts are Nan and Robert Ehrlich.

On an average Saturday, eight people will troop up twelve flights of stairs to the Ehrlichs' apartment near the synagogue. The Ehrlichs, investment bankers in their mid-forties, became observant about eight years ago. Both were born Jewish, but had limited religious education. Robert first went to Lincoln Square to say Kaddish, the prayer for the dead, when his mother died. He went directly to the main service, where the prayers are said in Hebrew. "I was moved by the sound, by the ritual," he says. "It felt very good to me." He wanted Nan to join him, but she wasn't interested. "I'd never had a good experience in a synagogue," she says. "I went in kicking and fighting."

But she went—and she liked it well enough to go back. "I still didn't think it was for me," she says. "I'd spent a lot of time before Robert and I got married living the life of a contemporary single person, and I couldn't imagine how I could change." Slowly, she did. "You don't just become Orthodox," she says. "On Friday night, you say, 'Okay, I'll light the candles and say the kiddush and then I'll go out with my friends, like I always have.' But you like lighting the candles, and you keep doing it, and eventually it takes on meaning." What you get, says Nan, is "a strong sense of family values. A sense of security. A sense of purpose. You no longer feel like you're just going through the motions. Life starts to have spiritual meaning."

For the Ehrlichs, having eight people for lunch on Shabbat, several of them total strangers, is their pleasure, as well as their *mitzvah*—their way of serving God. It is something of a miracle that, with three children under the age of ten and two difficult jobs, they find the time. "Shabbat gives you a new perspective," says Nan. "First you think, This is impossible; how will I get everything done? Then you find you don't have less time—you have more. Shabbat gives you peace and space, which I didn't have. You get rid of a lot of anxiety."

When the guests are assembled, Robert pronounces the kiddush holding a full cup of wine—at least 3.2 ounces, by Jewish law—ending with the words *borai pri hagafen*. During this prayer, the challah (braided egg bread) is kept covered. Then everyone lines up at the kitchen sink and pours water from a cup with two handles, first over the right hand, then over the left hand; before drying his or her hands, each person recites a benediction that is posted over the sink.

At the table, Robert uncovers the challah and, lifting the two loaves, recites the blessing of the bread. Slices are passed around the table, and Nan brings out platters of food: chicken glazed in a honey sauce, salad, vegetables, and an enormous crock of cholent, a meat-bean-and-potato stew. Nan prepared all the dishes before she lit the Sabbath candles on Friday night.

Between courses, guests sing *zmirot*—song poems from the Middle Ages. There is enthusiasm for "*Yom zeh m'hubod,*" because of its chorus—"Toot-Toot"—which sounds, when done correctly, like the horn on a Volkswagen Bug.

Because some of his visitors cannot read Hebrew, Robert Ehrlich provides books with the songs written out phonetically. Over lunch, people talk about the Torah and about Israel, where the Ehrlichs are building a home and intend to move in a few years. Everyone pays a great deal of attention to the children, who leap, shout, reach, sit on laps, and leave the table without asking permission. In Orthodox Judaism, the joyful noise of children is not suppressed.

What is noticeably absent is the kind of discussion one would expect to hear at any other gathering on the Upper West Side. Nobody speaks of work; that is not an acceptable subject for the Sabbath. Nor is money: Nobody says anything about the price of a co-op or the cost of sending four kids to school. Also missing is vicious gossip. That is *"lashon hara"*—bad-mouthing—and is forbidden by the commandments. When the meal is finished, there is a Sabbath birthday cake (with no candles) for Nan.

Most people, like Robert and Nan Ehrlich, become religious gradually. Others jump in and embrace Orthodoxy wholeheartedly. Those people make Rabbi Buchwald nervous. "It's a sign of trouble," he says, "when a real yuppie type—someone who has been spending his evenings in fancy restaurants—suddenly gets very involved in Orthodoxy without first having a good understanding of the learning behind the practice. A quick conversion goes out as fast as he goes in."

Buchwald worries about the strain that newcomers experience. He thinks that in a conflict between secular desire and a desire to serve God, God should win hands down. And he knows it doesn't always work that way with his *baalei teshuva*. Sometimes, Buchwald fears that there's no way his *baalei teshuva* can survive in a modern environment. If he had the chance, he'd take all his beginners and isolate them for a couple of years. He's seen the problems, the conflicts that inevitably arise. He's sent some of his *baalei teshuva* off to Israel for a year of study at a yeshiva, and others to Orthodox therapists. "Without the background," he says, "trying to be observant and live in the modern world can make you schizophrenic. It can eat you up alive."

There are exceptions. Sometimes, beginners manage to adopt the rituals and immerse themselves in learning without apparent adverse effect, although in David and Vivian Relkin's case, it may be too early to tell.

The Relkins, whose traditional wedding was shown recently on the TV program *1986*, became observant less than two years ago. David, 26, is from an affluent Reform family in Great Neck, the town he calls "the rest home for assimilated Jews." He works at his father's Manhattan law firm, Kreindler & Relkin, and is the only one of seventeen lawyers who wears a yarmulke, the only one who keeps kosher, the only one who sometimes rushes over to the afternoon service held at Republic National Bank, around the corner from his office.

Vivian, 25, was raised as a Conservative Jew in Asheville, North Carolina, where her parents, immigrants from Hungary, owned a chain of clothing stores. Her father came from a Hasidic family, but when he arrived in the United States, he gave up much of his religious practice.

After attending York University in Toronto, she came to New York to be an actress. She studied with William Hickey and Herbert Berghof and hung around with a theater crowd. Her parents were not pleased. They insisted she get a job with one of their friends in the garment district, and they installed her in a nice apartment a block from Lincoln Square. "They thought that if I had to stare at the synagogue every time I walked out the door, I might go," she says. They were right.

Vivian had attended the beginners' service for just a few months when she spotted David Relkin. He'd grown up, he says, in a family in which "religion was made into a dumb show, where everything possible was done to overlook the substance." After his second year at the Cardozo School of Law, David took a December trip to the Soviet Union with two good friends. They planned to spend some time with the "refusniks," people who continue to practice Orthodox Judaism despite the Soviet government's opposition.

"I thought people were born with a stamp on their heads," says David. "Reform, Conservative, Orthodox. But when I got there, I realized that some people made the choice to be religious in the face of adversity—that these people were willing to fight for the right to pray, to have a kosher chicken, even if it meant losing all their privileges." For the first time in his life, he started to feel Jewish.

He was in Russia for two and a half weeks. When he returned, he joined the beginners' service and a Bible class at Lincoln Square, where he met Vivian in October 1985. Eight months later, they were married. They are expecting their first child at the end of February.

During their engagement, they observed the code of Jewish law that prohibits premarital sex, and like many Orthodox couples, they limited their physical expression of affection to holding hands. To the Relkins, it was a sign of their commitment to the faith and to each other. "It was extremely difficult," says Vivian, "but it was worth it. It gave us an opportunity to exercise restraint."

After the wedding, the Relkins began to live an extremely observant life. Vivian is one of the few women at Lincoln Square to wear a *sheitel* (wig) when she leaves her apartment or is in the presence of anyone other than her husband. She dresses stylishly but with the utmost modesty: The short skirts and bright makeup of her acting days are no more. "I like it. It means I belong to my husband," she says, voicing a point of view that would make the more "modern" women at Lincoln Square shake their heads in dismay. "Covering my body means I'm not open to viewing. I love coming home and taking off my wig. It makes our relationship very private. It sanctifies it. I feel safe dressing modestly. I feel higher."

David prays three times a day, and three evenings a week he studies the Torah with other men at the West Side Kollel (an adult yeshiva), on West End near 91st Street. Vivian is surprised at how fast their commitment grew. She says she's happier—that she no longer wants, for experience' sake, to check out every possible situation. "I don't have to live through it to know it's not right for me," she says. "I don't have to talk to strangers on the subway anymore. It's amazing. Two years ago, you couldn't have paid me to go out with an Orthodox guy."

The Relkins—and other people who have become highly observant—occupy an awkward place at Lincoln Square Synagogue. Modern Orthodox don't feel comfortable with them. "They're zealots. They're not in the spirit of modern Orthodoxy," says one woman.

People who become more religious than Lincoln Square's general population often decide to go on to a synagogue where there are fewer beginners. They start to feel that Lincoln Square, with all its young, single, well-to-do people, is a very abnormal place. "It's too rushed, too modern, and much too crowded," says one young woman. "And because it's on the West Side, it's too professional-oriented. Status is too important." She and her husband are considering a move to Brooklyn so they can attend a more traditional *shul*.

Most *baalei teshuva* who leave Lincoln Square, however, choose another of the neighborhood synagogues. Brad Scher, 26, a commercial-mortgage broker who's working on an M.B.A., stayed at Lincoln Square for three years before moving to West Side Institutional last spring. "I got tired of Lincoln Square," he says. "I wasn't thrilled by what I considered the meat market. There was so much pressure to meet people, and that's not why I go to *shul*." "It got so we felt lost at the Lincoln Square," says Irene Gottesman, who with her husband and young son recently joined West Side Institutional. "It was anonymous. It was tough for the rabbis to know you, and lots of times, it was too crowded to find seats." Gottesman is getting to know some older members of the WSI congregation. "People aren't just trying to make impressions."

Rabbis at the other synagogues are delighted with the migration. Last February, West Side Institutional had 50 people on a good Sabbath; now there are 200. At the Jewish Center, Rabbi Jacob Schacter welcomed seven new families this summer. Rabbi Avrohom Marmorstein at Ohab Zedek sees a lot of young "*shul* shoppers" in his synagogue on Shabbat. Perhaps 100 people who are not members wander in and out. Shlomo Carlebach's *shul*, Kehilath Jacob, has never been silent. In the sixties, Carlebach's "learnings" and guitar playing drew a young, hip crowd. Though today he and his twin brother, Elichaim, maintain that relaxed atmosphere—including a vegetarian kiddush following services—young people in suits and ties are showing up as well.

As Orthodox Jews settle up and down the streets of the West Side, local Orthodox merchants and restaurateurs have started to prosper. Fischer Brothers & Leslie, the kosher butcher on West 72nd Street, sells almost $2 million worth of meat a year. Miller's Cheese—all kosher—at 78th and Broadway, does a huge business, as does Meal Mart, a kosher delicatessen at 77th and Broadway. "There's no deprivation to being kosher now," says

Hillel Gross, who grew up Orthodox on the West Side. "Now you can get hot dogs at Meal Mart and take them to the baseball game. You don't have to sit there and salivate." Neighborhood liquor stores stock kosher wines that do not resemble the sweet, syrupy stuff of the Passover table. The Famous dairy restaurant, on 72nd Street, is doing better than ever.

There is a growing recognition in the neighborhood that these modern Orthodox have money and want to spend it. David Eisner, 28, who does health-care finance at Bear, Stearns, and his wife, Karen, who makes industrial films, live in a spacious, elegant apartment a block from their synagogue. Their walls are hung with modern art. Their shelves and tables hold a collection of ceramics from the thirties and forties.

They take advantage of living on the West Side—they eat out often, and not just in kosher restaurants. They eat fish—but not shellfish—anywhere they like. "The West Side is just right for us," says David. "It allows us to be uncompromising in our religious life without seriously compromising our secular life."

In the last two years, three upscale kosher restaurants have opened, within six blocks of one another—Benjamin of Tudela, on Amsterdam near 74th Street; Levana, on 69th Street east of Broadway; and La Kasbah, on 71st Street east of Columbus. Six nights a week (they are closed on Friday), these places are hopping.

At La Kasbah, the diners are expensively but conservatively dressed. There are numbers of attractive courting couples, but there is no flirtatious behavior. They seem to be trying very intensely to get to know each other. There isn't much time. People don't date forever. It's not a sport that the Orthodox are willing to play for years. There's tremendous emphasis on marriage and family. For Orthodox Jews, being fruitful is serious business. Having four children under the age of ten in a West End apartment isn't unusual. It is regarded merely as doing your duty—making sure that Orthodoxy will continue to flourish.

Even among the newly observant, there's pressure to marry as soon as possible. "Many *baalei teshuva* have sown their wild oats," says Rabbi Buchwald. "They've done their drugs. Now they've come to an oasis of stability. They want to lock it in. And locking it in is marriage." Marriage is often what most disturbs the parents of *baalei teshuva*. They can cope with their children's aberrant behavior as long as they believe it's a passing fancy.

When they see them making plans for a traditional wedding and a life that will preclude Saturday visits to aging parents in New Jersey, they flip. "I do what I can with them," says Buchwald, who, with his wife, Aidel, invites dozens of sets of nervous parents to Shabbat lunch. "I promise them that if the guests aren't having fun at the wedding because men are dancing with men and women with women, they should tell me, and I'll tell the band to strike up a samba."

Most of the children of these orthodox marriages start their educations in yeshiva, or Hebrew day school. Jewish education starts early. There's an Orthodox play group for two- and three-year-olds in a West End apartment in the Nineties. For this, children are signed up at birth. When they reach three, there are several options. On the West Side, children can attend the Manhattan Day School, on 75th Street; Chofetz Chaim—for boys only—on 88th Street; or the more liberal Abraham Joshua Heschel School, on 89th Street. All three schools go through the eighth grade.

Whether *baalei teshuva*, most of whom went to public school or good secular private schools and colleges, will keep their children in yeshivas is yet to be seen. These days, Orthodox parents seem to want their children steeped in the Torah from the instant they can comprehend it. They roll their eyes at the popular secular concept of letting a child make his own choice about religion. "It's nonsense to say, 'I'm going to let my child make his own decision when he's seven,'" says one mother. "Tell me, how is a seven-year-old going to choose? By whether they give out good cookies?"

Jewish learning is a critical part of what goes on at Manhattan Day School. "Our Torah emphasis is traditional," says Rabbi David Kaminetsky. "It's about as right-wing as you can get." Accordingly, in fifth grade, boys' and girls' classes are separated, although their academic program is the same. "We find," says Kaminetsky, "that a high level of sanctity is present when the sexes are separated."

At Manhattan Day School, even the fun is religious. On the third floor, Ari and Shlomo are playing computer games during recess. The computer asks a question. Then a baseball diamond, bat, and ball appear on the screen, and the boys get a chance to hit a home run by answering the question. That's the hard part.

The question is not "How many homers did Babe Ruth hit?" but "Who said, 'Am I my brother's keeper?'"

On a lower floor, in kindergarten, boys are playing with chess pieces. The girls are busy rolling and braiding challah, which will be sent down to the school kitchen to be baked. Boys also braid challah.

After the eighth grade, most of these children will continue with religious education. The boys will go off to the Marsha Stern high school for boys, on the campus of Yeshiva University (known as YU) in Washington Heights. Most girls will attend the Tonya Soloveitchik high school, known as Central, on 38th Street, also part of YU. Many students will go off to Ramaz on the East Side, where the tenor of the education, while still Orthodox, is somewhat more liberal.

Elizabeth Wurtzel, now a sophomore at Harvard, started at Manhattan Day School in kindergarten. She stayed there through eighth grade and then went to Ramaz. She has nothing positive to say about yeshiva education. "Children aren't encouraged to develop their potential," she says. "There's nobody who says to them, 'Hey, you should be great, you should contribute to this world.'" She finds people her age who went through the yeshiva system startlingly unintellectual.

Irving Howe, the social historian and critic, though, doesn't believe that young modern Orthodox Jews suffer from restricted intellectual exploration—or that their children will. "As far as I can tell," he says, "a good number of these people are liberal-minded. They have the luxury of time to think. They read Kafka and Kundera. Then they perform a synthesis between what they know of their religion and what they see in the world." Most modern Orthodox parents—at least at Lincoln Square—seem not in the least interested in circumscribing their children's intellectual development. "The people I know," says Ellen Goldstein, "want their kids to go to Harvard, Princeton, and Yale. I can't say that they particularly want them to be rabbis."

There are problems with modern Orthodoxy, some of them endemic to the West Side, others to the foundations of Judaism. They are most keenly felt at Lincoln Square. Members of the congregation are young, and as their many children crowd their West Side apartments, they tend to move to Monsey or Teaneck or Kew Gardens Hills. There will always be more single young people to replace them, but singles are transient, and a synagogue needs an older, established contingent to make it solid and to supply it with funds.

There is other distress, felt acutely in the past few months. The discord at Lincoln Square stems from what has been labeled "the women's issue."

At best, Orthodoxy and feminism are incompatible. In the morning prayer, men thank God "who has not made me a non-Jew, who has not made me an ignorant person, and who has not made me a woman." The last of the three is explained and re-explained as thanking God for permitting the man the obligation to observe all religious rites, while women are exempt from religious duties that must be observed at fixed times, when they might be occupied with children or meals. Observant women of a feminist bent find this blessing more of an irritation. They do not wish to be excused from any of their religious duties.

Besides sitting apart from men in the synagogue (and farther away from the rabbi), women must cover their bodies and their heads. A woman must not have sexual relations with her husband while she is menstruating and for seven days afterward. Before they can begin having sex again, she must go to the *mikvah*, where she immerses herself in a ritual bath. The laws of family purity don't disturb modern Orthodox women nearly as much as one might expect. In fact, two weeks of abstinence is seen as a great boon to sex during the rest of the month. "*Mikvah* really does a lot for your sex life," says one woman. "Even rabbis say it keeps you going, keeps you fresh. Neither of you is as likely to say that you're exhausted when you're just bored."

Although women are free to work, by custom it is their task to take care of home and children. By the same law, they are not required to attend synagogue, nor are they expected to read the Talmud, which should be the main avocation of their husbands.

What bothers women most are restrictions on how and where they can pray. Only men can form a *minyan*, or prayer group (which requires a quorum of at least ten who are over thirteen), and only with a *minyan* can certain prayers be said. Women are encouraged to pray alone in the home, but many miss the camaraderie of a prayer group. Diane Sandoval is one of the leaders of the Women's Prayer Group, which meets every month or so on Shabbat with the backing of Lincoln Square's senior rabbi, Saul Berman. It never meets on the premises of the synagogue, however. That would further inflame the sentiments of the people who disapprove. Sandoval is cautious when she describes the effort. She is quick to say that none of the prayers they recite requires a *minyan*. "We are all committed to Halakah," she says. "Our desire is to join together for learning, to get and give sustenance."

It doesn't sound like a big deal, but it has upset some otherwise calm people. Hillel Gross, a longtime member of Lincoln Square, is violently opposed to women gathering separately for learning and prayer: "It's an explosive issue," he says, "with a terrible potential for divisiveness. Women need to occupy themselves with the real, essential nitty-gritty of Judaism," he says. "Women are entrusted with the very pillars of what Judaism is. The women who are demanding to be called up to read the Torah in *shul* should first learn the basics. They're going for the glamour instead."

Becoming an observant Jew as an adult invariably involves making sacrifices. It means giving up a way of life that most young, successful people consider their birthright. Not everyone who tries can do it. For some, the cost is too high. For others, the rewards are adequate compensation. They do not swallow the doctrine whole. They think and study. And sometimes they are consumed with frustration, angered by the rigidity of their ancient religion. They do not give up. Somehow, they find a way to stay with their faith.

"There's so much that Orthodoxy gives me," says Ellen Goldstein. "The things that bother me about it don't seem that important. I think it would be crazy to dump the whole thing because I don't want to cover my head all the time and I want to wear blue jeans. If I find it intolerable, I don't do it. Nobody's going to excommunicate me for it; that's not what Judaism is about. You can't expect things to change too fast. You're talking about a 4,000-year tradition that's been pretty good to women. Judaism was the first religion to prohibit a man from summarily dismissing his wife when he grew tired of her."

SPIRITUAL EXPLORERS[5]

When I left the Catholic church at 20, I was certain of two things. One was that God the Father, with his heaven, hell, and purgatory, was pretty ridiculous. The other was that there were forces larger than our lives and that the self didn't die with the body's death. But while there was plenty of support for the former belief in the left of the 1960s, there was little for the latter. I didn't know where to look for a structure for my deep, but vague, beliefs.

Politically, I moved from the left into the Women's Movement. By this time I'd separated my spiritual beliefs from my political ones, and there was nothing at first in the Women's Movement to suggest I should do otherwise.

I took a class in parapsychology and read a bit about Eastern religions, but nothing seemed to offer any framework for what, at that stage, was less a quest than a semidefined spiritual hunger. I did eventually discover a movement which, if it hasn't given me all the answers I'm looking for, has at least helped shape my journey.

The feminist spirituality movement began to emerge in the mid-1970s and has become one of the largest submovements within feminism. It's amorphous, blending in a surprisingly smooth amalgam radical feminism, pacifism, witchcraft, Eastern mysticism, goddess worship, animism, psychic healing, and a variety of practices normally associated with "fortune-telling." It exists nationwide and takes the form of large, daylong workshops, small meditation groups, and even covens that meet to work spells and do rituals under the full moon.

But to the women in feminist spirituality, witchcraft had even a more fundamental meaning. It is a women's religion, a religion of the earth, vilified by patriarchal Christianity, and now, finally, reclaimed. Witches seem to embody all that men fear and hate in women—strength and potentially destructive (to men) forces. Feminist historians have added another more poignant dimension to our understanding of the term: witch burnings have been

[5]Reprint of a magazine article by Karen Lindsey, a writer, teacher, and poet. *Ms.* 14:38+. D. '85. Copyright © 1985 by Karen Lindsey.

revealed as a form of genocide whose victims were old women, odd women, influential women, sexual women, and healers.

When I first discovered this movement, I was both intrigued and put off. Activists I knew expressed disdain for women who, they felt, were substituting new versions of old religious mumbo jumbo for useful actions. I couldn't blame them. When Susan Saxe, a former member of the Weather underground and a self-proclaimed feminist, was arrested and sent to Boston for trial, the feminist community here rallied to her support. Spiritual feminists formed "energy circles"—sitting in a circle, holding hands, projecting empowering thoughts her way. "That's all fine," one of Saxe's harried defense committee members told me bitterly, "but why don't they use their 'energy' to help raise money for her defense?"

I sympathized with my friend on the committee, but I also felt there was more to what these women were doing than we understood, and I set out to explore the possibilities. I took a class from a local spiritualist, Diane Mariechild, and learned how to meditate, to look for people's auras, to discover who I was in past lives, and to invoke the goddess.

The goddess, I learned, is central to feminist spirituality. But few see her as the literal equivalent of the Judeo-Christian god. Starhawk, currently one of the movement's prime figures, describes the goddess in her books *The Spiral Dance* (Harper & Row) and *Dreaming the Dark* (Beacon Press) as "immanence": all living creatures—male and female, human, animal, and plant—have the goddess within them. Others see the goddess as being both within living creatures and outside us. Karen Vogel, cocreator of the magnificent Motherpeace Tarot deck, told me recently, "I feel there's something in us, but some outside creator too—some force that's inexplicable. We all come from something, and it starts out female, the Mother." Vogel's vision of the creative force comes closest to my own.

Feminist scholarship examining prepatriarchal history spawned this goddess imagery. Merlin Stone's *When God Was a Woman* (Harcourt Brace Jovanovich) and similar works have provided a historical and an anthropological basis for assuming that God the Father was a relative newcomer. The assumption that goddess worship necessarily went hand in hand with matriarchy has been debated among feminist scholars, but feminist spirituality seems to accept it as a given—at least metaphorically. At times, it creates a gorgeous and necessary mythology whose usefulness transcends its literal truth. When I feel assaulted by our culture's insistence on the omnipotence of the male, I find the goddess image enormously healing.

Since these images are mythic, the way is left open for some interesting connections with feminists in traditional religions. In a recent interview, theologian Emily Culpepper noted that "a lot of radical Jewish feminists have made up their own symbol of the six-point Jewish star with the Amazon labrys" (double-edged ax). Other Jewish feminists use in their spirituality the image of the Shekhina, the female aspect of God. Emily Geoghegan, a minister in the United Church of Christ and wife of an Episcopal priest, sees no conflict between her ministry and her participation in goddess-involving ritual. "The feminine aspects of the godhead are very important and very deep in me," she says. "God the Father means something to me, but God the Mother hits my heart."

Feminist spirituality rejects the traditional Christian notion of living this life in anticipation of the afterlife, but most of its adherents talk in terms of cycles of life, death, and rebirth. "I always believed in reincarnation," says Starhawk, "long before I'd even heard of it." Years later, when she started studying witchcraft ("witchcraft has a far more complex theology than most people know"), she was pleased to learn that witches believed in reincarnation. "It's a very different version of reincarnation than Hindus believe in," she says. "It's not about working through till you can get off the wheel [of life]. It's about being reborn among those you know and loved before: it's about your connection with the planet. *This* world is the domain of the spirit; this world is paradise, or at least its potential."

For others, like Hallie Austen Iglehart, workshop leader and author of *Womanspirit: A Guide to Women's Wisdom* (Harper & Row), reincarnation doesn't take the form of a personal afterlife. "I think we're a mass of energy, and we all go back to a cosmic pool, and the energy comes back as parts of other forms. For example, I identify a lot with Virginia Woolf, and maybe that's because I, and others who connect with Woolf, have part of her in us, and so in that sense we all 'were' Virginia Woolf. It's as though we're a bundle of sticks tied together in one lifetime, and after we die the sticks break up and come back in other bundles."

Starhawk calls such belief "a sense of personal continuity in terms of past and future." We are part of what was, and we will exist, in some form, in whatever follows: we are intimately responsible to both.

A large part of feminist spirituality involves the use of "tools" to reach the psychic/spiritual depths. Many of these are also used in the occult arts: astrology, palmistry, Tarot cards, and gems and crystals. The tool I've used most, even before discovering feminist spirituality, is the Tarot cards, similar to playing cards but containing pictures of archetypal human images. There are many different decks, but predictably, most of them reinforce gender stereotypes. An exception is the 1983 Motherpeace deck, a feminist reinterpretation. (For example, the kings are replaced by shamans, who are both female and male.) Cocreator Karen Vogel's beliefs about the cards echo my own. "They're not about fortune-telling," she says. "Their primary function is to reveal what's going on for you right now. They're not outside of you. They can help you change your reality—if they show you a certain pattern in your life, they can help you change that pattern, like something you might learn in therapy."

Along with the tools of psychic journeying go rituals. Says Hallie Iglehart: "Human beings need ritual; we need practices that stimulate our senses, help us move into that spiritual place. Ritual helps us transcend our egos, to feel that heart connection with other people." For Starhawk, ritual provides "a very powerful means to communicate, to come together to make changes and transformations. It's not that ritual is wonderful per se—it's what you use it for."

Perhaps the strongest criticism of feminist spirituality is that it takes energy away from political work and puts it into forming energy circles or praying to the goddess. It's an accusation women in the spirituality movement react to strongly. They acknowledge that religion can be used as a modern opiate of the people but deny that it usually functions that way.

Starhawk notes that the notion of a spiritual/political dichotomy is a middle-class Western notion. "If you look into the cultures of people of color, you find that magic, spirituality, and politics aren't separate from each other." She discovered on a recent trip to Nicaragua that the Christianity of the workers was different from that of the church. "The Christ they invoke is an immanent Christ. The Missa Campesino [Peasants' Mass] says, 'Jesus is the truck driver changing his tire; Jesus is the man in the park buying a snow cone and complaining that he didn't get enough ice.'"

Other women point to Gandhi, to the black Christianity of the U.S. civil rights movement, to the Quakers in the suffrage and peace movements, and to the nuns recently killed in El Salvador. They view spirituality as the force that can make continued political struggle possible—a counter to the growing problem of burnout. Iglehart describes the rituals she has participated in at the end of violence-against-women conferences, when participants were exhausted by the horror of what they were dealing with and the enormity of the task of fighting it. "People who were drained would be energized and focused through the ritual, with a very clear idea of what they were going to do."

Reva Siebolt, who is active in feminist electoral politics, needs spirituality to enable her to continue her work. "The energy of Washington is so brutal I go numb," she says. Spirituality gives her not only the strength to go on working, but also new methods of working. "I'm learning to listen to my inner voice, to get ideas from deep inside me, not just from some logical structure outside." Warns Iglehart: "If there isn't a back and forth between political activists and women in spirituality, the political women are going to get burned out, and the spiritual women are going to be out in spaceland."

Other problems in feminist spirituality reflect those in the larger feminist movement. Spirituality has been accused, with some validity, of being a white woman's concern, centering on white pagan traditions and goddesses. But as more women of color have become involved, their traditions have transformed feminist spirituality. Hallie Iglehart created a slide show of goddess images that include goddesses from Asia, Africa, and Central America. The feminist Tarot decks—Motherpeace, Amazon, Thea—all use multiracial images. *Woman of Power,* a Boston area spirituality magazine, has a large number of black, Hispanic, and Native American writers.

Pat Camarena, a Mexican-American feminist involved in witchcraft, sees that involvement as an extension of her heritage. "The difference between Mexican and pagan witchcraft is that Mexican witchcraft isn't in opposition to Christianity—it takes the Virgin as its central figure. When you do a spell, you invoke Mary." She sees the Virgin as a manifestation of the goddess, and feels a strong connection to the spells and rituals her grandmother used when Pat was a child, and those she herself now uses.

Women in feminist spirituality seem to feel more comfortable working politically around other than specifically feminist issues. Starhawk traveled to Nicaragua this past winter as part of a Witness for Peace group. More typically, they work on antinuclear and environmental issues, sometimes getting arrested for passive resistance. They see this as an extension of feminism—men own Mother Earth as they own women. This parallels a complex phenomenon in the Women's Movement as a whole: the feminist newspaper *New Women's Times* suspended publication last year, attributing its difficulties in part to the "large-scale movement of women from feminist activism to peace and antinuclear work." Whether this is a hopeful or alarming phenomenon, it's clearly not limited to feminist spirituality.

Finally there are criticisms of the goddess concept itself. One is that the image of the nurturing Mother—the "female principle"—is simply a new version of an old male definition. As one activist complained: "The nurturer image is quite complicit with a very traditional notion of women that's being pushed very hard by the right. As feminists, it doesn't seem to be a good time to be confirming those images in any way."

At the same time, the image can lend itself to an assumption of natural male inferiority—the Goddess is Mother, the God merely consort and Son. Many women see this as ultimately no more satisfactory than God the Father with his compliant virgin, or Zeus lording it over the lesser deities. Lisa Leghorn, coauthor of *Woman's Worth: Sexual Economics and the World of Women* (Routledge & Kegan Paul), finds the goddess image problematic. "If you anthropomorphize Spirit, you impose on it all our hierarchical experience of power. For me, that limits the transformation of consciousness. My experience of Spirit has to do with the power of love and vision, and that power is genderless."

What place feminist spirituality has or will have in my own life, I'm not sure. I'm not wholly comfortable with the goddess. The image has power for me, a reclaiming of the birth image men stole from us when they invented gods capable of reproducing from their own bodies (Zeus creating Athena and Dionysius from his flesh; God the Father digging Eve out of Adam's body and later planting Jesus in Mary's incubator womb). But I don't see it justified by any superior female goodness operating in the world. Female nonviolence seems to me chiefly a function of being deprived of the tools of violence, and I'm not sure the Mother would end up being any less abusive than the Father has been. Whatever the creative force is, it's too large to be encompassed in human imagery.

Nonetheless, the existence of the movement is important in my life—and I suspect it's important to the survival of feminism itself. More and more, I see in women and men around me, as I've seen for so long in myself, a spiritual hunger. When political movements are new, or when they're making obvious or dramatic changes, that need can become submerged in the thrill of discovery or accomplishment. When the struggle is long and old and riddled with defeat, the strength to stay in it needs to come from deeper places. Feminist spirituality offers one way of reaching for those places. Even for women who may not choose it for their path, it offers the assurance that there *are* paths, and non-patriarchal images to bring to other existing spiritual modes. And because it's a spirituality based on political awareness, it creates a vital link between two modes of being that in Western intellectual culture are often dangerously severed.

Last spring, I went to a daylong workshop Hallie Iglehart ran in Boston. There were about 30 women, ranging from their early twenties to their early fifties, and from lesbian separatists to suburban homemakers. The rituals and meditations were fairly familiar to me. But this day gave me a taste of transcendence. Why that happened in this particular group I'm not sure. Part of it was Hallie's own clear, unjudgmental personality; part of it was the extraordinary combination of women who seemed to know, at that moment at least, that differences of lifestyle, need, personality, had nothing to do with who we were or what we were creating there. It strengthened me, taking me a step farther in my spiritual journey.

I know now that if I can't accept the goddess as my image of the creative spirit, I can at least accept her as a wise and valued friend—a useful companion who has opened doors to places I might never have seen without her. Feminist spirituality has given me something I'm grateful for.

HAWAII'S DOMESTICATION OF SHINTO[6]

An American flag waves briskly in the breeze beside a Shinto shrine on the major freeway leading from Honolulu to Pearl Harbor. Just five miles away is the spot where Japanese planes dropped their bombs on the American fleet. Few tourists rushing between Pearl Harbor and Waikiki realize the deep irony that flag symbolizes. But for those who fought in World War II or know the history of that encounter, the sight of an American flag at a shrine so closely associated with the adversary calls forth a whole complex of reactions.

It was Shinto, the native religion of Japan, that had not only given its wholehearted support to the war machine but had provided its very rationale: the myths and legends that led directly to the kamakazi pilots. Shinto taught that the emperor was a descendant of the very gods who had created their islands and that Japan thus had a mandate to rule the "world under one roof" (*Hakko Ichiu*).

The idea that such a religion could ever find a home in America would have seemed preposterous in the 1940s. In fact, at the close of the war one of the arguments used against statehood for Hawaii was that the Japanese population in Hawaii was so great and their loyalties so questionable that it would be risky to include them in our commonwealth.

Suspicion about the Japanese was building up long before Pearl Harbor, of course. In the 1930s, when Japan was invading China, Japanese women solicited funds on the streets of Honolulu for good-luck headbands for the soldiers. Imported films glorified Japan's conquests; when Hankow and Canton fell, victory services were held in Shinto shrines in Hawaii. The emperor's birthday was celebrated each year, and it was rumored that the Shinto god of war, Hachiman, was worshiped in one of Honolulu's shrines.

Once Hawaii was attacked, all of this changed. Japanese leaders, including Shinto priests, were rounded up and deported. It was impossible to resettle all of the Japanese, as California had

[6]Reprint of a magazine article by James Whitehurst, professor of religion at Illinois Wesleyan University. *The Christian Century.* 101:1100-1. Copyright © 1984, Christian Century Foundation. Reprinted by permission from the Nov. 21, 1984 issue of *The Christian Century.*

done, for they constituted nearly one-third of the population. The people of Hawaii simply had to learn to live together despite their qualms. Suspicions continued for a while: Shinto shrines were considered a hotbed of subversive activities by some and were vandalized; Japanese maids were thought to be spies; Japanese fishermen were believed to have directed the pilots of the emperor to their targets.

Nisei (second-generation Japanese) were eager to allay such suspicions. The 100th Reserve Officers Training Corps unit at the University of Hawaii was eager to fight in the war and prove that Japanese were loyal citizens of the territory. They soon got their opportunity as part of the much-decorated 442nd Battalion (all Japanese) that fought in Italy and France and, on VE Day, led the parade of Allied Forces.

Elderly Japanese did not find it so easy to shift allegiances. For years, their hopes had been pinned on the invincibility of the emperor; never in its 2,000-year history had Japan been conquered. One small group, the *Doshikai*, even refused to believe that the empire had collapsed in the summer of 1945. In October of that year, rumors surfaced in Honolulu that Japan had really won and that Prince Takamisu was on his way to Hawaii to negotiate a surrender. It was even whispered that President Harry Truman was going to Tokyo to apologize for the bombing of Hiroshima and Nagasaki.

In light of the persistence of such beliefs among a people nurtured with Shinto myths, it is understandable that many Americans felt it necessary to crush the Shinto faith once and for all. General Douglas MacArthur was in a quandary. Though he believed firmly in the freedom of religion, he saw the hold that fanatical Shintoism had on the Japanese mind. He pondered the matter for weeks; the solution finally came in the Allied Directive of December 15, 1945. Shinto was to be completely disestablished: it could not be taught in Japan's public schools, state funding would be eliminated, and the emperor would be persuaded to denounce his divinity (to "de-god" himself, as the GIs called it). On January 1, 1946, Emperor Hirohito shocked Japan with a radio announcement—broadcast repeatedly, so there could be no misunderstanding—stating that it was a mistake to think of him as a descendant of the gods or that the Japanese were a superior people.

That such a nationalistic religion could be found on American soil was a shock to me when I first encountered it 20 years ago, shortly after Hawaii became a state. I discovered that Shinto had come to Hawaii with Japanese workers looking for jobs on the sugar plantations a little more than a century ago. When they found they liked Hawaii and decided to stay, the workers sent word home for brides. Parents arranged marriages, and soon boatloads of "picture brides," as they were called, landed in Honolulu. Although marriages had been meticulously planned, the missionary-educated Hawaiians had qualms about their legality. To satisfy the public outcry, hasty weddings were arranged. At the Izumo Tai Shi shrine in downtown Honolulu, there were as many as 100 weddings a day. From these unions issued a population explosion that soon flooded the islands.

The immigrants brought with them their godshelves (*kamidana*) and the numerous festivals (*matsuri*), primarily associated with the agricultural cycle. As they became prosperous and moved to the cities, they constructed Shinto shrines. Their celebrations, especially the New Year's festival, became a part of the Hawaiian landscape.

America prides itself on its religious pluralism, its hospitality to all races and religions. But how did a religion which was so much a part of the distinctive Japanese way of life manage to survive on U.S. soil?

My search for an answer took me first to an investigation of the postwar status of Shinto in Japan. In an interview with Professor Naofusa Hirai at the Kokugakuin University (a Shinto institution) in Tokyo, I learned that Shinto is a religion of nature; its deities (*kami*) are personifications of natural forces such as rivers, seas, mountains, fire and wind—powers that create a sense of awe and wonder in the human spirit. Professor Hirai regrets the way Shinto became a tool of the state, a part of the war cult. "Shinto is eager," he said, "to shake off these nationalistic accretions and move strongly in the direction of internationalism." He, with other Shinto leaders, would interpret the phrase *Hakko Ichiu* (the world under one roof) as pointing to the goal of democratic world government. Far from being supernationalistic, Shinto priests today are often active in peace movements.

In returning to Hawaii, I wanted to see how this new interpretation was working in the States. I interviewed Bishop Kazoe Kawasaki, head priest of the Daijingu Shrine on Pali Highway in Honolulu. Kawasaki was himself a victim of wartime prejudice and spent most of the war years in the relocation center at Camp McCoy in Wisconsin. From him I learned how easy it is for Shinto to adapt to new situations, since one of its major teachings is just that: to blend with the social and cosmic environment. Kawasaki, a skillful communicator, employs numerous Western teaching methods such as flip charts and object lessons to get his point across. Although Shinto has generally been viewed as polytheistic, Kawasaki's flip charts show a decidedly monotheistic emphasis, which undoubtedly communicates better to a Western-educated audience. One Creator God, *Hitori Gami*, is shown as the source of all lesser *kami* manifestations.

Kawasaki held up a fun-house mirror at the center of the sanctuary near the large, round mirror that symbolizes *Amaterasu*, the sun goddess. "We should be perfect mirrors, clean and without blemish," he said, "and not distort things as this fun-house mirror does." Later he displayed a group of billiard balls in a triangular rack and showed how each ball moves in relation to the others. Comparing them with a display of square blocks, he said, "These cubes are too individualistic; they can't move well with their surroundings." A beautiful illustration of accommodation!

In the shrines of Hawaii, I found many examples of survival through adaption. Shinto has not yet succumbed to the Sunday-morning service, as has Buddhism: it celebrates in the evenings on specified days of each month, such as the 10th, 15th and 29th. But a sermon has been added to some services: wooden chairs often replace tatami mats with rounded pillows on the floor: tape-recorded music sometimes replaces the sound of drums, wooden blocks and bamboo flutes. Instead of a bamboo dipper at a basin of flowing water for purification at the entrance to a shrine area, one finds a water faucet, paper cups and a paper-towel dispenser! So far, there is no sign of Bingo, but shrines do regularly have their raffles. Stacks of rice flower, sake and fruit are often placed at the altar; after the gods have consumed the "essence," the food is given away at the end of the service as door prizes.

Through such adaptions, Shinto has made itself at home in its American setting. But Americanization is usually a two-way street. Is there anything to be learned from a religion as alien as Shinto?

Through the years, I have come to respect and appreciate it in ways that would seem impossible for one who grew up during World War II. For one thing, Shinto offers a needed corrective to our domineering attitude toward nature; it maintains a fine-tuned sensitivity to the "ground of Being," an intuitive awareness of the mystery which created and sustains us. Shinto shrines, with their unpainted surfaces and natural beauty, conjure up a feeling of sacred space as well as provide a place for quiet withdrawal. Passing under a *torii* arch and washing one's hands creates an atmosphere of readiness and receptivity. And when one arrives at the portal of the shrine, the simple clapping of the hands and bowing deeply helps one to restore a cosmic balance. Note that it is not an attuning of oneself to nature, as though nature is something outside the self; the Japanese have no word for "nature" in that sense. Yet it would be overly romanticizing to say that everything in modern Japan shows a perfect blending of humans and the environment; that is more likely a private achievement, expressed more in one's enclosed garden than in the public arena—witness the beer bottles littering the pilgrim's path up Mt. Fuji!

Is nature mysticism impossible in a secular age then? Alfred Bloom of the University of Hawaii's religion department thinks not. He insists that Shintoists, for all their love of nature, are still firmly grounded in the mundane world of business and economics. A Shinto priest sees nothing incongruous about waving his *harai-gushi* (purification wand with paper streamers) over the nose cone of a Boeing 747 and blessing it for secular use. Even in the machine he senses something that is more than just machine, since the divine is at the heart of all matter, even the technological products humans create. Perhaps there is something here that Westerners can appropriate.

If there is something to be gained from Shinto, there is also a pitfall to beware of: the peril that comes from too closely associating religion and culture. Shinto now regrets its close wartime associations with an imperialistic state, when it was used as a tool by the warlords.

I grew up in a church in Ft. Wayne, Indiana, where a prominent stained-glass window portrayed a cross before an American flag—as though there were no conflict between the two. And as a young pastor in Rockford, Illinois, I found that an American flag simply could not be removed from the sanctuary without splitting the church. My experience tells me that in a good many churches it would be easier to remove the cross. Are our temptations really so different from those that faced Shinto? We have our own myths of divine origin as a nation blessed by God with a "manifest destiny" to bring a large share of this continent "under one roof." A better knowledge of Shinto's history might save us from a "cultural Christianity" which tells people only what they want to hear.

In my youth, "Japs" were pictured as slant-eyed terrorists with bombs in their hands and daggers between their teeth; today the former enemy has become a friend. In wartime Hawaii, Japanese leaders were deported; today, the *nisei* Daniel Inouye represents our 50th state in the U.S. Senate. And in the short period of 25 years, the despised religion of Shinto has become domesticated: it is just another sect listed in the Yellow Pages of Hawaii's telephone books.

An American flag flying beside a Shinto shrine on the freeway to Pearl Harbor! An incredible sight one can encounter only in America. And only in Hawaii could it happen at such breathtaking speed.

III. THAT OUR CIVIL RIGHTS SHALL HAVE NO DEPENDENCE ON OUR RELIGIOUS OPINIONS

EDITOR'S INTRODUCTION

With so vast a range of religious groups operating within the borders of the United States, a high degree of tolerance is essential to prevent society from dissolving in conflict. The devastation that religious hatred can work on a country is plain to anyone with a minimal knowledge of world history, or, indeed, anyone with a television set, for whom scenes of murder in India, Ireland, and the Middle East will be all too familiar. It is for this reason that the neutrality of the government with respect to religion is considered so important, and why attempts to "Christianize" the government are widely regarded as a threat. (Interestingly, a recent study of a midwestern American community, *All Faithful People* [1983], found that a strong religious commitment correlates closely with a high level of religious tolerance.)

The founders of the American republic were eager to protect it from the religious conflict that had made Europe a killing ground for centuries. In "The Bicentennial of the Virginia Statute," William Lee Miller, writing in *Christian Century*, closely analyzes the text of the famous bill, drafted by Thomas Jefferson and sponsored by James Madison, that established religious freedom in formerly Anglican Virginia and that influenced the development of the Bill of Rights. The actual religious beliefs of Jefferson, Madison, and their colleagues—a subject of much recent misinformation—is clarified by Robert P. Hay's article, "The Faith of the Founding Fathers," reprinted from *USA Today*.

It has been a constant challenge to Americans in the two hundred years since the signing of the Constitution to uphold the founders' ideals of religious freedom. Nor has it been easy to agree on what forms these ideals should take in law and public policy. In "Religion and a Neutral State: Imperative or Impossibility?," a speech made to the Christian Legal Society, Carl H. Esbeck meditates on the dilemma posed by the constitutional requirement of keeping government and religion autonomous without impairing the functioning of either. Samuel Rabinove's "Religious Freedom for All: A Jewish Perspective," an address to the Second World Congress on Religious Liberty, considers the problem from the viewpoint of a religious minority whose existence has repeatedly been jeopardized. Both pieces are reprinted from *Vital Speeches of the Day*. "Voices of Reason, Voices of Faith," originally published in *Time* magazine during the 1984 presidential campaign, is a collection of remarks on the issue of church-state separation by scholars, clergy, and activists from a variety of backgrounds.

THE BICENTENNIAL OF THE VIRGINIA STATUTE[1]

The Bicentennial music has not played as loudly as it might have during the period just drawing to a close (1984–86), for one of the distinctive achievements of the American revolutionary period: the Virginia Statute for Religious Freedom. When Thomas Jefferson returned to Virginia from Philadelphia in 1776 he turned his attention to the cause of religious freedom. However, his bill of religious freedom, drafted in 1777 as part of a comprehensive revising of the Virginia law code, stalled in the Virginia Assembly in 1779.

By 1784 Jefferson was in Paris as U.S. minister to France and James Madison assumed primary sponsorship of the bill. The bill was opposed by Patrick Henry, the most popular political figure in the state. Henry's proposal for a general assessment for religion almost won—in fact *did* win in a vote of the committee as a whole—before Madison managed to postpone further action on the issue to the following year. The climax of the debate came in the legislative session that began in the fall of 1785, just 200 years ago. Madison guided the bill through a complicated parliamentary struggle and against considerable opposition in the House of Delegates. After succeeding there, he had to overcome the objections of the Senate. Finally, on January 16, 1786, the two bodies reached a compromise, and three days later Jefferson's great bill

[1]Reprint of a magazine article by William Lee Miller, chairman of the department of rhetoric and communication studies at the University of Virginia, Charlottesville. *The Christian Century*. 102:1171-5. Copyright © 1985, Christian Century Foundation. Reprinted by permission from the December 18-25, 1985 issue of *The Christian Century*.

became law. A landmark in the history of the struggle for religious freedom, the Virginia statute was a model for other states and, most important, for the guarantee of religious liberty incorporated in the U.S. Bill of Rights.

In a letter to Jefferson a week after the legislative session had ended, Madison wrote: "I flatter myself that [the enacting clauses] have in this country extinguished for ever the ambitious hope of making laws for the human mind." One way we can honor this accomplishment and begin to appreciate its significance is by taking a look at the wording of Jefferson's statute.

When you look at the Virginia Statute for Religious Freedom, you find an interesting form. It is rather like an introduction to a waltz. The actual enactment itself is quite short. It is preceded by a long and passionate preamble, four times as long, one full clause-crammed page, that sets forth the argument, and is intellectually the important part of the statute. The short paragraph of the enactment itself then is followed by a concluding paragraph that might be said to be rather amusingly un-Jeffersonian, of which more below.

Here's the way Jefferson, working on the revisal in 1777, had started out:

Well aware that the opinions and belief of men depend on their own will, but follow involuntarily in the evidence proposed to their minds; that Almighty God hath created the mind free, *and manifested his supreme will that free it shall remain by making it altogether insusceptible of restraint*;

The Senate of Virginia, in those exchanges with the House of Delegates that Madison described, deleted the two clauses in italics and a later one of the same tendency. This later deletion appears in the clause, perhaps strategic in its piety, about the "holy author of our religion" who chose not to propagate that religion by coercion, "as was in his Almighty power to do"—here comes the deleted part—"*but to extend it by its influence on reason alone. . . .*" Surely it will come as news to some that Christianity spread across Europe and the world by that means alone.

These three deletions plainly were not stylistic only, although a stylistic case certainly can be made for them. They take out the most sweeping of Jefferson's assertions about the ineluctable sovereign sway of human reason—"follow involuntarily the evidence proposed to their minds"; the free mind "altogether insusceptible of restraint"; "extend it by its influence on reason alone." Madison wrote to Jefferson, in the letter that we have been quoting, that the amendments voted by the Senate "did not affect the substance though they somewhat defaced the composition," but one may argue that exactly the reverse is true. They *improved* the composition by eliminating some of Jefferson's cluttering effort to say too much, leaving the strong phrase "Almighty God hath created the mind free" in its ringing clarity as the beginning.

But deleting those clauses certainly did affect the substance. Dumas Malone wrote that as a result of the Senate's action—to which Madison and the House of Delegates in the tired ending of the session had to agree—"the Statute does not rest on quite so broad a base as the one its author had designed." You can say that, or you say it no longer asserts so insistently rationalistic a foundation for its program, but allows implicitly for the nonrational elements that many—certainly Madison's indispensable allies the evangelical "enthusiasts"—see to be important, alongside "reason" in the making of human convictions.

As these suppressed clauses indicate, Jefferson held an intellectualistic picture of belief, grounded in the ineluctable power of *argument* and *evidence*. His friend Madison held such a view also. Madison had written in his *Memorial and Remonstrance*: " . . . the opinions of men, depending only on the evidence contemplated by their own minds, cannot follow the dictates of other men."

This view of religion is rather at odds with the religion of "enthusiasm," conversions and revivals—religion that, whatever its connection with reason, argument and evidence, was certainly linked to passion and will—that had furnished the chief popular support for the statute, and was to spill out across the country once again during Jefferson's presidency, and Madison's, and many times thereafter. These spillings were to shape a rather different kind of religion, and religious liberty—a rather different country—than Jefferson and Madison, one may presume, expected. For the American system of religious liberty, as for the American system of government, Jefferson, Madison and a small group of other heirs of the Enlightenment furnished much of the brain power, but the religion of revival furnished the troops. . . .

Well aware that Almighty God hath created the mind free, that all attempts to influence it by temporal punishments or burthens, or by civil incapacitations, tend only to beget habits of hypocrisy and meanness, and are a departure from the plan of the holy author of our religion, who being lord both of body and mind, yet chose not to propagate it by coercions on either, as was in his Almighty power to do; . . .

Long after these events, Jefferson wrote in his "Autobiography," a short piece composed for his family in his 77th year, that an amendment had been proposed, way back then in 1786, inserting the words "Jesus Christ" before the phrase "holy author of our religion," thus making it read "the plan of Jesus Christ the holy author of our religion, who being . . . " and so on. "The insertion," he added, "was rejected by a great majority, in proof that they meant to comprehend, within the mantle of [the statute's] protection, the Jew and the Gentile, the Christian and the Mahometan, the Hindoo, and infidel of every denomination." Whether or not a great majority of the Assembly meant any such inclusiveness, the older Thomas Jefferson certainly meant it, and the younger one no doubt would have liked to have meant it too, except that as he composed the bill he used a phrase, no doubt for strategic reasons, that sounds otherwise: "*the* holy author of *our* religion. . . . "

Let us start over again with the long preamble, the argument of which has a biting fervor not usually found in Jefferson's cool felicitous writing—not found even in the Declaration of Independence, except perhaps in the indictments of King George.

Well aware that Almighty God Hath created the mind free, that all attempts to influence it by temporal punishments, or burthens, or by civil incapacitations, tend only to beget habits of hypocrisy and meanness, and are a departure from the plan of the holy author of our religion, who being lord both of body and mind, yet chose not to propagate it by coercions on either, as was in his Almighty power to do; that the impious presumption of legislators and rulers, civil as well as ecclesiastical, who, being themselves but fallible and uninspired men, have assumed dominion over the faith of others, setting up their own opinions and modes of thinking as the only true and infallible, and as such endeavoring to impose them on others, hath established and maintained false religions over the greatest part of the world and through all time. That to compel a man to furnish contributions of money for the propagation of opinions which he disbelieves, is sinful and tyrannical . . .

. . . In Jefferson's draft, he had written, in the last clause quoted above, "that to compel a man to furnish contributions of money for the propagation of opinions which he disbelieves *and abhors,* it is sinful and tyrannical. . . . " He thus made explicit the fact, all too evident from the history of the human race, that our differing beliefs are not always the amiable companions taking different paths up the Mount of Truth which, in the multifaith nation Jefferson helped to found, it is often prudent to pretend they are. They can *abhor* each other. The use of the strong word *abhor* betrays again a considerable warmth on Jefferson's part, and a perception about the underside of the contest of beliefs not always present in the genial and harmonious optimism of his line of intellectual descent.

The Senate of Virginia took out that word, and Madison and the House did not fight for it.

Jefferson held not only to religious liberty but to the separation of church and state, and a strictly voluntary way in religion as the means to achieve it. Of course it was he who was later, in 1801, in his often quoted letter to Baptists in Danbury, Connecticut, to coin the metaphor of a "wall" of separation that has haunted this subject ever since, but though participants in this Virginia struggle had not yet been favored with that subsequently ubiquitous metaphor, they had arrived at the practical point of policy it described. Through the complexities of Virginia politics from 1776, when the established church effectively collapsed, down to the enactment of Jefferson's statute, the issue had been effectively reduced to these two alternatives: a "general assessment" for religion, under which citizens would pay their tax for the denomination of their choice, and a complete separation. Jefferson's bill of course was the expression of the second position. He opposed using government's power even on behalf of a religion a citizen believes in; this was the concrete point of policy to which Virginia politics had maneuvered itself at the time the statute was enacted.

 . . . that even the forcing him to support this or that teacher of his own religious persuasion, is depriving him of the comfortable liberty of giving his contributions to the particular pastor whose morals he would make his pattern, and whose powers he feels most persuasive to righteousness, and is withdrawing from the ministry those temporary rewards, which proceeding from an approbation of their personal conduct, are an additional incitement to earnest and unremitting labours for the instruction of mankind; . . .

He made plain that sharp division between the *civil* and the *religious* that he and the dissenters held in common. One of his assertions most often quoted puts it this way: " . . . that our civil rights have no more dependence on our religious opinions than our opinions in physics or geometry."

Some religious folk may draw back a little from the implications of the way that point is put: that for the purposes of the state and of society—of our living together—our religious opinions have no more significance than our opinions on physics or geometry. Not so, says the believer, and maybe others as well; "opinions" about the ultimate issues of life and death, good and evil, and the meaning of existence *do* have considerable civic significance—more than "opinions," if such there be, about right angles and squares.

> . . . that our civil rights have no more dependence on our religious opinions than our opinions in physics or geometry; that therefore the proscribing any citizen as unworthy of public confidence by laying upon him an incapacity of being called to offices of trust and emolument, unless he profess or renounce this or that religious opinion. . . .

The orthodox interlocutor of Jefferson may find a further touch of latitudinarianism in that rather shoulder-shrugging phrase "this or that opinion" about religion. Such an outlook— the dominant modern outlook, to be sure—is more evident still in another Jeffersonian observation, perhaps the most often quoted of all he made on this subject. It comes not from the statute but from his *Notes on the State of Virginia*: "But it does no injury for my neighbour to say that there are twenty gods, or no god. It neither picks my pocket nor breaks my leg." The orthodox have historically responded: But it does do me and my children and my neighbors and the society we all share much injury, more substantial injury perhaps than pocket-picking or leg-breaking, though of a less tangible kind, to say there is no God. Think not only of what one of our modern television evangelists might say—with his attacks on the "humanists" who "pull down God from the skies" (quite a concept, that one) and on "Godless" this and that, but also of what a G. K. Chesterton might say. Your no-Godliness affects the fabric of our shared world. But a "fastidious atheist" (to borrow a phrase from Justice William O. Douglas, who said humorously that such a one might even object to "God save this honorable court") could of course retort that your Godliness pollutes our shared world. And so we have to live together, with these counterclaims of injury. The Jeffersonians say— exactly because we disagree so directly—that the outcome should be left to free choice; it should not be determined by the power of law.

Jefferson's statute mingles pragmatic with principled arguments, as advocates do in the heat of rhetorical battle. His fundamental claim, however, rests on substantive human rights, as he will insist in the most extraordinary way, at the end of the statute itself. Though he believed that voluntary religion is best for all concerned, and thus may be justified by arguments from utility, his position at its foundation did not rest on a calculation about what would prove to be "best," but on an intrinsic claim of natural right, freedom of "conscience" or of "mind."

Or perhaps on two natural rights, closely interwoven. The claim of the right for every person to believe and profess whatever he does believe resounds through the whole document. Not only the many styles of believers in one God but also the believers in 20 gods or in none may rightfully claim full freedom to hold and to profess their belief. There is in addition a closely related "natural right," referred to in the passage that follows, the right of every person to full, unlimited participation in civic life—to hold office, to receive honors, to be a citizen in every particular—without regard to religion.

> . . . that our civil rights have no dependence on our religious opinions, any more than on our opinions in physics or geometry; that therefore the proscribing any citizen as unworthy of the public confidence by laying upon him an incapacity of being called to offices of trust and emolument, unless he profess or renounce this or that religious opinion, is depriving him injuriously of those privileges and advantages to which, in common with his fellow citizens, he has a natural right; . . .

These two rights, or two aspects of the one right, represent the two dimensions, personal and social, of civil liberty in general and of religious liberty in particular. The moral grounding of religious liberty in a democracy rests upon the recognition that the human being transcends every social order, most especially in his most fundamental convictions. But it rests also on the need of the society, and the benefit of society, of uncoerced consent of the governed.

Jefferson did make an argument about the benefit to religion at least from the negative side: Compulsion, he pointed out, damages religion at its core. Already he has said that attempts to coerce belief "tend only to produce habits of hypocrisy and meanness." Now he adds further:

> . . . that it tends also to corrupt the principles of that *very* religion it is meant to encourage, by bribing, with a monopoly of worldly honours and emoluments, those who will externally profess and conform to it; that though indeed these are criminal who do not withstand such temptation, yet neither are those innocent who lay the bait in their way; . . .

Jefferson did not ordinarily exhibit the full awareness of the inclination of a man's interests to warp his thought that his friend Madison was to remark a few years later in Federalist 10 and 51. But on the subject of religion, Jefferson took for granted that any magistrate would "of course" make his own "opinions" the sole rule of his actions.

> . . . that to suffer the civil magistrate to intrude his powers into the field of opinion and to restrain the profession or propagation of principles on supposition of their ill tendency is a dangerous fallacy, which at once destroys all religious liberty, because he being of course judge of that tendency will make his opinions the rule of judgment, and approve or condemn the sentiments of others only as they shall square with or differ from his own; . . .

Pursued further, that assertion—that any person elevated to the civil magistracy would "of course" make judgments strictly to promote his own commitment—might call into question the social functioning of Jefferson's own rationalism and optimism. Just how is it that truth is to prevail in combat with error if none of us can recognize a piece of the former that goes against our prior opinion? Or the rights of persons to hold the latter? Perhaps even "civil magistrates" can do better, even in the field of "opinion," than Jefferson here allows—or Jefferson's own world of rational argument could scarcely function.

In any case, say the Jeffersonians, the state's purposes are fully served by intervening only when an *act* occurs. The statute contains this sentence, quoted at important moments thereafter by the U.S. Supreme Court, when that body made a distinction, in the "free exercise" of religion, between "belief," which should be completely free, and "action" based on religious belief, which cannot always be so: " . . . that it is time enough for the rightful purposes of civil government for its officers to interfere when principles break out into overt acts against peace and good order . . . " Jefferson put the whole point succinctly (he was not always succinct) in a straightforward sentence that was perhaps too blunt for Virginians with their establishmentarian hangover, because the Assembly struck it out: "the opinions of men are not the object of civil government, nor under its jurisdiction."

For Jefferson, religious liberty was a part of that larger liberty (larger to him—larger and also smaller to many believers), freedom of the *mind*, which it takes no search to discover to be the center of Jefferson's life: founder of the University of Virginia, most prominent early advocate of universal education, defender of freedom of the press, enthusiastic supporter of science and friend of scientists, aristocrat only in his belief in a natural—intellectual—aristocracy. That list of achievements that Jefferson chose for his epitaph showed again that freedom of the mind was central for him—more central, alas, than it was to prove in practice for the nation of which he was intellectually the most significant of the founders. His great oath, which now encircles his memorial in Washington, is "I have sworn upon the altar of God eternal hostility against every form of tyranny over the mind of man."

The most important passage in the Virginia statute is the climax of the argument in the preamble, which spreads the claims hitherto restricted to religion out into a broader territory. The famous passage, to which we will return in a moment, might almost be presented as the quintessence of Jeffersonianism:

. . . that truth is great and will prevail if left to herself; that she is the proper and sufficient antagonist to error, and has nothing to fear from the conflict unless by human interposition disarmed of her natural weapons, free argument and debate; errors ceasing to be dangerous when it is permitted freely to contradict them.

Jefferson's sharp condemnation of all compulsion in this domain is compressed in the enactment itself, now stated as the Law of Virginia:

Be it enacted by the General Assembly [or: We the General Assembly of Virginia do enact] that no man shall be compelled to frequent or support any religious worship, place, or ministry whatsoever, nor shall be enforced, restrained, molested, or burthened in his body or goods, nor shall otherwise suffer, on account of his religious opinions or belief; . . .

Then comes the other side of this thoroughgoing repudiation of all compulsion—the securing of unfettered freedom:

. . . but that all men shall be free to profess, and by argument to maintain, their opinions in matters of religion, and that the same shall in no wise diminish, enlarge or affect their civil capacities.

It is one of the familiar effects of a thoroughgoing social achievement that those who come afterward, and live their lives taking its benefits for granted, have a hard time believing it ever was much of an issue. Yesterday's battle cry has become today's commonplace. But the issue of religious liberty had been of great moment, and still was (still is) elsewhere in the world. With this statute Virginia became the first state to end by law all forms of official religious persecution and exclusion and compulsion—to break with the whole ugly history of the use of state power to punish, enforce, suppress and enact religious beliefs.

Now the final paragraph, which was described above as rather amusingly un-Jeffersonian.

And though we know well that this assembly [has] no power to restrain the acts of succeeding Assemblies, . . . and that therefore to declare this act irrevocable would be of no effect in law; yet we are free to declare, and do declare, that the rights hereby asserted are the natural rights of mankind, and that if any act shall be hereafter passed to repeal the present or to narrow its operation, such act will be an infringement of natural right.

May we not find in this paragraph an implied wariness that error, in this field, just might make a comeback after all? And that truth, even equipped with its natural weapons, might still have something to fear? More clearly one can discover in this last paragraph the un-Jeffersonian desire, suppressed but real, to bind the future.

Jefferson is distinctive among the American founding fathers, and indeed perhaps among thinkers about politics anywhere, in the thoroughness with which he wanted to free the present from the encumbrances of the past. He was, of course, one of the purest products of the Enlightenment, a man who took the institutions of human societies intellectually in hand, put them under the clear-glassed microscope of human reason, and found many of them defective. They were defective by reason's test—the degree to which they provided for human freedom and human happiness. Therefore, repair them, for the earth belongs to the living. . . .

Jefferson had a remarkable view about the discontinuity of generations: "one generation is to another as one independent nation to another," he wrote. Here is an elaboration of his view on this point by the historian Edmund Morgan:

He liked to think of generations as nations, and he sought independence not merely of Americans from England but of every generation of Americans from the preceding one. At the risk of putting words in the mouth of a man who could speak quite well enough for himself, I would say that Jefferson's public career focused on securing for Americans a right of expatriation from the past.

Expatriation from the past! *By right!* Each generation a nation to itself! Ah, yes, but now when something deep and central in him is touched—freedom of religion, as he understands it—he wishes he could prevent any expatriation. On this matter he wanted with his own dead hand to reach out from the past and to shake an admonitory finger at any future Assembly, at any future American generation, that would diminish this statute. Don't do it! In his statute something final, eternal, permanent, beyond all generations, applying to all generations, had been captured: a natural right of man. Freedom of the mind.

THE FAITH OF THE FOUNDING FATHERS[2]

For myself I fully and conscientiously believe, that it is the will of the Almighty, that there should be diversity of religious opinions among us.
—Thomas Paine, *Common Sense* (1776)

The rights of conscience we never submitted, we could not submit. We are answerable for them to our God. The legitimate powers of government extend to such acts only as are injurious to others. But it does me no injury for my neighbor to say there are twenty gods, or no God. It neither picks my pocket nor breaks my leg.
—Thomas Jefferson, *Notes on Virginia* (1781)

The religion, then, of every man, must be left to the conviction and conscience of every man; and it is the right of every man to exercise it, as these may dictate. This right is, in its nature, an unalienable right.
—James Madison (1785)

Full-page spreads appearing in more than one American newspaper recently have quoted some of the best known of America's Founding Fathers on things religious in a purported attempt to make it clear to everybody that those men of the Revolutionary Age were preeminently men of faith. [For the purposes of this article, the term "Founding Fathers" is being used in a broad sense to include those men of the generation of 1776 who participated in or provided the rationale for the American Revolution, who fought for reforms in their own states, who attended the Philadelphia convention of 1787, or who served the young nation in a diplomatic post abroad. In other words, "Founding Fathers" as here defined are not just those who helped draft the

[2]Reprint of a magazine article by Robert P. Hay, associate editor of *USA Today* and associate professor of history at Marquette University. *USA Today*. 114:80–3. My. '86. Copyright © 1986 by the Society for the Advancement of Education.

Constitution *per se*, but those as well who made any major contribution to the establishment of the American Republic. Certainly, John Adams is best thought of as a Founding Father, even though he was American Minister to England at the time the Constitution was being drawn up. Similarly, Thomas Jefferson is also clearly a Father of the American creed, even though he represented the U.S. in France from 1784 to 1789 and was not—as George Washington, Benjamin Franklin, Alexander Hamilton, James Madison, and others *were*—physically present at the Constitutional Convention.] Similarly, not a few people prominently associated with the religious and political right have intoned that a speedy return to the first principles of some ancient and hallowed American faith *is* indeed called for in this morally benighted age of communistically inspired materialism, godless schools, and abortion on demand. From numerous pulpits, political forums, and editorial pages, the theme crescendos throughout the land.

Human affairs are ever filled with irony, and there are many little ironies—and some greater ones—involved in these pious and impassioned invocations of the faith of the Founding Fathers by the firm of Falwell, Helms, and (numerous) Associates. Not the least of these ironies is that some of those men of Revolutionary War vintage who most prided themselves on their liberalism and even their radicalism on religious questions are being metamorphosed into devotees of fundamentalism or persons somehow sympathetic to its social and political goals; or, at the very least, such an attempt at metamorphosis is being made.

From a historian's point of view, what we have here is a most interesting example of historical revisionism, one all the more engaging because it is being done on a broad cultural scale instead of in the narrower academic setting that so often serves as the context for historical reinterpretations. Historical revisionism—whether of the broadly cultural or the more narrowly academic variety—is often desirable; and it is, in any case, virtually inevitable. Merely to think about the past is, in some important ways, to revise it. There is no way for us humans to have a pure and undiluted history, the absolute truth in and of itself, for the past is always called up to be called on—that is, called on to serve, in one way or another, the present generation and its multitudinous (and often conflicting) interests. Surely, however, such revisionism has its outer limits of legitimacy, and any thesis which suggests that the views of George Washington, Benjamin Franklin, or Thomas Jefferson have much in common with the preachments of today's socio-politico-religious right wing simply will not wash. As a distinguished and largely self-taught Canadian paleontologist of the early 20th century used to say, the particular theory of development is nothing without the fossil. As any serious student of that evolution which is the American past could add, the historical thesis is nothing without facts.

Religious Individualism

What is the truth? Just what are the most salient facts about the faith of the Founding Fathers? One of the most fundamental facts is that there were among them many faiths and not just one. Religion was, for them, largely an individual affair. Religious truth was not something to be imposed by the community, by the government, by tradition, or by creed so much as it was something the individual must choose (or choose not to choose) for himself. Let each and every person decide. In a real sense, the American Enlightenment represented the Reformation carried almost to the nth degree.

If, as some have posited, the inner logic of Protestantism was to make each soul a church unto itself, then several of our Founding Fathers would be fit candidates for the title of the quintessential Protestant type. To be sure, Washington and Jefferson were formally Anglican (or Episcopalian), but in matters of doctrine and dogma, each man was the sole communicant of a church of one. Franklin also self-consciously fashioned his own creed, and there were many others in late-18th-century America who did the same thing.

Religious individualism was a cherished principle to these enlightened types, partly because it seemed a thing clearly dictated by Nature and Nature's God. Conceivably, as the skeptical Thomas Paine once wrote, Almighty God had had the power to force all of his creatures to see religious matters in exactly the same way. Quite obviously, given the diversity of opinion throughout history, the Almighty had not exercised any such divine prerogative. To Paine and to others, this meant that God intended as well for the mind of man to remain forever unfettered in the presence of merely earthly power. Throughout history, unfortunately, lords temporal and spiritual have conspired to fetter the human mind, the better to enslave the human frame. In this modern age, however, increasingly enlightened people were on to all the little tricks of priests and popes and kings and feudal lords. Humankind was walking out of the darkness of ignorance, superstition, and persecution, marching inexorably into the glorious light, it was believed.

For many of the Founding Fathers, the key to all future human progress lay in always remembering that a worthy faith was not a thing to be blindly accepted, but was, instead, something to be reasoned about by each and every individual believer. Everything possible needed to be done to secure this individuality of belief that was deemed so vital for the future of a republican order, so essential to the liberty of humankind. What the Founding Fathers did was a radical thing, and the time in history when they did it made it far more radical than it would have been in a later, more secular age. They created, in a land of countless churches, a nation that officially had no church.

Some of these individual and very individualistic Fathers went further still. Not only did they succeed in disestablishing Anglicanism in post-Revolutionary Virginia and in constitutionally eliminating the possibility of the establishment of any one faith in the nation as a whole, but they also, in the inner sanctum of their own minds, dismantled Christianity in its traditional form.

Since Nature and Nature's God had made freedom of religious opinion an inherent and inalienable right of man, that right must not be tampered with, in the Fathers' own time or in any age that was yet to be, by any minority or even by any majority, however moral or right it might think itself. Thus, if he chose to do so, each American of the future could be—like Washington, Jefferson, Franklin, and Paine—a faith unto himself. The Constitution itself guaranteed it because an even higher law than that— the law of Nature—guaranteed it.

Another of the numerous ironies is that, when these intensely individualistic American Fathers reasoned about religious matters, they found themselves agreeing on certain basic precepts. This was a circumstance, however, that surprised them less than it pleased them, for this meant that their own personal experience was serving to confirm their deeply held conviction that a community of shared belief need not be imposed on people by force of arms or threats of eternal hell-fire and damnation, but could, instead, be arrived at voluntarily. When Thomas Jefferson and John Adams found themselves agreeing on some elements of belief (and, admittedly, agreeing to disagree on others) and when, to an even greater degree, Jefferson found himself thinking many of the very same thoughts that James Madison thought, it bore ample testimony that a community of individuals need not be merely a contradiction in terms. Looking back upon history, enlightened spirits beheld civil discord, wars between nations, and endless strife—all flowing naturally from attempts at enforced uniformity. On the other hand, they saw, as if in a vision unfolding about them, a far more genuine community of skeptical, but rational, men.

If, over time, endless numbers of complex creeds and countless bodies of dogma had been concocted to bind the faithful together, now just a few simple ideas served as the necessary cords of enlightened connectedness. It seemed undeniable that there was balance and regularity in the natural world. The passing seasons suggested this to the farmer (and Washington, Jefferson, and Adams all liked to think of themselves as farmers). In its more formal way, Sir Isaac Newton's *Mathematical Principles of Natural Philosophy* furnished those who read it with the very same message—there was order in things universal. Such order meant design, and such design meant a designer. To a man, then, the Founding Fathers began with a belief in the existence of God the Creator.

One of the most striking differences between the American Enlightenment and its French counterpart was the utter absence in the former of that atheistical streak clearly evident in the latter, a tendency which especially manifested itself during that stage of the French Revolution when an attempt was made to do away with organized religion and to set up, in its stead, the worship of a man-made goddess of pure reason. Americans of the late 18th century continued to worship God, even if liberal thinkers insisted on worshipping the deity in their own way. After all, to use one's head was one of the best forms of worship.

Having created—and having done so perfectly—there was little need for their Creator to constantly intervene in the affairs of enlightened men. Instead, the deist's God worked mainly, if not entirely, through the laws built into the universe at the moment of creation. The blatant providentialism of 17th-century American Puritanism had obviously receded as a concept, although it had not entirely disappeared. Some of those who still cherished the old idea of an intervening Providence now made that force one less whimsical and capricious, one much more bound somehow by its own rules of order.

Thus, even among many who frequented the churches in an era when the percentage of church memberships was down, the idea of a wrathful Jehovah had steadily lost ground to a kind of "reasoned providentialism." Admittedly, even in men who saw God as a somewhat more remote Moral Governor of the Universe, there was still at times the very human tendency to make God anthropomorphic. Sometimes they also imagined, as so many before and after them have, a *father*; not a father enraged at the endless transgressions of an ungrateful and utterly depraved progeny, however, but, rather, a loving father smiling down benevolently on all his children, wishing universal humanity well.

Rules and Reason

This Benevolent Protector of the World, that spirit that was God, had shown his concern for human beings by creating them, by building in rules of order for their benefit, and by giving them minds rational enough to perceive these natural principles and hearts good enough to want to follow them. Not only had God ordained rules for the universe as a whole, he had created laws as well for all the little spheres of human activity—for the realms of religion, politics, economics, education, science, and so on. What was true in macrocosm, then, was just as true in microcosm. As the Founding Fathers believed, all those investigators, regardless of field, who perceived God's rational principles most clearly, who pointed them out to others, and who thereby benefitted others deserved to be seen as heroes and as godly men besides. Thus, Jefferson declared Francis Bacon, Isaac Newton, and John Locke, men of science and liberty, to be the three greatest men who had ever lived. Many 18-century American skeptics would have joined Jefferson in putting these three, among others, in the Enlightenment's Pantheon.

The essence of morality for non-dogmatic souls lay not in following every jot and tittle of some set of senseless thou-shalt-not's, but, rather, in serving humanity. The greatest service that could be rendered in their own day, they concluded, was not in the pulpit, but in the ministry of public-interest politics. While

Nature and Nature's God may have intended freedom, tyranny had been humankind's fate almost since the dawn of time. The great work still remaining to be done, then, was to see to the creation of a political order in which man would be as free in a state of society as he had been in the state of nature. Such a republican society in the U.S. could be an example to universal humanity, inspiring the downtrodden everywhere, and in time doing nothing less than changing the course of human history. Freed at long last from tyranny, man would be as happy here below as he had always had a right to be. Freed from the superstition of the ages, man would now worship primarily by using his God-given reason. Reason would discover the truths of science. Science would lead to progress and progress would lead, if not to perfection, then at least to a steadily improving life.

This, in essence, was their creed, the faith of the generation of Founding Fathers. It was for this faith that a weary Washington sacrificed most of that retirement at his beloved Mount Vernon he had so long dreamed of. It was this faith that again and again wooed a thin-skinned Jefferson (who was always ambivalent about political involvement) off his little mountain and into the thick of the political fray. Both these men, and others like them, offered up their time and energy and resources and devotion on the altar of this faith. "By their deeds ye shall know them," says the Bible. By their works we have long known the Founding Fathers, and by their works we know them to this very day—a Revolution made, nationhood declared, a Constitution written, republicanism secured, an offspring warned to be eternally vigilant, a reputation gained among the friends of liberty throughout the world that has lasted down to the present hour. It was a challenging enterprise and a noble work, and only a mighty faith could have sustained it.

Why, it may be asked, have we as yet said nothing of those staples of so many American creeds both of the past and present—revelation, tradition, the incorrigibly sinful nature of man, the literal truthfulness of the Bible, the divinity of Jesus of Nazareth, the Trinity, and so on? On all of these matters, members of the Founding Father generation disagreed. However, if they disagreed on these particulars, they did so without completely losing the sense of community that resulted from the sharing of the broader principles of their enlightened faith.

Some clung to revelation, but Ethan Allen, for one, celebrated pure reason as "the only oracle of man" and penned an influential pamphlet on that subject. On the other hand, John Adams, though enlightened, could never free himself from the idea that man is often best characterized by his penchant for folly and error. As Alexander Hamilton saw it, man was always self-interested. It was simply man's nature to be. For his part, Jefferson, finding most of the Bible objectionable, discarded all of the Old Testament and most of the New, extricating only what he regarded as the authentic teachings of Jesus himself. Jefferson also denied the divinity of Jesus. Franklin doubted it. It is in Franklin's own words that we have a most intriguing listing of specific enlightened beliefs, including some that men who thought themselves just as enlightened as the good Dr. Franklin would have challenged. His credo, in the form of a letter to the Reverend Ezra Stiles, the president of Yale, was written a few months before Franklin's death in 1790:

Here is my creed. I believe in one God, creator of the universe. That he governs it by his Providence. That he ought to be worshipped. That the most acceptable service we render to him is doing good to his other children. That the soul of man is immortal, and will be treated with justice in another life respecting its conduct in this. These I take to be the fundamental principles of all sound religion, and I regard them as you do in whatever sect I meet with them. As to Jesus of Nazareth, my opinion of whom you particularly desire, I think the system of morals, and his religion, as he left them to us, the best the world ever saw or is likely to see; but I apprehend it has received various corrupting changes, and I have, with most of the present dissenters in England, some doubts as to his divinity; tho' it is a question I do not dogmatize upon, having never studied it, and think it needless to busy myself with it now, when I expect soon an opportunity of knowing the truth with less trouble.

As Franklin's letter indicates, the Founding Fathers, unlike some of their gloomier descendents, could laugh about religion and make quips and jokes about it. People who did not agree on every article of faith could still be lighthearted in their discussions of this whole business. God intended human happiness even when weighty religious matters were under review.

Toleration

The Founding Fathers' inability to agree on every particular of doctrine and dogma seemed, in a way, a fitting recapitulation of the previous 200 years of American history. To them, the story of colonial America as a whole had been the story of religious diversity and the attendant inability of any one of the numerous sects to so dominate the others as to be able to establish itself as the one true religion for the entirety of English America.

Despite the strenuous opposition of 17th-century Puritans and others, in time there had developed a toleration that was born first mainly of necessity. By the middle of the 18th century, however, this pragmatic toleration was, more often than before, becoming a principled toleration. The Founding Fathers' contribution here was first to see and then to argue that the diversity which human societies had for so long regarded as a flaw or a weakness was actually a great strength, and something eminently serviceable for nation-making as well.

It was only out of a people that thought for themselves that a self-governing republic had any chance at all of being fashioned. Thinking for oneself in matters of religion and morals was part and parcel of thinking for oneself generally, and thinking for oneself was a necessary precondition for governing oneself. The literalness with which many of the Founding Fathers took the principle of self-government—and the free thought clearly implied in it—was quite revolutionary in terms of its potential. It remains so to this very hour. It is perhaps still far too revolutionary for some contemporary American types.

In fact (and this is another of our ironies), many of the American people have been a trifle ill at ease with the Fathers' radical thinking and with their religious skepticism almost from the first days of the Republic. Thus, it is hardly surprising to learn that the revisionism of today has had its earlier equivalents. History has often been rewritten with a view to making the Fathers more pious and orthodox than they in fact were. Especially when the waves of fundamentalism and soul-saving evangelism began to sweep over the land at the very end of the 18th century and in the first half of the 19th, the patriotic children of the Fathers attempted to recast their Fathers' images, to make the patriots of 1776 over in their own likeness.

Again finding it comforting to believe that a superintending *and intervening* Providence sustained the American Republic, the sons often transformed the deistical Fathers into self-conscious agents of the Almighty. When Washington died in 1799, his grief-stricken national progeny eulogized him everywhere. He was, popular opinion held, greater than Alexander, greater than

Caesar, greater than Cromwell. He was, asserted orators using a theme that was to have a long history, nothing short of "the American Moses," sent by God himself to lead "the modern Israel of the Lord" out of "the worse than Egyptian bondage of Great Britain" and into "the Promised Land" of American peace and prosperity.

When Jefferson and Adams both died on the Fourth of July, 1826, the 50th anniversary of the American Republic, patriots calculated the odds against such a coincidence and declared that it must obviously be providential, that America's God had called "the two Patriarchs" home in a blaze of glory. By a sheer act of will, it was further argued, both these aged and ailing Fathers had actually held onto life until this special Fourth of July in order to show their willingness (and America's) to cooperate fully with the designs of Providence.

The deistical beliefs of the Fathers were clearly beleaguered in this fundamentalistic America of the 19th century. They did not, however, entirely pass from the scene. Some later presidents, including such important ones as Andrew Jackson and Abraham Lincoln, continued the Founding Fathers' tradition of religious individualism, skepticism, and indifference to the fine points of dogmatic theology. Although oratory, eulogy, and public sentiment would transform the assassinated Lincoln into the good "Father Abraham" martyred on Good Friday, the living Lincoln, like the Washington and the Jefferson whom he so much admired, was really a freethinker in religion, a deeply private man who chose to be religious in his own very personal and even unique way.

The tension that undeniably exists between the faith of the Founding Fathers and that creed of some of their more fundamentalistic American sons and daughters has manifested itself in a number of ways in eras earlier than our own. In the past, the nation has endured despite its falling away from the faith of the Fathers. Perhaps it will do so again, thereby lending further credence to the Jeffersonian dictum that neither a babel of voices nor a multiplicity of creeds can undo the republican order of things—not even when some of those voices are too strident and not even when some of those creeds are filled with utterly far-fetched and erroneous propositions.

Still, two points are well worth making in this year of our Lord 1986. It is only a relatively short distance, as the crow flies, from Thomas Jefferson's Monticello to Jerry Falwell's church. Philosophically speaking, however, the two places are much, much farther apart, and one gets to the latter not so much by returning to the faith of our American Fathers as, instead, by repudiating that faith.

The second point also speaks directly to the question of the relationship (or the lack thereof) between Falwell and company on the one hand and the Founding Fathers on the other. Specifically, calls have been made in our day and generation for a new constitutional convention, one that would most probably have a rightist social agenda. One wonders just who it is that will serve as the new Washington at such a time as this or as the sagacious and pragmatic Franklin. Who among us, we may well inquire, is Madison enough to "father" a constitution and Jefferson enough to see and articulate the need for it to have a Bill of Rights?

Such questions are many and the answers to them alarmingly, distressingly few. Nevertheless, while there is a veritable array of philosophical, religious, practical, patriotic, social, and other reasons to oppose these latter-day fundamentalistic designs to improve upon the work of the Founding Fathers, perhaps the very best reason of all is, surprisingly enough (but yet fittingly enough, given the themes of this article), one that may best be categorized as *providential*. After all, if God had intended Jerry Falwell to be a Founding Father, would he not have made him one? Instead, in the fullness of time and for the Almighty's good purposes, we were furnished with a Washington, a Jefferson, and a Madison. Enough said. Enough written. Hallelujah! Praise the Lord!

RELIGION AND A NEUTRAL STATE: IMPERATIVE OR IMPOSSIBILITY?[3]

We have long been vexed by the proper relationship between church and state. Tension between the two is indigenous in the very nature of these institutions: the state making powerful claims on its citizens and the church asking uncompromised loyalty of

[3]Address by Carl H. Esbeck, professor of law at the University of Missouri–Columbia, at the Christian Legal Society's Freedom and Faith '84 Conference, April 5, 1984. *Vital Speeches of the Day.* 50:548–53. Jl. 1, '84. Reprinted by permission.

the selfsame individuals who are religious adherents. This dual citizenship suggests that there is an area of overlapping jurisdiction by church and state. The church has a sphere of influence in which it is autonomous and operates unhindered by the state. The state too has a sphere of responsibility in which it attends to its temporal or secular duties in a manner impartial toward the many competing religions. To complete the illustration, the two spheres interlock signifying an area of shared jurisdiction over certain matters within society, although they differ concerning their role in shaping and enforcing cultural choices in the area of overlap.

Apportionment between these three areas—the autonomous church, the secular state, and the area of concurrent jurisdiction—is one of the enduring issues of public debate. Of recent note is the claim, originating from a theological base, that the state can be neither neutral nor neglectful about values of first order, such as the nature of humankind and the purpose of life. The argument begins with the premise that God is sovereign over all of life. To those who acknowledge this sovereignty, it is asserted that there can be no separation between man's religion and other areas of life, including the political and legal. A person's religious presuppositions go with them wherever they are, whatever they are doing in life. This total unity, it is said, exists not only within each individual but also at corporate levels, including government institutions. Government cannot be dualistic, for it too holds a *Weltanschauung* or worldview. The deduction follows that state neutrality is not only impossible and thus a myth, but worse, it is a cover-up to use the state to advance philosophies that are antithetical to Christianity. In short, the argument concludes, either the state favors Christianity or it favors an opposing philosophy. There is no neutral ground.

This myth-of-neutrality assertion deserves attention, for if its proponents are correct there can be no separation of church and state as presently exists in America. Rather, in this view the state can only cling to the existing orthodoxy or reject it and embrace a new one. The current cultural pluralism is cited as evidence of the American state in the very throes of such a transition.

The thesis of this paper is that the myth-of-neutrality argument is partially right and partially wrong. For reasons of religious liberty the state can and should avoid any involvement with matters of religious worship, propagation and teaching which together comprise the very heart of one's belief concerning the nature and destiny of humankind. Conversely, the paper argues that the state cannot retreat from the regulation of certain conduct which is arguably immoral and still claim its neutrality concerning the rightness of the conduct. The very decision by the state to withdraw its regulation leaving the morality of the conduct up to each individual is a value-ladened choice. In sum, the state cannot be neutral on moral issues, but it can and should be neutral on questions central to religions' faith.

Having stated the particular issue that is the subject of this paper, the myth-of-neutrality argument is best discussed in a larger context. The assigned task of this paper is to define the proper juridical relationship between church and state. In short, the charge is to postulate what the law "ought to be," or perhaps what was intended at certain formative moments in American history. It is useful to approach this task by beginning with what the law "is," and then to discern points, if any, where the reality of what "is" and what "ought to be" are at variance.

The current case law of the federal courts concerning religion and the first amendment can usefully be classified into three areas:

1. Freedom of religious expression and association, presently addressed in the courts under the speech, press, assembly and petition clauses.

2. Government's respect for religiously based conscience (herein of the right to conscientious objection), presently addressed in the courts under the Free Exercise Clause.

3. The appropriate relationship between church and state (popularly known as the separation of church and state), presently addressed in the courts under the Establishment Clause. The word "church" is understood to embrace all parachurch and other religious organizations.

These three—freedom of religious expression, respect for conscience, and separation of church and state—in sum comprise religious liberty, at least liberty from oppressive government as distinct from private offenses.

A frequently forgotten aspect of any analytical task is to identify areas which are not part of the controversy. At the juridical level, two of the three subdivisions of first amendment religious liberty, namely, freedom of religious expression and respect for conscience, are not in serious disarray in American law. Freedom of religious expression, indeed, all speech and press regardless of the content, is protected constitutionally to a very high degree. So long as religious expression is protected at the same high level as is expression of philosophical, political, economic or artistic content, there need be no fear for the legal rights of religious adherents of all persuasions to believe, speak, publish, assemble and associate relative to matters of faith.

This is not to suggest that the current law of religious expression is perfectly as it ought to be. That two federal circuit courts have denied student-initiated high school groups authority to voluntarily meet in classrooms to discuss religious matters before or after school hours is shamefully discriminatory when science or literary student clubs are permitted. Governmental discrimination against religious expression remains isolated, however, and there is cause to hope that this invidious treatment will be corrected in the courts or by the Equal Access bills before Congress.

When it is said that religious expression is not controversial, one must be certain to distinguish between the juridical and the prudential. Here we speak juridically only. Although the first amendment amply insures religious speech and association, that does not mean that every use of the legal right is prudent. For example, one may think it never wise for a minister to use the pulpit to endorse a candidate during a partisan election, even though it is a cleric's legal right to do so.

One of the interesting developments in the religious landscape is that many churches which earlier separated themselves from American public life have now awakened to a call to be stewards of culture, science, environment, education, law, and, yes, even politics and government. A single-minded concern for private virtue has been supplanted by an increasing penetration into matters of civic virtue and the struggle for a more just world. Many churches are no longer willing to silence themselves. This shedding of extreme pietistic beliefs which caused privatization of faith and withdrawal from culture has been politically controversial. But emphatically it is not unconstitutional. A church separated from the state need not be a silent church.

Likewise, governmental respect for individual conscience grounded in religious belief is accorded high protection under the Free Exercise Clause. When a religious belief is sincerely held and places an individual in the "cruel choice" of either obeying his religious convictions or the state's mandates in positive law, the courts have held that the law must give way and exempt the religious devotee. Only when the government's interests are compelling may the state subordinate human conscience.

To be sure, the constitutional protection of conscience under the Free Exercise Clause is not all it ought to be either. In a few recent cases the United States Supreme Court has been seemingly guided more by expedience than principle in discovering reasons of state which are deemed of such exigency as to push aside conscience. Here too, however, one does not see in America evidence of a widespread intolerance to religious practices being sanctioned by law (licensing of fundamentalist schools in a few states and home education by parents excepted).

The third subdivision of first amendment religious liberty is the Establishment Clause which embraces the concept of the separation of church and state. Here the controversy is full-blown at the juridical level, and there is little common ground even among churches on what the law ought to be.

The matter should be approached by first clearing away the underbrush of widely held misconceptions. The first misconception is the simplistic idea that the Free Exercise Clause is pro-religion and the Establishment Clause is anti-religion. If one were to follow this notion, in every first amendment case involving religion these two clauses would be at war with one another. The judicial task, then, would be to determine if the Establishment Clause eclipses Free Exercise, in which case the anti-religious forces prevail, or if Free Exercise prevails over Establishment producing a win for religion. That line of reasoning is utter nonsense, for it presumes that the First Congress which drafted the first amendment in 1789 placed side by side two phrases each contradicting the other. It would be as if the selfsame statesmen had written, "Congress shall make no law . . . abridging the freedom of the press, but Congress may censor all newspapers for reasons which on balance seem sufficient." The proposition of an intentional, built-in contradiction is so preposterous as to suggest to the rational its improbability.

The manner of reconciling the Free Exercise and Establishment Clauses is clear. Both clauses advance religious liberty. The Free Exercise Clause protects the religiously informed conscience. Concomitantly, the Establishment Clause mediates the relationship between church and state. The nature of that relationship is for the mutual benefit of both. That is, religious liberty is served when the Establishment Clause protects civil government from overreaching by dominant religious organizations that seek to use the offices of state to advance their religious causes. Reciprocally, the Establishment Clause protects churches from intermeddling by the state and undue entanglement with its army of administrators and their battery of regulations.

Refreshingly, the Supreme Court has not been confused about this matter, for the second and third parts of the Establishment Clause test require that government action not have the effect of advancing or inhibiting religion (note the reciprocity), and that such action must not lead to excessive entanglement between the two. In short, some separation of church and state properly understood is protective of churches as well as the state and thus advances the liberty of believer and nonbeliever alike.

The second misconception concerning the Establishment Clause, one of the enduring fictions of first amendment law and American historical lore, is that the matter of separation of church and state was settled at the time when our Constitution was adopted and the first amendment ratified (1789-1791). Hence, there are repeated appeals to the intent of the Framers or the Founding Fathers. That notion may have a vestige of credence if one is referring to religious liberty vis-a-vis the federal government. The first amendment, however, was not applicable to state and local governments until the mid-twentieth century. It is common knowledge that the Bill of Rights applied only to national government, at least, that is, until the Warren Court in the 1940's and 1950's selectively applied its prohibitions including those of the first amendment to the states and their political subdivisions.

Since the first amendment had little to do with the separation of church and state until this century, just when and why did America embark upon this unique experiment? It was indeed an experiment for the American colonies were the first to separate church and state. The development took place differently in each of the colonies and spanned a hundred year period. Rhode Island, Delaware, Pennsylvania and New Jersey never had established churches, although certain religions were favored in their laws. In a well-known struggle, Virginia disestablished the Anglican Church in 1786, but the Old Dominion had been preceded by disestablishments in North Carolina (1776), New York (1777) and Vermont (1779). The Puritan's Congregational Church was not affected by the Revolutionary War and did not yield to disestablishment until 1818 in Connecticut and finally 1833 in Massachusetts. For present purposes it is sufficient to note that the separation of church and state was a state law development resulting from changing local attitudes. It was not a juridical development from the top down as would be the case if the first amendment had required it of the entire nation beginning in 1791. Thus, until *Everson v. Board of Education* in 1947, the separation of church and state was almost entirely a matter of state constitutional law.

This is pointed out not to suggest unhappiness with the liberties taken with judicial review by the Warren Court. Rather, the effort is to be wholly candid about what the courts and lawyers are doing—namely, reading substantive values into the Establishment Clause which were not placed there by its authors in the First Congress.

Returning to the myth-of-neutrality assertion, it is a helpful generalization to classify those active in church-state litigation into three schools of thought. First, there are those who argue for the increased privatization of religious beliefs, harboring a conviction that theistic religion is largely irrelevant, even dysfunctional, in matters of public discourse. Out of reasons of conscience, of course, the religious beliefs of individuals should be tolerated so long as those beliefs are not brought to bear in any serious way on public policy and matters of state. This group shall be referred to as the "secularists."

A second group is made up of "separationists" who for the most part desire a benign or benevolent separation of church and state. Although a few adjustments in rhetoric, rationale and result would be made, separationists generally subscribe to the position of the United States Supreme Court from *Everson v. Board of Education* in 1947 to *Larkin v. Grendel's Den* decided in 1982. Churches descendant of Anabaptists are most often separationists today, and the mainline Protestant churches generally have been persuaded to this view. The historical position of Baptists is separatistic.

Finally, a third group argues for a closer, organic relationship between church and state wherein the government has a proper role in preserving the unity and integrity of the Christian faith. Like the secularists and separationists, this third group would stop short of utilizing the coercive power of the state to deny right of conscience to religious dissenters and nonbelievers. Short of coercion, however, this third group envisions that the state should side with and foster "true religion." No doubt, it is implicit that the state is wise enough to select as the "true religion" their religion. Adherents of conservative Calvinism heavily populate this third group, as well as many holding the classical Roman Catholic position. The literature has left this final group unnamed, at least in any satisfactory manner. Because this group believes that a state to be legitimate must acknowledge that its authority to govern is from God, this third category shall be designated the "theocentric" position. Theocentrists are not theocratic, which would be a complete melding of church and state. Nevertheless, theocentrists do charge the state with certain covenant obligations to God which for them supersede the social contract in a democracy to follow the will of the majority.

Under severe financial pressures to fund their ministries, particularly schools, a moderate strain of theocentrists have proposed that the state support all religions impartially, Christian and otherwise. This not only affords a more attractive package to present in the political arena, but it keeps the state out of the thorny business of choosing among competing faiths for the one "true religion." Still, the state advances religion over nonbelief and remains theocentric in that it is accountable to an ambiguous God-in-general, an all-purpose generic god.

The myth-of-neutrality argument appears most prominently in the literature of the theocentrists, both the moderate strain and those unabashedly pro-Christian. Moreover, the efforts of the theocentrists in the courts and legislatures on church-state issues are often opposed by the combined efforts of the separationists, for theological reasons, and by the secularists, because of their view on the disutility of theistic religion.

The point to be decided is whether the concept of a neutral state is realizable and imperative for reasons of religious liberty, or is it an impossibility and a subterfuge promulgated by some secularists to further their own ideology and social agenda. That ought to prompt the more specific inquiry, "Neutral about what?" The secularists, separationists and theocentrists have responded quite differently to that question depending on whether the subject matter was (1) personal virtue and morality, or (2) religious worship, propagation and training. The secularists would insist on state neutrality as to both matters, while theocentrists claim the impossibility of neutrality as to either. The separationists, however, argue for state neutrality only concerning religious worship, propagation and training. On matters of virtue and morality many separationists have long been active in urging state prohibition of vices, thus non-neutrality, such as gambling, alcoholism, drug abuse, prostitution, pornography and the like. (A few separatists groups, notably the "peace churches," have even resisted use of the coercive power of law to prohibit immoral behavior damaging to community.)

Is the separationists' position defensible in any principled way? Can a line be drawn which insists on state neutrality as to religious worship, propagation and training, while seeking to use the force of civil law to encourage and compel, if need be, their understanding of proper moral behavior? The separationists have responded "yes" to this challenge, and their apologia appears formidable.

The separationists reject the secularists' position that Christian moral claims (and those of other religions) should be a matter for one's personal conduct only, not that of the political community. A state may and often does legislate concerning morality, whether it be against graft, racism, child abuse, incest or sodomy. Freedom of choice to do what is morally wrong cannot be justified in the same way as freedom to do what is morally right. The secularists have adopted the Enlightenment's mistaken view concerning the freedom of conscience. From the agreed upon premise that all people have equal dignity, many secularists have erroneously reasoned that all persons' ethical views are of equal validity. This misunderstanding is due to a one-sided view of humanity which enthrones free will in human action. The new moral norm becomes, simply, to do your own thing and try to hurt as few people as possible in the course of doing so. Secularists have often ignored the ill effects that individual action may have on the entire society. The notion that what consenting adults do in private has no social effect is a fiction, for when enough consenting adults harm themselves the result is a social problem regardless of whether consent was involved. When it comes to personal conduct many secularists have doubted the validity of truth or the possibility of perceiving it and embraced a situational morality. Once truth is denied, these secularists are without fixed standards to make judgments concerning the acts of others. Where there are no norms, there can be no law. Thus, they argue, the state must be morally neutral. In contrast, traditional religions hold that truth exists, is knowable, and does not change. And therefore the acts of people can be judged morally wrong.

The implementation of religiously based morality through positive law is to be sought by believers and churches through persuasion and consensus with others. This is to be pursued by ample use of the legally protected rights of religious expression and association. It makes little sense for the secularists to concede to religious adherents the freedom of speech, and then to argue that the separation of church and state is violated when religious adherents win the debate leading to enactment of moral legislation consistent with their religious views. Separation of church and state does not disqualify the government from legislating against immorality simply because the moral principles concerned were derived from religious presuppositions. If they hope to defeat moral legislation, the secularists will have to proceed by the same means: speech, persuasion and consensus. There need be no neutral state on matters of virtue and morality by reason of the Establishment Clause. The clause separates church and state, not the religious believer from the state. The latter is possible only by death or exile.

To be sure, not all morality should be codified into positive law. Any effort must avoid a new moralism backed up by a coercive legalism. In addition to civil rights other than religious liberty, there are limits on what legal processes can accomplish, and the civil and criminal law should be called upon only to restrain acts where harmful or disorderly consequences emerge in the community.

Now, what of the theocentric position that the state cannot be neutral on matters of religious worship, propagation or teaching? This is the crux of the matter dividing the religious community. The choice is between a theocentric state or a secular state. Many separationists and theocentrists alike desire to live God-centered lives and to dwell in and work for a theocentric society, but it is quite another matter to insist on a theocentric state. For reasons of religious liberty, separationists desire a secular state, meaning the government's authority to rule comes in the first instance from the people holding citizenship, not from God.

The separationists' arguments which command state neutrality on core religious matters entail both pragmatic considerations and reasons of principle. At the practical level America is at present a religiously diverse nation. Given our republican form of government, federal, state and most local governments cannot hope to represent the desires of their multi-religious and non-religious citizens and still openly favor Christianity, even least-common-denominator Christianity, should anyone want it. Whatever one's interpretation of history concerning the "Christian America" debate, the stark reality of the present is that only a slim majority of Americans are polled among those on church membership rolls, and even if "churched" may still not be Christian, and even if Christian hardly agree on the theological implications of the scriptures. Of necessity the state must be neutral concerning confessional differences.

"All of that is not true," say some in the theocentric group, or, if it is partly true, the matter can be turned around, perhaps with the assistance of a state more supportive of Christianity. However, even if a theocentric state became possible at some future time, the pragmatic objection is secondary. At the very foundation of the rift between separationists and theocentrists concerning the proper role of the state are differences in certain theological presuppositions. Not only do these groups differ on their theology of the state, they also view differently the nature and role of the church. Accordingly, they necessarily differ on how church and state are to relate to one another.

The separationists' arguments from theology which counter the myth-of-neutrality assertion are fourfold. First, beginning with the Reformation there slowly has evolved a definition of religion which presupposes voluntary adherence, not coercion, with a zone of personal spiritual autonomy withdrawn from the reach of any civil authority. In Christian theology humankind is given free will concerning the claims of God on individual lives, including the possibility of choosing unbelief and disobedience. Deity is understood to be a personal God desiring fellowship and communion with people. If God was to force that relationship rather than draw individuals to Himself, the objects of His favor would be changed into a kind of impersonal machinery, mere automatons. By the very nature of religion, churches are left to attract members by force of persuasion and the appeal of their doctrine, not by privilege and the imprimatur of state. Most certainly, then, the state cannot become the agent for achieving sectarian preservation and propagation.

The Danish theologian, Niels H. Soe, draws from his country's folklore this illustration. It is told that a man won a lady's love by means of a magic charm. In winning her she was changed and was no longer what the man loved. Hence the winning was a bitter disappointment, for the man got hold of his lady's body but not her heart. As Soe concludes: "Love is inseparable from respect of the other's personality. Divine love, strange as it may seem, is not different in this sense. God wants communion with man. And therefore wills that man remain man, a personal, responsible being."

There is a second, correlative principle at work here. Religious liberty is not a gift of the state. The state is limited in its authority, having no jurisdiction over the confessional beliefs which comprise the very heart of religion. The natural consequence of religion being voluntaristic is that government has no competence in the matter nor is the state equipped to determine any one system of belief as religious truth or to be the judge of orthodoxy. In Reformation theology all things are fallen or imperfect, including the state. To suggest that the state is competent in matters at the core of a given faith is to uncritically exalt the state in contravention to the very doctrinal position of an imperfect state.

A third reason of principle militating for state neutrality concerning religious worship, propagation and training is the danger of cultural religion. Cultural religion is the elevating of certain ceremonies, holidays and other traditions of a nation to the level of the sacred. In its extreme form it is referred to as "civil religion," which comes about when predominate religious groups have identified so closely with government and the politics of the country that patriotism and nationalism go hand-in-hand with spirituality. Civil religion can deprecate the integrity, vitality and independence of churches, which by their commission transcend present-day society, politics and national boundaries. The role of the church is global; it is not a department of state to be seen and utilized as a tool to serve the aims of state. Civil religion is dysfunctional when it anesthetizes individuals from confronting the choices to be made between the ways of the world and the teachings of their church. Culture cannot convert people to Christianity. Indeed, American civil religion can be more than ceremony and ritual, but an alternative, competing religion.

Fourth, and finally, where churches have become unduly involved with the agencies of government, they risk being subverted in that their programs become redirected to meet ends chosen by government. Having lost their independence by allying with government, churches become compromised in their efforts to act in accord with their higher calling. State aid to religious programs, conditioned on conformity to the proverbial bureaucratic "strings," can slowly sap all spiritual content from a ministry. In the extreme, a church may be so hobbled that its mission is altogether thwarted. Moreover, when a church believes it is called to speak prophetically and critique the state, its expression is rendered tepid under the chill of real or apparent threats from government. When a religious organization is influenced in this way, its spontaneity is dulled and the fervor and allegiance of its members wane.

In summary, the state can and in many cases should enact laws which both positively and negatively serve a peoples' need for moral order and virtue. However, respect for the transcendent character of human responsibility and the need to safeguard the integrity of churches will inevitably carry with it neutrality by the state concerning religion.

The most serious challenge by the theocentrists to the neutral-state position of the separationists is the contention that there is no easy duality between religion and moral obligations. If the state is bound to enforce a moral duty by positive law, it is difficult to insist that it ought to do so severed from the religious faith which gives rise to that moral obligation. The rejoinder is this: admittedly at the individual level human nature is not dualistic, able to separate virtue from its religious presuppositions. This does not, however, hold true at the corporate level. Given that people hold a world and life view which does not separate the secular from universal transcendent beliefs, the error is to generalize from this precept and uncritically apply it at the corporate level of government. The modern nation-state does not require an official religion to supply a dominant and unifying world view to govern effectively. Indeed, in the West today nations rule by consensus politics drawn from a mix of competing interests, only some of which have traditional religious bases. True, a pluralistic democratic state cannot long survive without some integrating beliefs which operate at the political and social level and define the commonweal. For example, society should recognize that law has transcendent origins which are higher than the state, thus affording a point of reference for judging the state and placing restraints on its power. The requisite social glue, however, need not be a state-sanctioned mode of worship and religious dogma. The democratic state can be sustained if churches measure up to the calling to reach their people with a faith which among other things teaches a responsibility to preserve and nurture society, including political institutions. The path to securing a state that abides by ethical behavior is through a godly people. Such a people as citizens—citizens with the religious vitality and discipline to use their free will responsibly—will comprise the needed social cement for America or any republic. Alternatively, experience has shown that state endorsement of and aid to a common religion risks a compromising and theologically sterile church.

For the theocentrists to raise the specter of a republic collapsing into totalitarianism if the state does not favor Christianity is to misplace the role and priorities of the church. The church does not exist to sustain political order. To be sure, the political benefits of the work of the church are great. But a virtuous people with the discipline to be self-governing is derivative of the church's task, not its foremost purpose.

What does this mean for the United States Supreme Court's tripartite test presently used in Establishment Clause cases? The three-part test announced in *Lemon v. Kurtzman* (1971) has not proved sufficiently durable to reach results consistent with the principles of church-state separation discussed above. One is tempted to propose no substitute, for the bald language of Black-Letter-Law cannot be divorced from its underlying principles. Still, the Supreme Court's verbal map can be improved upon, for one cannot expect every judge and lawyer to have an indepth appreciation of the foundational principles underpinning church-state relations which maximize religious liberty. Simple formulations can be helpful.

A formulation which folds the first two parts of the *Lemon* test into a single factor and which chooses better terminology is as follows:

First, the Establishment Clause requires that government be neutral toward religion, but not indifferent and never hostile. Second, the Establishment Clause prohibits government action which compromises the independence or integrity of a religious organization, absent some truly exigent threat to public health, safety, peace or order.

Remember, coercion of conscience is already protected by the companion Free Exercise Clause. Further, the Free Speech

Clause protects religious organizations which engage in social action, even when it causes political division along religious lines. The same clause insures access for religious speech to a public forum. The Establishment Clause addresses quite a different problem where both church and state are to be shielded from improper involvement with each other. As with the *Lemon* test, under this proposed formulation both the motive of the government and the consequences of its actions are scrutinized. If a consequence of government action is to foster excessive entanglement with churches, that would violate the independence of the church. Discrimination among denominations would be prohibited as contrary to neutrality, for such unequal treatment would advance the interests of some while inhibiting others.

In practice this proposal would yield results not substantially different from the existing three-part test of *Lemon v. Kurtzman*, but with a good deal more logical consistency to the exact language of the test. For example, state regulation of religious schools would be permitted only to the extent of health and safety standards, and to verify, through attendance records and achievement tests, that children are receiving an adequate education. Any additional regulation would compromise the independence and integrity of religious schools. Prayer in public schools, Christmas nativity scenes on public property, and legislative chaplains would not be constitutional. Admittedly, there is some historical and cultural tie to these forms of religious expression, but matters such as prayer and the nativity of Jesus are profoundly worship. It borders on desecration and is a step toward civil religion to strip these symbols of their central religious content and palm them off as a mere slice of Americana drained of religious significance. Finally, many recent attempts at government regulation of religious organizations by the Department of Labor, National Labor Relations Board, Equal Employment Opportunity Commission, and Internal Revenue Service would be rebuffed by this proposed test. Absent some truly sustantial threat to public health, safety, peace or order, regulation of the internal operation of religious organizations compromises their integrity.

Initially, it must be perplexing—devout separationists making common-cause with the exponents of a secularized society, together urging separation of church from state. As must now be apparent, however, their motives for doing so are widely divergent: the secularists want to privatize traditional religions so that they not influence affairs of state, and the separationists desire to protect the integrity and vitality of their churches. Moreover, this old alliance which brought separation of church and state from theory into political reality for the first time on American soil has its limits. As separationists and theocentrists increasingly emerge from their self-imposed cloister and bring their religious beliefs to bear on public policy in matters as divergent as nuclear weapons, the environment and economic policy, the secularists, although hardly routed may at least be observed backpedaling.

There is danger in overconfident assertions concerning subtle and complicated matters, especially concerning as ancient a problem as church-state relations. So it is with the solution suggested in this paper to adhere to a separation of church and state where the church is independent, voluntaristic and not silent, and the state is neutral and secular. One observation can be made with safety. The oft-lamented tensions between church and state are not all bad. Rather, the presence of tension is symptomatic of something healthy. Each "power" is sharpening and offsetting the other. For those who would defend the free church, this tension is evidence that the churches are neither so worldly as to be indistinguishable from the aims of state nor so withdrawn from the world as to be irrelevant to it.

RELIGIOUS FREEDOM FOR ALL: A JEWISH PERSPECTIVE[4]

Throughout history—and throughout the world—religious minorities of *all* faiths generally have not fared very well at the hands of religious majorities. Sadly, that has been the norm, rather than the exception. And the Jews were always a religious minority in every country in which they lived. The 17th century French philosopher, Blaise Pascal, in his *Pensees*, spoke from knowledge and personal experience when he said: "Men never do evil so completely and cheerfully as when they do it from religious

[4]Address by Samuel Rabinove, legal director of the American Jewish Committee, at the Second World Congress on Religious Liberty, September 6, 1984. *Vital Speeches of the Day*. 51:59–62. N. 1, '84. Reprinted by permission.

conviction." Even today, we need not look very far for illustrations: events in India, Iran, Lebanon and northern Ireland come to mind swiftly.

In fact, it is only within the past 200 years that the concept of religious liberty for all has gained widespread, though by no means universal acceptance. For example, religious liberty is denied to Jews in the Soviet Union today. In medieval Europe, where the interests of church and state were intertwined, the non-Christian was a virtual outcast. To hold unorthodox religious views was perilous. Heresy was to be extirpated, and Jews, the major non-Christian group, were subjected to many kinds of repression, from civil restrictions to slaughter. The official Roman Catholic Church view of Jews was codified by the Fourth Lateran Council, convened in this city in 1215 by Pope Innocent III, which decreed, among other things, that Jews should be distinguishable by their dress, not appear in public on Good Friday or Easter, and not hold any public office where they might exercise authority over Christians.

Although certain protections for Jews were afforded by some popes and some rulers, Jews had little recourse when religious fanaticism was aroused. During the First Crusade in 1096, for instance, the participants massacred, robbed and forcibly converted Jews in the Rhineland. When the crusaders took Jerusalem, they herded Jews into a synagogue and burned them alive. Other massacres of Jews occurred elsewhere, for example, in 1348 in Switzerland and Germany during the Black Death plague, which Jews were accused of causing by poisoning the wells. It should be stressed that Jews were viewed by many Christians not at all as ordinary human beings, with human strengths and weaknesses, but rather as creatures of the Devil. (This view persists in some quarters to this very day.)

The persecution of Jews in Spain offers a dramatic illustration of the savagery that could be perpetrated under the union of throne and altar. In 1391, massacres took place in the largest cities—4,000 Jews were killed in Seville alone—and forced conversions were prevalent. Converted Jews were known as New Christians, and their number grew steadily, fostered by frequent killings. Those who refused to convert were expelled in 1492.

Those who remained as converts were nevertheless discriminated against by exclusionary legislation that, for example, banned all those of Jewish descent from public office and made their testimony in court against Old Christians inadmissible. New Christians were accused of being insincere in the conversions into which they were coerced (sincerity, of course, was often tested by torture); the Inquisition, controlled by the Spanish monarchs, was set up in Seville in 1480 to ensure religious orthodoxy by those who had converted to Christianity. Nobody knows the precise number of victims of the Inquisition, but we do know that tens of thousands were burned at the stake.

Spain's union of church and state was emulated elsewhere in Europe with the coming of the Reformation in the 16th century, which brought with it neither freedom nor any move away from union of church and state. Martin Luther and John Calvin viewed religious orthodoxy as a legitimate concern for the state and heresy or deviation from the one true faith as intolerable. Thousands of Christians were put to death in subsequent years simply because they held religious convictions different from those which prevailed in the countries where they lived. As with the Jewish victims in the First Crusade, barbarities occurred because religious tolerance was scorned and because the state enforced its own religious beliefs. By the time of the Peace of Westphalia in 1648, which ended the Thirty Years War, an estimated three to four million Catholics and Protestants had been slaughtered. In the words of Sidney Hook, chairman of the Department of Philosophy at New York University: "God has been enrolled under all banners, including those arrayed against each other."

As a direct result of religious intolerance in Christian Europe, tens of thousands of Christians who belonged to minority sects in their homelands fled to America—Puritans (who have been termed Old Testament Christians), Lutherans, Quakers, Baptists, Catholics, Huguenots, Mennonites and many others. The first Jewish settlers in America arrived in New Amsterdam in 1654, having fled the Inquisition which, in effect, had pursued them from Portugal to Brazil when the Portuguese conquered Brazil from the Dutch. Some of the early settlers of America, ironically, carried with them the virus of intolerance and were prepared to deny to others in the new land the very freedom of conscience they so passionately had demanded for themselves in Europe. The Puritans in Massachusetts Bay Colony, for example, savagely persecuted Quakers and Baptists, as a result of which, Roger Williams fled and established in Rhode Island not merely the first Baptist church in America, but also the first American colony to rigorously separate church and state.

Rhode Island's charter contained the broadest grant of religious liberty ever given by an English monarch. It read:

No person within the said colony, at any time hereafter, shall in any wise be molested, punished, disqualified, or called into question for any difference of opinion in matters of religion: every person may at all times freely and fully enjoy his own judgment and Conscience in matters of religious concernments.

Not surprisingly, Rhode Island soon became a haven for Jews from Barbados, who established a congregation in 1678. The Touro Synagogue in Newport, R.I., today is a national historic shrine. In sharp contrast to Rhode Island, a Maryland law concerning religion, enacted in 1649, prescribed the death penalty for any person who denied that Jesus Christ is the Son of God or who denied the Holy Trinity. Jews in Maryland were not permitted to hold public office until 1825.

It was no accident that the Constitution of the United States contains no mention of Jesus Christ. In fact, it contains no mention of God either. The Founding Fathers, led by James Madison and Thomas Jefferson, painfully aware of the bitter fruits of church and state entanglement, sought to avert religious oppression and conflict by separating religion and government. In Article VI of the Constitution, in a provision that was revolutionary for its time, they stipulated that there shall be no religious test for national public office. In the First Amendment, they barred the Congress from establishing religion or prohibiting the free exercise thereof. Their wisdom and foresight were truly extraordinary.

The fact is that the religion clauses of the Constitution of the United States have been a blessing for freedom of conscience in general and for American Jews and other minorities in particular. The First Amendment has been America's Magna Charta of religious liberty and church/state separation. Because of it, for example, the U.S. Supreme Court has ruled that it is not the business of government to compose prayers or to sponsor prayers for American children to recite. Nor, the Court has held, is it the business of government to pay for schools whose chief reason for being is to propagate a religious faith—whether that faith is Protestant, Catholic, Jewish or whatever. This is not to suggest, however, that there have been no problems. Indeed there have been, the letter and spirit of the Constitution notwithstanding.

In 1843, in New York City, religion was an accepted part of public school curriculum. When a group of Jewish parents took issue with the use of a particular textbook, *American Popular Lessons*, for religious instruction, the Board of Education appointed a committee to look into the matter. The committee rejected the protest, reporting to the Board that it has "examined the several passages and lessons alluded to and had been unable to discover any possible ground of objection, even by the Jews, except what may arise from the fact that they are chiefly derived from the New Testament and inculcate the general principles of Christianity." That some citizens might reasonably object to having their children indoctrinated with "the general principles of Christianity" evidently did not even enter the minds of the committee members.

In 1844 in Philadelphia there was a major riot. Twenty-four people were killed, two Roman Catholic churches were burned to the ground, and it took Federal troops using cannon to quell the rioters. What was it all about? Nothing trivial. It was about whether Catholic pupils in Philadelphia public schools would be allowed to read from the Catholic Douay version of the Bible rather than the Protestant King James version. In fact, a major factor in the establishment of Catholic parochial schools in America during the last century was the quite accurate perception on the part of many American Catholics, both clergy and laity, that the public schools were Protestant-oriented and that textbooks often referred to Catholicism in disparaging terms, such as "popery."

Now, what about Jewish perspectives concerning religious liberty for everybody? In a recent issue of the *Quarterly Review* published by the Union Theological Seminary in New York City, a Protestant institution, John E. Smith, professor of philosophy at Yale University, made an interesting observation. In his article entitled "Tolerance as Principle and Necessity," he cited John Locke, as follows:

In arguing against the possibility and the legitimacy of a Christian theocracy, Locke makes a telling point in connection with ancient Jewish tradition which we would do well to ponder in the midst of twentieth-century conditions. The ancient Jews, as Locke correctly points out, never did require that "foreigners" and "sojourners" among them obey the Mosaic law. Insofar as there was a Jewish theocracy, idolatry among the Jews could be and was punished in accordance with that law. But insofar as one was not a member of the Jewish community, neither judgment nor punitive action could be taken.

Nothing would please me more than to be able to maintain that Jews and Judaism throughout the ages invariably have upheld the principles of religious liberty and freedom of conscience for all, Jews and non-Jews alike. But, alas, that has not quite been the case. What has been the case, however, is that our most respected rabbis and scholars (Judaism at its best) have indeed championed these human values, rooted in Biblical teaching, which translate into individual liberty and justice for all. In Leviticus, we hear the voice of the Lord: "Proclaim liberty throughout the land unto all the inhabitants thereof"; in Deuteronomy, we are admonished: "Justice, justice shalt thou pursue."

It is true that the great philosopher, Baruch Spinoza, was publicly excommunicated by the Jewish community of Amsterdam in 1656. The motive for this drastic action, however, which historically has been a comparative rarity in Judaism, must be understood. It was less a concern for enforcing religious conformity than it was a well-founded fear that Spinoza's affiliation with the Jewish community, many of whose members had so recently escaped to Holland from the Inquisition in Spain and Portugal, would be tainted and jeopardized by harboring a heretic whose expressed beliefs were seen to be threatening to all traditional religion.

One of the finest elucidations of the predominant attitude within Judaism toward religious liberty stems from Conservative Rabbi Robert Gordis, Professor of Bible and of the Philosophies of Religion at the Jewish Theological Seminary in New York, in an article in the Spring 1964 issue of the publication, *Jewish Education*, as follows:

Judaism accepts the existence of differences within the Jewish group and the right of dissidents to their own outlook and practice. It recognizes the existence of other religions and their inherent right to be observed.

There inheres a measure of naivete, as there is of oversimplification in Albert Einstein's utterance, "I thank God that I belong to a people which has been too weak to do much harm in the world." But more than mere incapacity inheres in the Jewish attitude toward religious liberty. The balance between the universal aspirations of Judaism and its strong attachment to the preservation of its group-character impelled it to create a theory that made room in God's plan—and in the world—for men of other convictions and practices.

Moreover, the deeply ingrained individualism of the Jewish character, its penchant for questioning, its insistence upon rational conviction, have made dissent a universal feature of the Jewish spiritual physiognomy. As a result, all groups (within Judaism) have achieved freedom of expression and practice, though efforts to limit or suppress this liberty of conscience have not been totally lacking and undoubtedly will reoccur in the future. Finally, the millennial experience of Jewish disability and exile in the ancient and medieval world has strengthened this attachment to freedom of conscience among Jews. In addition, the modern world had demonstrated that the position and progress of Jews, individually and collectively, is most effectively advanced in an atmosphere of religious liberty.

Another trenchant exposition of the meaning of religious freedom for all appeared in an article by Orthodox Rabbi Elieser Berkovits of Boston in the magazine *Congress Weekly* in 1955. Rabbi Berkovits declared:

When I assert that I believe in Judaism, it means that I do not believe in Buddhism, Mohammedanism, or Christianity. I believe in Judaism because I am convinced that it is the only true religion. Of course, I understand that the Buddhist, the Moslem, or the Christian has the same kind of faith in his own religion as I have in mine. . . . For how dare I claim for myself the right to live by my ultimate convictions without at the same time claiming the right for all mankind! . . . We consider the Church opposition to Copernicus and Galileo distasteful, not because it condemned what later proved to be valid astronomy, but because it opposed ideas with dungeons. . . . Freedom, democracy, indeed mankind as a whole, are not in need of levellers; not of those who would level all men through the powers of intimidation or coercion they possess, nor of those who would level by cajoling us into the surrender of individuality and into the watering down of all faiths and convictions. . . . The essence of tolerance is the appreciation of the fundamental truth that to live is to be different.

Which reminds me of an observation by Heinrich Heine: "Monopoly is as injurious to religions as to trades; they are only strong and energetic by free competition."

Noble words, but what about the actuality, what about Israel, the only Jewish state in the world? To state the obvious, Israel is by no means monolithic—there are numerous religious, ideological and cultural differences which inform the sensibilities of Israelis today. On May 14, 1948, when the state of Israel was created, the Israel Declaration of Independence proclaimed:

The State of Israel . . . will foster the development of the country for the benefit of all inhabitants; it will ensure complete equality of social and political rights to all its inhabitants irrespective of religion, race, or sex; it will guarantee freedom of religion, conscience, language, education and culture.

Has this promise been fulfilled? According to the U.S. State Department, essentially it has, even though in Israel religion and the state are not separate. (A good many Israeli Jews wish they were separate.) In any event, the U.S. State Department's annual reports on human rights practices in countries throughout the world confirm that Israelis of all faiths enjoy freedom of religion, expression and assembly. Yet it is also true that some Israelis, in the light of the bitter Jewish historical experience, deeply resent and oppose efforts of Christian missionaries to convert Israeli Jews to Christianity. This resentment notwithstanding, however, the Israeli Ministry of Religious Affairs pays the salary of every Christian minister in Israel, as it does of every Orthodox rabbi and Muslim imam. What the government does not do, ironically, is pay the salary of rabbis of Conservative and Reform movements of Judaism, which are denied official recognition. Non-Orthodox rabbis, for example, are not authorized to perform marriages in Israel or to serve as chaplains in the armed forces. It is important to note that many Israeli Jews, particularly those who emigrated from Asia and Africa where traditional Judaism held sway, are not well acquainted with alternate forms of Judaism.

While Orthodox and non-Orthodox Jews have co-existed in Israel since its inception, tensions have risen over the question of how religious a society Israel ought to be. Ultra-Orthodox Jews (referred to by one Israeli journalist as the Moral Minority) are steadfast in their determination to remodel Israel into what would amount to a theocratic state based on ancient Jewish law, or Halakha. They are angered by what they believe to be widespread desecration of the Sabbath and other impious behavior by Israeli Jews. Their views on such issues as abortion, birth control, conversion, autopsies, the status of women and use of motor vehicles on the Sabbath are not generally shared by most Israelis, who do observe many religious traditions, but not nearly as strictly as the ultra-Orthodox would require. The heart of the problem has been that, since Israel has been almost evenly divided between two major political blocs, the ultra-Orthodox, although only a small fraction of the population, have been able to use their political leverage to impose their will on others on a number of issues. And, perhaps regrettably, the intensity of religious feeling has been on the rise. Some of the ultra-Orthodox go so far as to deny the legitimacy of the existence of the State of Israel because the Messiah has not yet come.

"Only too often," complained a woman Member of Parliament in the Labor Party, Tamar Eshel: "we find that Orthodox Jews, according to their very deep beliefs, feel responsible for my sins. And they feel obliged to stop me from sinning and to force on me a style of life that, according to them, is the right one. That is definitely against basic freedoms."

In an article in the *Journal of Reform Judaism* this past winter, entitled "Liberal Judaism in Israel: Problems and Prospects," Rabbi David H. Ellenson, Professor of Jewish Thought at Hebrew Union College in Los Angeles, observed: "In short, the Orthodox establishment is unyieldingly antagonistic to non-Orthodox varieties of Judaism in Israel and, in light of the political power it wields, it will certainly be able to prevent Knesset recognition of the legitimacy of Reform and Conservative Judaism for the foreseeable future." There is, however, an active coalition in Israel, the Movement Against Religious Coercion and for Separation of State and Religion, comprising Reform and Conservative rabbis, scientists, doctors, educators, and women's rights activists, which is seeking equal status for all currents of Judaism.

Whether in Israel, the United States or anywhere else in the world, what are the proper limits of religious freedom for all? Sometimes the answers are relatively easy for most of us, but at other times they may be quite problematical. Consider, for example, a hypothetical case: A man named Abraham tells his wife that he has heard the voice of the Lord directing him to build an altar and sacrifice their 10-year-old son, Isaac. His wife promptly telephones the police, Abraham is arrested, examined, and eventually is placed in an institution for the criminally insane. Is this a violation of Abraham's religious freedom? Nobody in his right mind, Jewish or non-Jewish, would say so. In fact, back in the 1920's, in New York State, a man who did slay his young son, because he believed that God had ordered him to do so, was incarcerated as insane.

But there is a somewhat similar, though much more difficult issue, which actually arises not infrequently in the United States. Jehovah's Witnesses believe, as a matter of religious conviction, that the Bible prohibits blood transfusions. Some Jehovah's Witnesses, in fact, have accepted death, as God's will, rather than receive a transfusion which might have saved their lives. A good many people, including Jews, would say that religious freedom means that they have the right to make even such a fearsome decision, and that the state has no right to force a sane adult to undergo a procedure which profoundly violates his religious faith, even if the alternative is death. But what about a desperately ill

8-year-old child of Jehovah's Witnesses? Do her parents have the right to impose their religious convictions on her, and refuse to allow a blood transfusion, even if that is the only treatment that would save her life? Almost all Jews, I believe, would answer "no." In fact, American courts have ordered blood transfusions in such cases, the deep religious convictions of the parents notwithstanding.

A different kind of religious liberty problem arose some years ago in the state of Wisconsin, which pitted the right of the state to require that children attend school until age 16, against the right of Amish parents to limit their children's education to age 14. In this conflict situation, the U.S. Supreme Court ruled, in the case of *Wisconsin* v. *Yoder*, in 1972, that the right of the Amish parents should prevail. My own organization, the American Jewish Committee, joined with others in a friend-of-the-court brief in the Supreme Court upholding the religious rights of the Amish parents. But what about the rights of the Amish children in such a situation? In our complex, technological society, is it really acceptable, for *any* reason, to permit parents to halt their children's school education at age 14, thereby effectively restricting their children to becoming farmers or laborers like themselves? This is a challenging and difficult question as to which reasonable persons of intelligence and good will, Jewish or non-Jewish, may well differ.

I will conclude this presentation, which I purposely entitled "A Jewish Perspective," rather than "*The* Jewish Perspective" (There is, of course, no single Jewish perspective) with two quotations which, perhaps more than any, encapsulate my own personal convictions. One from Thomas Jefferson: "It behooves every man who values liberty of conscience for himself to resist invasions of it in the case of others, or their cases may, by change of circumstance, become his own." The other from a distinguished American jurist, Judge Learned Hand: "The spirit of liberty is the spirit which is not *too* sure that it is right."

VOICES OF REASON, VOICES OF FAITH[5]

As the debate deepened last week over the proper relation between religion and politics, *Time* invited a number of religious leaders and scholars to offer their reflections on the issue. All were asked just how the wall of separation between church and state should be defined, and whether they viewed the current campaign controversy as salutary or harmful. Among the responses:

HARVEY COX, professor at the Harvard Divinity School, Baptist minister and author of *The Secular City***:** The contribution of religiously committed people to the public arena should not be viewed as a nuisance or a threat. It is a potential source of energy and enlivening of the discussion of public issues. Religion has had an influence on political life in the U.S. from the beginning. Sometimes it has been a positive and constructive one, sometimes negative and destructive; but it has always been there, and the idea that it should not be seems rather idle. We have to realize that in the past couple of years one of the major new actors in public political discourse has been the black churches. Jesse Jackson's campaign is simply not comprehensible unless it is seen as the voice of the religious traditions and values arising from the black church, especially the concern for the poor and the marginal of our society, which is a very biblical message.

Although I disagree with the fundamentalists and evangelical preachers on almost everything, I welcome their participation in the larger political discourse. It is healthy that they are there. If Walter Mondale wants to disagree with Jerry Falwell or Jimmy Swaggart, that's fine. He has a right to do that, and when they begin making political statements they open themselves to that kind of criticism. It is very precarious for religious leaders to back a particular candidate, because their credibility as religious leaders is at a somewhat more basic level, formulating moral principles. But that is a matter of prudence.

The waiver I want to introduce is that people have very strong feelings about religious convictions. Therefore when we enter into a debate like the one we are now having, there is a special responsibility for restraint, for civility, for affirming the right

[5]Reprint of an article compiled by the editors of *Time*. *Time*. 124:28-9. S. 17, '84. Copyright © 1984 Time Inc. All rights reserved. Reprinted by permission from *Time*.

of the other person to have a position that differs from yours and to avoid accusing people of being in bad faith. Religious spokesmen have a responsibility to remember that overheating the conversation is not going to contribute to what any of us want. But an elected official has the most sensitive kind of responsibility for nurturing the diversity that is the most remarkable thing about American religious life.

THE REV. RICHARD JOHN NEUHAUS, Lutheran pastor and director of the Center on Religion and Society: It is important to make a distinction between religiously based values in the public square, and the role of institutional religion. What is properly thought of in legal terms as Jefferson's "separation of church and state" deals with the role of institutional religion in the public arena. Unfortunately, in the past several decades, a new and unhealthy situation developed, where it was assumed by many people that the separation of church and state meant the exclusion of religiously grounded values from the public arena. Now the religious New Right has kicked a trip wire, alerting us to the fictional character of a proposition that many Americans have been bamboozled into accepting: namely, that this is a secular society.

The religious New Right has shocked the cultural elites of America, because the elites assumed that "those people" had been thoroughly dismissed and discredited, going back as far as the Scopes trial of 1925, the so-called monkey trial. But beginning after World War II, with the emergence of the neo-evangelicals, those people have come back from the wilderness to which they had been consigned by the educational, media and mainline religious leadership.

We can do one of three things in response. We can say, O.K., let's have religion in the public square, and embark on head-on clashes and open-ended religious warfare. That would be disastrous for American society. The second thing is send all those people back to the wilderness. That, I think, is not possible. The third possibility, and this is the work of many years ahead, will come from recognizing that America lacks a coherent, morally grounded public philosophy. We do not have the vocabulary to debate moral issues in the public square. This could be severely damaging, if not fatal, to the American democratic experiment. The present confusion, however, *can* turn out to be a watershed moment in American political and cultural life if we begin to reconstruct a public philosophy, one that is responsible to, and in conversation with, the religious-based values of the American people.

SEYMOUR MARTIN LIPSET, professor of political science and sociology at Stanford University: The U.S. is the most religious country in the world. Some 95% to 98% of Americans say they believe in God. In most European countries it is less than half that. One of the explanations is precisely the separation of church and state. Churches must go out and recruit their membership. With state support, a religion doesn't have to work to maintain itself.

All of this has never meant that religious people do not take part in politics. The abolitionist movement was very much a religious movement. So, too, were the prohibition and anti-gambling movements, as were the anti-Catholic nativist movements of the 19th and early 20th centuries. We have issues dealing with civil rights, war and peace, abortion, homosexuality, crime. All of these are seen by some religious people as reflecting religious beliefs.

So having religious people foster political views is not new. If you take the view that abortion is murder, you can't expect that not to be expressed in the political arena. People have a right, and a moral obligation, to push what they believe to be true. If one uses religious arguments, one has a right to do that, just as one has a right to oppose them. It may be dangerous for the nature of the [church-state] debate, but I don't see how you can stop it.

RABBI ALEXANDER M. SCHINDLER, New York City, president of the Union of American Hebrew Congregations: Our understanding as Jews of what the First Amendment is all about is that the state does not in any sense favor one religion above others. That does not mean church groups should not be involved in the political process or should not compete in the marketplace of ideas. American Jews have always claimed that right and exercised it forcefully. But when the state begins the process of favoring one religion, the wall of separation is broken.

At the Republican Convention, fundamentalist ministers were conspicuous. There was the letter by Senator Laxalt, suggesting that God wants Americans to vote Republican and that the Christian thing to do is re-elect Ronald Reagan. The President himself suggested as much. It all amounts to saying that what is desirable is the establishment of a Christian religion. What made matters worse was the implicit assertion that these views alone are true and have God's blessing, and that those who oppose them are not just misguided, but sinful, intolerant and unpatriotic as well.

This issue is a crucial one for the Jewish community, and transcends partisan considerations. For we Jews are not just a minority in this country, we are a minority with a history. We suffered greatly in our wanderings across the globe. We were subject to continuous exile, religious conversion, economic appropriations, legal persecutions, anti-Jewish riots and genocide. These were the hazards faced by our people as they traveled the world. But they are hazards that are utterly absent from the American landscape. The reason is the principle of separation. In all other countries, there was a state religion. Here, there is none. This explains the unanimity and the fervor with which we uphold this principle, and wish to maintain it inviolate. Anything that attacks it may in itself not seem like a great matter—What's a crêche paid for with public funds? one might ask. But add them all together, and you begin to see the erosion of the wall that in our judgment is the cornerstone of liberties in America.

JESUIT FATHER JOSEPH O'HARE, former editor of *America* **magazine and newly installed president of Fordham University:** The important distinction is not between public policy and private religious beliefs. You can't have politicians who are schizophrenic. I think the line that must be drawn is between what one believes are moral and human values that should be protected by the law, and the very particular judgment that has to be made about what is the best kind of law, given the social realities of our society. On abortion, for example, one must consider the fact that there are many people who will try to have abortions even if they are declared illegal, that the matter is seen by different groups as an extremely important exercise of their personal rights. The judgment about what is the right law is a judgment on which good people, who share opposition to abortion, can disagree.

I think our religious leaders should enunciate the values and clarify the moral principles involved in public policy issues. But when they get down to the question of particular laws and candidates, our religious leaders would do well—as certain of our Catholic bishops are doing—to say they do not support any specific legislation or candidate.

The President—and nearly everyone else in politics in this debate—has expressed himself poorly. By some of the things he said when he spoke in Dallas, he seemed to suggest that those who oppose prayer in the schools are being intolerant of religion. That kind of arguing is very dangerous. My quarrel with the new religious Right is that they do not simply want to disagree with their opponents, they want to excommunicate them. The idea that there is one Christian position on issues like prayer in the schools violates the rules of debate in a pluralistic society. At the same time, while I understand how much the Jews have suffered from established religion, I think they are being overly cautious about attempts to accommodate religion generally. I am opposed to compulsory prayer in the schools, for example, but I think the idea of giving different religious groups access to school facilities should not be dismissed out of hand.

CLAIRE RANDALL, general secretary of the National Council of Churches: As I understand church and state separation, it does not say that religious bodies or people of belief cannot articulate their own convictions as they relate to societal issues. There has long been an understanding in this country that they not only can, they should. The difficulty comes when those ideas put forward by religious groups become narrow, sectarian views. Certainly, you can put such ideas before the rest of the society and say, "This is our contribution to the moral thinking of this society, and to the public debate on a given issue." But if you put the ideas out and say, "This is the way you *must* go," and everyone *must* go this narrow way, that is totally different.

So the problem really comes when Government officials want to make laws that are based on the more narrow religious tenets or sectarian positions, and try to impose them on the entire society. That is what people are struggling with now. It seems as if there are some religious groups that want the Government to behave in that way, and there are people in Government who agree. At issue are laws that would require activity in the public place that borders on or is a religious activity. That's the school prayer problem.

There is no question that this country has felt a powerful impact from the Judeo-Christian tradition. A great deal of the impact on the founding of this country, on the Constitution, and on people like Thomas Jefferson came from the Enlightenment, which offered a rational, ethical approach to government. If you push that back, it would take you to many Jewish and Christian roots. But it would be a mistake to believe that this country was founded on strict Jewish-Christian faith principles alone, because the Enlightenment influences were broader than that.

THE REV. JERRY FALWELL, founder of Moral Majority and chancellor of Liberty Baptist College, Lynchburg, Va.: I don't believe that the "wall" exists in the Constitution. It has been a "practical" wall that has been a good thing for the U.S. during its history. However, we have never had in this country a separation of church and state. There never was a time in American history when politics and churchmen haven't merged and blurred, including the evangelical ministers of the abolitionist movement who broke the back of slavery and on up through the civil rights movement. The wall is an imaginary wall intended to keep government off the back of the church, to prevent the officialdom of the church from coercing their followers. But it was never intended to keep churchmen from voicing an opinion or asserting moral values.

It is impossible for a person with sincere religious convictions to divorce his daily actions from those convictions. Our personal convictions always translate into our votes, our life-styles, our words. Just as it would be impossible for a labor activist to vote for a right-to-work law, so does a person's private beliefs on the right of the unborn translate into policy.

All civilized society is governed by legislation of morality by consensus. In America, you can't commit murder or rape or robbery [with impunity] because some time back there Americans decided that that was a good moral way to live. So it is today.

Intelligent men and women who care about each other have to seek what the founders called in their documents "the general welfare" without oppressing the rights of minorities. Responsible legislation and judicial practice is and always has been morally informed. The general principles of American democracy have always been Judeo-Christian moral principles. That same generation of Americans who came out of the bondage and darkness of the Old World to found this nation, when they framed a Constitution and wrote the Declaration of Independence, referred to their creator with a capital C, they created a chaplain of Congress, they had prayers in their school from Day 1. Throughout all these 200-plus years, there has been a commitment to basic values. That's what we're coming back to now.

I could be offended by a President who tried to create a Christian republic, or a Jewish President who tried to create a Judaic republic. But regardless of a President's faith, if he were promoting Judeo-Christian values, I would say amen to him. Yes, there is a sense of secularism in the nation and always will be. But this is also a religious society, always has been and always will be. I applaud that, so long as there is the absolute guarantee of total civil rights for the nonbeliever. I could never be offended at the assertion of those basic values as long as there is a clear commitment to pluralism. It is a fine line, but it is not too great a risk to reassert that we are a nation under God.

IV. LIBERTIES IN CONFLICT

EDITOR'S INTRODUCTION

Religious liberty has been an issue in American society since the beginning of European settlement in New England. American national mythology holds that the Puritans came to America in search of religious freedom; it is perhaps less well known that the freedom the Puritans sought was for themselves alone, and that the colonial authorities vigorously persecuted dissenters.

This divided heritage has remained with us to the present day. The debate over prayer in the public schools, for example, may be a bitter one, but it is hardly as bitter as the dispute that arose during the nineteenth century over which version of the Bible to use for moral instruction in the public schools, the Protestants' King James Version or the Roman Catholics' Douay Bible. In 1844, twenty people died in riots in Philadelphia over this issue, and there were more deaths in other cities.

Or consider the outcry over religious cults, which are reported to brainwash recruits and take control of their labor and property. Similar charges were leveled against the Shakers of the late eighteenth century; their early leaders were attacked by mobs for breaking up marriages when they convinced new members to join their strictly celibate communes and to yield all their possessions to the church. Judicial efforts to identify the difference between a cult and a religion are discussed in the first article in this section, "Marginal Movements" by Thomas Robbins, reprinted from *Society*. It is followed by "On the Different World of Utah" by James L. Clayton, a portrait of the members of the Mormon Church, once vilified as a cult, now well assimilated into the mainstream and gaining thousands of converts yearly.

An equally complex problem is the conflict between the "public interest," as defined by the federal government, and the religious freedom of a minority. To what extent may government agencies intervene against activities such as the animal torture and sacrifice practiced by adherents of Santeria and Candomble? In the case of Native Americans, whose use of hallucinogens in religious ritual violates antidrug laws and whose sense of the holiness of nature is often at odds with commercial interests, the government has shown an unusual willingness to override minority rights, as Robert S. Michaelsen demonstrates in his *Society* article.

On the other end of the spectrum are groups whose theology attacks the very legitimacy of the federal government. Such groups, described in Richard N. Ostling's *Time* magazine article, "A Sinister Search for 'Identity,'" are prosecuted by the government not for their beliefs but for the violent acts they commit to achieve their goals.

In a society as diverse as that of the United States, attempts to reorganize relations between church and state and to destabilize relations among different populations are regarded with suspicion. In "What the Fundamentalists Want," Richard John Neuhaus, writing in *Commentary*, eloquently explains why the right-wing Christians, much feared for their claim to represent the dominant and, indeed, the only true religion, should nevertheless be accorded the religious tolerance they find it hard to give to others.

MARGINAL MOVEMENTS[1]

In the United States, the traditions of religious liberty and separation of church and state create a unique context for conflicts between religion and public authority. The growing tension along the increasingly ambiguous boundary of church and state can be related to two trends: the phenomenal expansion of the modern state with permeation of governmental prerogatives through nearly all socioeconomic and cultural processes; and the consequent increasing fragility of the state and precariousness of its provision of both services and legitimation. A third key trend, the expansion of the activities and functions of churches, is partly a consequence of the fragility of the overexpanded state. The convergence of diversifying "religious" operations and an expanded scope of public authority operates to maximize the potential for conflict.

[1]Reprint of an article by Thomas Robbins, a writer on contemporary religious movements. Published by permission of Transaction, Inc., from SOCIETY, vol. 21, no. 4, May/June 1984. Copyright © 1984 by Transaction, Inc.

Public authority increasingly regulates all manner of nonreligious organizations in the United States. The privileges and exemptions enjoyed by religious institutions are made more conspicuous and controversial, and churches increasingly appear as isolated privileged enclaves. Entrepreneurs and leaders hasten to label their operations "religious" to partake of privileges and exemptions, thereby fueling popular resentment against clerical prerogatives.

The consequences of what might be termed the "regulatory gap" between church-related and secular enterprises are mitigated to the extent that religious groups are highly specialized in their functions and do not compete with other institutions and groups. The phenomenon of secularization in the twentieth century and the much touted privatization of modern religiosity have entailed the specialization of religion and its detachment from other social realms. This inhibits the potential for conflict in the interface of the privileged churches with the increasingly expanded, centralized state. Some aspects of secularization are presently being reversed, and the boundaries of the religious "specialization" are becoming less distinct. Religious organizations frequently appear to be seeking to expand the scope of their functions and authority. They come into conflict with both the state and other institutions and groups such as the family, businesses, medical practitioners, teachers, social workers, and minorities. Dean Kelley of the National Council of Churches notes, "The churches are let know that [if] they venture out of their hallowed precincts of chapel, croft and chantry into the 'real' world, they will have to brave the rigors that their 'secular counterparts' (supposedly) have to meet."

The heavily regulated and bureaucratic nature of American society, particularly its social service processes, encourages the functional diversification of religion as a means of evading regulatory constraints. In their introductory essay to *Religious Movements in Contemporary America*, Irving Zaretsky and Mark Leone argue that today's religious ferment is "typically American" in its "entrepreneurial" quality. "As a people we have a built-in incentive toward individualism and innovation, and we are reaping the consequences of that tradition today in religion. If it is gone from the small businessman in the economy, it is alive and well in religion." In America, according to Zaretsky and Leone, religion is "the only place where social experimentation is possible. It is the folk answer to a system that is over-diplomaed, over-certified, too specialized, and too conscious of where one receives certification."

An observer sympathetic to religion may be uncritically enthusiastic over the innovative and entrepreneurial quality of today's religious esotericism. Perhaps it was innovative and dynamically entrepreneurial for the Reverend Jim Jones to have his followers adopt children who were wards of the state of California and thus become eligible for welfare benefits to be paid to the church. The religious claims of the Church of Scientology and Synanon might be viewed as end runs around the constraints of accreditation and professional standards for psychotherapists. Such evasions provoke resentment and movements to expand state authority to protect the "religious consumer." These movements crack down on alleged fraud, deception, and malpractice by gurus and others said to be "practicing therapy without a license" by promising specific psychic benefits for established fees. Such demands are met by arguments affirming the priority of religious freedom and the inadmissibility of state intervention in this realm. The diversification of religious entrepreneurship, protected by the First Amendment, conflicts with trends toward broader public regulation of organizational behavior and increased liability of professionals for harmful practices.

Fragility of the Expanded State

The expansion of the apparatus and regulatory mandate of the state has contributed to church-state tensions. Paradoxically, the same can be said of the fragility of state authority and operations, which is now increasingly apparent, and which is perhaps in part a consequence of the state's overexpansion. The state's ability to manage the economy and mitigate both inflation and unemployment is more and more in doubt. The conflict between containing fiscal deficits and enhancing military preparedness is particularly acute. The contraction of public services may imperil key social values such as equal opportunity or the elimination of poverty. The foundations of public revenue may be seriously threatened by tax revolt. The ability of the state to cope with crime and terrorism, with or without an erosion of civil liberties, has been questioned. The state cannot deliver the goods, services, and meanings essential to an elevated "quality of life." (The Great

Society motif of the 1960s, as well as the dissident sociopolitical currents of that period, entailed a demand or promise that the state should or would create an elevated quality of life for the general populace.) A widespread skepticism has crystallized regarding the ability of state power to solve social problems and bring about the good life for all.

As the state falters, social movements and groups attempt to fill the vacuum. The Guardian Angels claim to be combating crime and are resented and allegedly persecuted by the police. Religious groups are particularly adept at seizing opportunities arising from a vacuum. Religious symbols and mystiques of fellowship provide broad and unbounded legitimation for expanded activities and services; constitutionally grounded church autonomy provides a barrier to the intrusive state and its constraining regulatory apparatus, which is prohibited from becoming "entangled" with ecclesiastical affairs. The communal provision of diversified services by totalistic cults such as the Unification Church is an extreme example of this development. On a more mundane level, some Protestant parents send their children to Catholic parochial schools because they believe that the teaching is superior and drug use and knife fights are less frequent than in public academies. Other Protestants send their children to evangelical Christian schools where parental values will be transmitted and interracial contacts minimized. The growth of religious surrogates for public services such as public schools produces conflicts with both traditional providers of services—such as licensed doctors, teachers, or social workers—and with groups that feel dependent upon public services. Those groups—often disadvantaged—fear that nonpublic services will not be accessible to them and that the surge of private surrogates will diminish the resources available for public services.

These tendencies contribute to the increasing range, intensity, and salience of issues involving churches and religious groups in public, legislative, and judicial debates. Stigmatized movements such as Scientology and the Unification Church are at the cutting edge of church-state boundary disputes because they are so highly diversified and multifunctional. Their religious shield against federal regulation enables them to consolidate what Richard Ofshe calls "protected empires." I think many issues involving "cults" are closely related to broader issues of church autonomy vs. public prerogatives in various areas including labor and employment, health, education, commercial practices, and financial accountability. With the notable exception of the mystified "mind control" issue, the conflicts in which cults are involved are similar to conflicts and controversies involving less stigmatized religious groups. The esoteric beliefs and rituals of cults, their frequent messianic intolerance, and their lack of community and grass-roots support, render them particularly provocative and vulnerable. The broader reality is the ongoing diversification of religious activities conflicting with the expansion of the state's regulatory mandate.

Religious Diversification and State Regulation

In the fall of 1983, the Reverend Sun Myung Moon appealed his conviction for tax fraud. The appellate brief written by Laurence Tribe notes that the prosecution relied heavily on the assertion that Moon had expended funds for "personal" and "business," rather than "religious," purposes. This established that they were Moon's taxable personal funds, not tax-exempt church funds. Tribe's brief argues that the distinction between "the religious" on the one hand and "the economic" or "the personal" is "itself a constitutionally protected religious distinction" such that "the jury was bound to accept the Unification Faith's *own* definition of what was religious." The judge allegedly erred in empowering the jury "to decide, on whatever basis it wished, whether various expenditures 'were' religious." Moon is also the beneficiary of an *amicus curiae* (friend-of-the-court) brief filed by the National Council of Churches, the United Presbyterian Churches, and other mainline church groups. The *amicus* brief complains that evidentiary rulings by the trial court prevented the defendant's attorneys from eliciting testimony indicating the relationship between the defendant's commercial enterprises and the financial needs of the church's spiritual mission. The *amicus* brief expresses "sharp distress" at the horrendous "breach of religious liberty."

The question of who determines what economic involvements or financial allotments are for religious or nonreligious purposes is of crucial importance to highly diversified movements with far-ranging operations and investments. Cults are egregious but not unique in their diversification, hence the support given to the claims of the generally detested Mr. Moon by more respected religious groups, which may also have investments and commercial enterprises.

In 1978, Joey P. Moore argued in "Piercing The Religious Veil of The So-called Cults," in the *Pepperdine Law Review*, that the economic diversification of some movements is so extreme that such organizations further "secular purposes which are not enumerated by Section 301(e) of the Internal Revenue Code." Much of Moore's concern is directed to the social programs of movements such as the Unification Church, Scientology, the People's Temple, Synanon, Hare Krishna and the Children of God. Moore doubts that the "underlying goals and policies" of these movements are truly religious. The agendas of the movements, he argues, included altering the nature of the family, creating a utopian society, revolutionizing sexual mores, fighting communism, or bringing about socialism. "Can the inference be made that [these movements'] attempts at securing formal recognition are merely efforts to conceal their social programs?" Cultist "programs of this nature . . . have uncertain, if any, religious import" and should be carefully scrutinized as to whether they disqualify a group from having the status of a tax-exempt church.

Moore's implicit definition of an authentic religion is narrow and would exclude, for example, millenarian sects, which create visions of "a better world" and whose members often try to live in accordance with such visions. More interesting are the implications for the expanding social programs of conventional churches, for example, the Catholic bishops' agenda on arms control, conservative sociopolitical activism of evangelicals, Jewish support for Israel, and Catholic agitation against abortion and gay liberation. As James Beckford recently noted, the protests within churches against American involvement in Vietnam in the late sixties and early seventies were relatively low-key compared to "today's religiously inspired campaigns against abortion, euthanasia, and the teaching of evolutionary theory in public schools." The conflicts in which both conventional and deviant groups are enmeshed seem similar. Fundamental issues cut across the sometimes ambiguous line separating reputable churches from stigmatized cults.

The Worldwide Church of God was founded almost fifty years ago. Still under the leadership of its elderly prophet and founder, Herbert Armstrong, the movement may be on the borderline of respectability. Acting on complaints from church dissidents of serious financial mismanagement, the attorney general of California began an investigation and sought to examine the church's books. To prevent the records from being destroyed, the attorney general obtained a court order appointing a receiver, who was forbidden to interfere with "ecclesiastical affairs." The receivership lasted for nearly three months in 1979 until loyal church members raised a $2 million bond and obtained a stay of the court order.

The theory under which the attorney general acted is that church finances constitute a "public trust." The status of a church as a charitable trust or corporation gives the state a special mandate to investigate mismanagement and to ensure that tax-exempt funds are spent in accordance with the stated purposes for which the exemption was granted. Under this doctrine, church funds are "public funds" and the attorney general, who represents the public, has a greater regulatory mandate regarding church finances than for the affairs of private businesses. This theory is anathema to officials of the National Council of Churches and other groups, who insist that what is essential is not that a given church is also a charitable trust, but that a particular charity has a special status as a church. This severely limits the power of the state to interfere since the First Amendment gives churches a greater protection from state regulation than is afforded private companies. Concerned denominational spokespersons also repudiate what appears to them an overly facile distinction between financial and ecclesiastical affairs of churches. According to Dean Kelley this is a dichotomy that religious bodies cannot afford to concede. "How a religious body raises, invests and expends its funds cannot be divorced from its religious purpose, ministry and mission, and Government cannot intervene in the one without affecting the other." The "religious freedom lobby" would cover diverse financial and commercial endeavors under the blanket protection of freedom of worship.

The concern of conventional church leaders over both the public trust doctrine and the financial/ecclesiastical dichotomy is not mitigated by the likelihood that the state will apply these doctrines primarily to esoteric groups with charismatic prophet-leaders. The churches with charismatic leadership, as Richard Ofshe has noted, have not developed built-in bureaucratic mechanisms to promote financial accountability. The implications are substantial for more stable groups. Protestant and Catholic church groups collaborated in a successful campaign to amend the California statutes to nullify the power of the attorney general to take future action similar to that taken against the Worldwide Church of God.

In 1977, the Equal Employment Opportunity Commission (EEOC) sued the Southwestern Baptist Theological Seminary in federal district court to compel the seminary to file form EEO-6, which seeks to obtain data on the number and duties of several categories of employees concerning their compensation, tenure, race, sex, and national origin. According to regulations of the EEOC, submission of this form is mandatory for all institutions of higher learning with fifteen or more employees. The commission's authority in this area is ultimately grounded in Title VII of the 1964 Civil Rights Act.

The government's contention regarding the applicability of the EEOC rules was disputed by the seminary, which argued that there was never any congressional intent to apply the Equal Employment Opportunity Act to religion or religious activities. The seminary is wholly owned and operated by the Southern Baptist Convention, and it has the exclusive purpose of training people to serve the denomination. The district court agreed with the defendant and in January 1980 issued an opinion denying EEOC jurisdiction over the seminary, which has a right to make what it views as "divinely guided assessments of each employee's suitability" without state interference. The district court opinion also argued that an unconstitutional burden on the free exercise of religion is presented by the application of Title VII to any aspect of the seminary's employment practice or policy. In July 1981 the circuit court of appeals partly reversed the decision of the district court and ruled that administrators and support personnel of the seminary, who are not ministers, are subject to the regulatory jurisdiction of the EEOC. While the Baptist seminary was entitled to the status of a church, only personnel directly involved in teaching or supervision of teaching could be viewed as ministers and be excluded from the EEOC's jurisdiction. The circuit court rejected the opinion of the district court that a determination by the state as to which employees are performing religious roles threatens the separation of church and state and burdens the free exercise of religion. In the spring of 1982, the Supreme Court declined to review the circuit court's decision.

The Southwestern Baptist Theological Seminary case presents a clear conflict between claims of religious liberty/church autonomy and the expansion of the scope of state regulation in pursuit of a key social value—equal opportunity. The substantive area of labor and employment policies is one in which cults are under attack. The multifunctional diversification of some religious movements may render participants highly dependent upon the group, which provides a range of services for the participant, who is relatively powerless to affect group policy. There are implications for exploitation of the participants, who may derive more spiritual than material benefit from their labor in church owned enterprises. Other issues involve implicit contracts in which the participant surrenders his own property in return for a nonenforceable promise of lifetime care, which is conditional upon the whim of a guru or prophet. There are also questions arising from the training of professionals and paraprofessionals in religiotherapeutic movements. The alleged noncertification of the trainees renders them dependent upon the movement, outside of which they cannot practice their trade. There are allegations that labor patterns in exploitative totalistic cults constitute instances of slavery in violation of the Thirteenth Amendment. To what extent can the state interfere in "religious" practices involving labor and employment? This question bears upon churches as well as cults.

There are numerous allegations of fraudulent practices and substandard care with respect to a range of social services operated under the auspices of religiotherapeutic movements. Particularly likely to be affected are quasi-medical institutions such as baby clinics or nursing homes, as well as facilities for delinquents or drug addicts. Fierce controversies over licensing have erupted. In this respect excoriated cults are often in the same position as born-again groups, although the latter have considerably more political clout and grassroots support. Several years ago, the attorney general of Texas made strenuous efforts to subject to a licensing requirement homes for incorrigible girls operated by Brother Lester Roloff, an ally of erstwhile Governor Clements. Although corporal punishments and one attempted murder (of an inmate by other inmates) allegedly transpired in these establishments, the state's nominal victory was nullified by a formal transfer of ownership to a church.

In the recent landmark Supreme Court decisions involving Bob Jones University and The Goldsboro Christian Schools, the Supreme Court rejected the claim that withdrawal of a tax exemption from church-linked schools practicing racial discrimination unconstitutionally burdens the free exercise of religion. Justice Burger's majority opinion represents a broad and sweeping application of the "public policy doctrine" whereby tax exemptions are conditional upon the exempt organization's conformity with public policy. This doctrine has also been used by the Internal Revenue Service (IRS) against the Church of Scientology. In arguing for the withdrawal of Scientology's tax privileges, the IRS produced a lengthy list of transgressions against public policy, ranging from theft of public documents (for which several Scientologists have been convicted) to brainwashing. The litigation continues, but an appellate court has drastically reduced the list of actionable transgressions.

Burger's opinion affirms that all tax exemptions are fundamentally granted in consideration of the charitable quality of the organization's activity. The petitioning schools had claimed that an institution was entitled to a tax exemption if its purposes were religious or charitable or educational—i.e., there are three alternative, coequal qualifications. Justice Burger rejected a literal reading of the Internal Revenue Code and affirmed that all tax-exempt organizations must be "charitable" in the common law sense of the term, serving a public purpose and not contravening public policy and community standards. Logically, a "charitable" interpretation of religious tax exemptions should strengthen the activist "public trust" doctrine. This would affirm the government's responsibility for overseeing church finances, as claimed by California in placing the Worldwide Church of God under receivership. Additional implications of the Burger opinion may include claims that exotic cults have jeopardized their tax privileges through authoritarian, antisocial, and antifamily practices which contravene community standards (e.g., the IRS cites brainwashing as one of many reasons for challenging the tax exemption of the Church of Scientology). Alternatively, politically active church groups may risk their tax privileges in challenging public policy. In a concurring opinion, Justice Powell expressed unease with the sweeping nature of Burger's public policy emphasis, and reminded the Court that one aim of our system of tax exemptions is to subsidize diversity and dissent.

The Issue of "Mind Control"

There is one respect in which conflicts over the alleged use of "mind control" by cults are continuous with conflicts embroiling less esoteric religious groups. Presently the range of groups that are targets of both brainwashing allegations and attempts at physical abduction of converts is expanding. Increasingly, born-again, fundamentalist, and Pentecostal groups are being targeted. An aspect of what Robert Wuthnow has called today's "religious populism" is the diffusion of religious patterns such as fundamentalism, glossolalia (speaking in tongues), and faith healing—once associated with rural, southern, or lower-class persons—among the educated middle classes. New Christian fellowships are arising and developing campus ministries. Such groups, as well as older fundamentalist or Pentecostal groups, appear alien and antimodern to many parents of converts, who are prone to label these groups "cults" and apply to them a conceptual framework developed by the opponents of the Unification Church and Hare Krishna. The growth of these latter groups has leveled off. Consequently there appears to be a cadre of professional deprogrammers and auxiliaries that cannot be supported merely by operations against the classic "destructive cults." Recent deprogrammings have involved "Christian" groups such as the Maranatha Fellowship, the Champaign-Urbana Fellowship, Hobart Freeman's Faith Assembly (which rejects modern medicine), Jews for Jesus, and even the respectable and rapidly growing Assemblies of God. As Ted Koppel was told on a "Nightline" program by a deprogrammed ex-member of the Faith Assembly, "it is not only the Moonies or the Krishnas wearing orange robes who brainwash people, it is also the groups which are so close to Christianity that no one wants to fight them, but they're the real danger" [approximate quote]. The line separating stigmatized "mind controlling cults" and acceptable high-commitment groups is becoming increasingly indistinct.

The interface of the diversification of putatively protected religious activities and the expanding regulatory mandate of the state is presently heightening the tension between church and state. Cults such as Scientology and the Unification Church are egregious (though hardly unique) in their diversified aggrandizement and are thus on the frontier of church-state conflict. The conflicts in which stigmatized cults are enmeshed are not qualitatively distinct from the conflicts involving more reputable groups. The basic conflict can be conceptualized as a claim of church autonomy clashing with a claim that public authority is responsible for enforcing a certain value (e.g., racial equality) which is allegedly contravened in a commercial, financial, educational, healing, social service, or political operation linked in some way to a church. The most absolutist defenders of church autonomy would cover all manner of enterprises with the shield of the First Amendment, thereby equating with freedom of worship the right to pursue profitable activities without public accountability. Not only can one make money for God, but that process must be deemed a religious one. At the other extreme is the doctrine of the California attorney general in which the state may interfere with the finances of a bona fide church more freely than it can intervene in the affairs of a private corporation because church money is held by church officials as a public trust. The traditional proscription of governmental "entanglement" in the running of churches allegedly pertains mainly to "ecclesiastical" affairs, not to church finances.

Integral to debates about church and state is the traditional distinction between religious belief, which is generally interpreted as receiving an absolute constitutional protection, and religious action or behavior, which receives a more limited protection. The degree of protection afforded verbal behavior involving direct expression or acting out of beliefs is generally viewed as substantial, since freedom of belief must entail affirming and teaching beliefs, praying, chanting, and performing other rituals.

The belief/action distinction is currently under attack by both proponents and opponents of enhanced state regulation of churches. The defenders of church autonomy fear that diminishing the sanctity of religious behavior relative to the sacred subjectivity of belief will lead ultimately to effective state control of religion via control of religion's practical implementation. "'Exercise' is an *action* word, used expressly in the First Amendment solely to characterize freedom of religion" notes Dean Kelley. A rigid adherence to the belief/action dichotomy will "render the free exercise clause a dead letter, conferring no independent rights to act or practice and no collateral sanctions where beliefs were unpopular enough to incur the wrath of repressive legislation." Some of the opponents of cults have questioned whether the belief/action dichotomy is applicable to the

context of cultist religiosity in which religious beliefs are allegedly inculcated by coercive persuasion and are thus not held voluntarily. The constitutional guarantee of "free exercise of religion"
may be inapplicable to cults, in which religion is supposedly not
"free." This perspective differs from the conventional view that
perceives a constitutional proscription of any state interference
with religious beliefs, notwithstanding how those beliefs are generated.

The radical quality of the concepts of "brainwashing" and
"mind control," which are used to legitimate public or private action against cults, elevates the challenge to church autonomy
from the level of religious action to religious belief. Cultist brainwashing syndromes are said to include as key components repetitive chanting and the teaching of converts that loss of faith will
result in eschatological harms such as being reincarnated as a
worm or being cast into a lake of fire. (Both ritual chanting and
eschatological warnings figured in a recent trial in which the
Hare Krishnas were ordered to pay an ex-devotee and her mother $32.5 million in part for "false imprisonment" through brain-
washing of a fourteen-year-old girl.) Elements of sectarian
ideologies such as absolutist and polarized thinking are interpreted as aspects of mental impairment produced by cultist mind control. Attributions of mind control often entail transvaluations of
items (e.g., indifference to nonreligious matters, suddenness or
apparent irrationality of conversion, dualistic thinking, stereotyped discourse, chanting) that might otherwise be viewed as simply demonstrating the intensity and dogmatic quality of the
devotee's faith. The convert's belief is used as a sign of incompe-
tence or victimization.

Some "remedies" for cultist mind control appear to involve
constraints on religious belief, teaching, and ritual. The most per-
vasive remedy is "coercive deprogramming," toward which the
courts have often been permissive. The process involves forcible
confinement of a devotee who receives counterindoctrination,
which often entails direct attacks on the convert's beliefs. Legislation has been introduced in several states to directly legitimate
and facilitate such procedures through court-ordered guardian-
ships or conservatorships. Such proceedings will directly impli-
cate the state in the deconversion of minority believers. In my
view, the introduction of "mind control" into legal discourse has
implications for shifting the focus from religious action to religious belief.

Mind control additionally shifts the focus of inquiry and control to the murky area of individual consciousness of which reliable knowledge is lacking and inferences are highly susceptible to subjectivity and bias. Even though "free will" is a metaphysical concept, the legal system has generally assumed that individuals are autonomous and responsible. If peer pressure, perhaps accompanied by repetitive chanting, rituals, intolerance, dogmatism, and fire-and-brimstone intimidation, is treated as a demiurge that inundates free will, the result will be a radically innovative reinforcement of a disturbing trend to erode the assumption of personal autonomy as a premise of legal action.

In my view the ultimate sources of hostility to authoritarian cults lie in their extreme diversification and aspiring omnicompetence. These tendencies can also be seen somewhat in more reputable groups. In the process they have provoked various groups such as clergy, parents, and mental health workers whom they compete with or seek to displace. Legal constraints on religious movements should be developed within the framework of the duality of action and belief. Substantial constraints can be imposed on abusive movements without undermining the sanctity of religious belief and verbal expressions of belief.

ON THE DIFFERENT WORLD OF UTAH: THE MORMON CHURCH[2]

Utah is widely perceived—both nationally and locally—as a "different world," a state out of step with the rest of the nation. "Crossing its border is like riding along a wrinkle in time," said *The Denver Post* in a 1982 series of articles on Utah. "It's strange, weird, dizzying: a land where everything seems just a few degrees out of plumb." The Mormon Church "wields irrefutable influence" in virtually every aspect of life, *The Denver Post* claimed, and the Church "does not take kindly to dissent." The pluralism of the other 49 states does not apply in Utah, the articles maintained, because Utah is "the Church State," and that

[2]Address by James L. Clayton, Provost, University of Utah, at the National Collegiate Honors Council's 20th Annual Conference, October 31, 1985. *Vital Speeches of the Day.* 52:186–92. Ja. 1, '86. Reprinted with permission.

means "authority, obedience and control" have become the hallmarks of Utah. Robert Gottlieb and Peter Wiley, in their more recent book *America's Saints*, speak of increasing authoritarianism within the Mormon church and the shrinking space for the independent scholarly Mormon within this "self-contained" and somewhat "mysterious" community. A "siege mentality prevails" in Mormondom, they believe, and the tension between Mormons and the rest of America and between liberal Mormons and authoritarian Mormons "promises to intensify in the years to come." The bizarre bombings in Salt Lake City earlier this month, where two persons were killed and a third seriously injured in three separate incidents, has reinforced this image of Utah as indeed a "different world," particularly since these tragic incidents seem to be related in large part to activities and issues which could only be possible in the Mormon culture.

The purpose of this presentation is to examine the accuracy of the view that Utah and the Mormons are "a different world." I will argue that although "The Church State" thesis has some validity, it is largely a caricature of life in Utah today. I shall also maintain that despite the recent, bizarre, and baffling murders in this city and the increasing authoritarianism within the Church itself, the measurable evidence and the long-term trends are toward greater accommodation between the Mormons and other Americans. Finally, I shall contend that in contrast to the increasing accommodation between Mormons and non-Mormons there is increasing tension—some would call it paranoia—between Church leaders and historians of Mormonism, a tension as unnecessary as it is unwise. Some suggestions for diminishing this tension will be presented in my concluding remarks, suggestions which emphasize building on the essence of Mormonism rather than defending its excesses.

The perception that Utah is a different world stems largely from the fact that Utah is 68 percent Mormon and that no other state is dominated by any single religion to this degree. Rhode Island's population is 64 percent Catholic, a close second, but even in the South, where Southern Baptists are strong, no state quite reaches the level of domination of the Mormons in Utah. Ironically, the majority of Salt Lake City residents is non-Mormon, and has been ever since World War I. The domination of the state by Mormons is evident in a variety of ways: Utah's governor is a Mormon, most of Utah's mayors are Mormon, as are all of Utah's congressmen and senators. All of the superintendents of Utah's school districts are Mormon and about 90 percent of the state legislature belongs to that faith. There are "Mormon seats" held by church authorities on the boards of many of the state's major corporations as well as a Mormon apostle on the State Board of Regents. All of the state's university and college presidents are Mormons, as is the state's Commissioner of Higher Education.

Utah is different in other ways. Utah's birth rate and the percentage of children under 10 years of age is the highest in the nation; the state's abortion rate is among the lowest. Because of this high birth rate and the state's limited resources, its level of per capita income has been trending downward for many years and is now near the bottom in state rankings (49th in 1984). Violent crime rates in Utah are also very low, a fact that should be underscored in light of the recent bombings, as is the percentage of the population who are in prison. This latter figure may be low because Utah tends, according to prison authorities, to keep only the more violent criminals locked up. Alcohol and tobacco consumption are lower in Utah than the national average, and the average Mormon male lives six years longer and the average Mormon female three years longer than other Americans. The state also has extraordinarily low rates of cancer, cirrhosis of the liver, heart disease, syphilis, and gonorrhea; but a much higher rate of obesity. The percentage of the population living in urban areas is very high, as is voter turnout. The percentage of students who complete high school and college is also near the top nationally but very few leave the state to go to school.

Utahns are also politically more conservative than the rest of the nation, although this is a relatively recent phenomenon. Utah led the nation both in 1980 and in 1984 in the percentage of votes cast for President Reagan. Utah county, the home of Brigham Young University, also cast a higher percentage of votes for President Reagan in 1984 than any other county in the nation—over 80 percent. Utah's senators and congressmen (there are no women) are also among the most conservative in Washington.

Undoubtedly the Mormon Church has played a major role in shaping political attitudes within the state. The Church has taken strong public stands against abortion, the Equal Rights Amendment, premarital sex, pornography, artificial insemination of single women, homosexuality, and to a lesser degree, women who are employed outside of the home. It has also opposed liquor-by-the-drink in Utah, the showing of X-rated films, and efforts to repeal right-to-work laws. Utahns have generally agreed with the Church on abortion, the ERA, pornography, and homosexuality, but not on X-rated films, right-to-work, and women employed in the work force.

A typical picture of the Mormon Church leadership by those who see Utah as being "out of step" with the rest of the nation is one of an ultraconservative, anti-intellectual, male gerontocracy determined to preserve the status quo and fearful of the trends they see in contemporary society. This image is further buttressed by the tendency of Church leaders to see the media as an "enemy" and their reluctance to be interviewed by reporters.

The average Mormon, as distinguished from the Church leadership, has a somewhat more positive image among those critical of Utah. *The Denver Post*'s lists of descriptive adjectives of Mormons generally include words like: "organized, middle-class, cliquish, frugal, earnest, clean-living, industrious, optimistic, pragmatic, obedient, conservative, anti-intellectual and prolific. They want to be liked; worship heroes and celebrities; worry about being accepted, and tend to think the rest of us are doomed."

There is, of course, a positive side as well, often overlooked or underemphasized by those with preconceived notions about life in Utah. Most objective observers would agree with the Mormons' description of themselves as very family-oriented, law abiding, and honestly concerned for each other's welfare. Most Mormons find real satisfaction in their weekly gatherings, exhibit sincere interest in improving their communities, and are viewed by themselves and others as a wholesome and genuinely happy people. They are world renowned for their welfare program, offer a wide array of leadership opportunities to their youth as well as adults, and the advice church members received for successful living from their leaders is, on the whole, admirable and sound. Women who choose to be homemakers and shun careers are genuinely respected, even though more women work outside the home in Utah than do nationally. Mormon temple marriages are remarkably stable and the work ethic is very much alive in the Beehive State. The opportunity to turn to God for divine guidance in all aspects of their lives is perhaps what Mormons cherish most, while not denying that right to others, and nowhere in America is spirituality held in greater esteem. Perhaps nowhere is it more in evidence as well.

There is much truth in these critical insights, but they need to be balanced with positive insights, and a deeper, more accurate, and more judicious understanding is possible with a little more data. Take the most common generalization about Utah, i.e., Utah is a Mormon state. Nominally, members of the Mormon Church represent 68 percent and Christians (including Mormons) 75 percent of the population of Utah. In total church membership this is almost exactly the same as Rhode Island and North Dakota. About 60 percent of the residents of the state consider themselves "very" or "somewhat" active in the Mormon faith, but this is a self-identification figure. About 80 percent of Americans identify themselves as Christians, but according to *The Gallup Poll* half of these people do not know who gave the Sermon on the Mount. A more realistic approach to real commitment is to measure what Mormons in fact do. Considerably less than half of them attend church regularly, pay tithing, or participate in Mormon temple rituals, three key litmus tests of authentic Mormon behavior. Committed Mormons actually number no more than about 40 to 45 percent of Utah's population. Put another way, *most* Utah residents are either non-Mormons or inactive Mormons and are largely indistinguishable in their religious behavior from other Americans. The majority of Utah residents are therefore really indifferent to Mormonism, at least in terms of their personal commitments.

Within the active Mormon culture there are several distinguishable subcultures, obvious to those who live within the state but less obvious to those from outside. There are "orthodox," "authoritarian," and "liberal" Mormons as well as a small number of "heretics." Each group has its own quite different set of characteristics, which will be described shortly, and there is considerable cross over by individuals among these groups depending on the issue in question. Generalizations about these groups are therefore risky, and many individual exceptions must be allowed for, but these general persuasions or intellectual inclinations do exist and it is necessary to understand these subcultures in order to understand just how different Utah really is and precisely where these differences are focused and to what degree they really exist. I shall begin by describing the most typical kind of Mormon—the orthodox Mormon—and then analyze those groups to the right and to the left of that group.

"Orthodox" or mainstream Mormons believe that God directs the Mormon Church and no other, they fully accept current Mormon doctrine and seriously attempt to practice the officially approved teachings of their faith. Orthodox Mormons attend meetings regularly; pay a tenth of their income to the Church; abstain from tobacco, liquor and stimulants; seldom question Church doctrine or policy; and are comfortable if not serene in their faith. Most of them are not comfortable with those who advocate "blind obedience" no matter how high their office, and most are appalled by religious fanaticism.

As Gottlieb and Wiley suggest in their book, *America's Saints*, mainstream Mormons are not very thirsty for information and therefore are not much disturbed by historical controversy. Orthodox Mormons are conservative and conventional, committed but not especially aggressive, deeply religious but not especially intolerant. Orthodox Mormons believe in the possibility of and even the necessity for compromise with secular culture, as for example when the Church was forced by the U.S. government to cease the practice of polygamy and when, under growing pressure from the civil rights movement, it more recently broadened the category of those eligible for the priesthood to include all black males. But, unlike their more liberal brethren, orthodox Mormons view these changes as God-directed, not man-directed, and any religious compromise as limited and infrequent.

Perhaps half to two-thirds of the active membership falls into this orthodox category as measured by church attendance, payment of tithes, temple worship, abstinence from stimulants, and other obvious indicators of Mormon religiousness. But half to two-thirds of the active Mormon population is less than one-third of the state's population.

To the right of the "orthodox" Mormons are what Gottlieb and Wiley call "authoritarian" Mormons. Authoritarian Mormons are generally described as more rigid and less compromising than orthodox Mormons, much more inclined to submission to authority as opposed to individual freedom of thought. As Gottlieb and Wiley suggest, they are much more willing "to internalize and obey leadership signals" and to assert the absolute correctness of their own views. Authoritarian Mormons emphasize to a far greater extent than the orthodox their belief in the existence of a great cosmic battle between God and Satan, good and evil. They believe that a really committed Mormon should, if the

occasion requires it, be "belligerent" in the cause of righteousness, or in other words "stand up and be counted." Those who
think this way are inclined to dwell more on the "good" side of
Mormon history, more on those events which promote faith than
those which promote skepticism, for to do otherwise is to promote Satan's cause, they believe. When in doubt those in authority should decide what is best—hence the authoritarian label.

Authoritarian Mormons seem to be more conservative politically than mainstream Mormons. Virtually all of them are Repub-
licans. A few but not many subscribe to the ideals of the Liberal
Party, the Freeman Institute, or the John Birch Society. Many authoritarian Mormons are also opposed to the theory of evolution,
not so much because of a belief in the literal accuracy of the Bible
(which Mormons deny), but on the ground that it denies there is
order and design in the universe.

Authoritarian Mormons place great emphasis on obedience
to authority because they believe their leaders are divinely inspired, in secular as well as religious matters. Accordingly, they
are openly intolerant of critics of the Church, and are proud to
be considered God's "chosen people."

The prime motivating force that has engendered the recent
authoritarian mentality in some Mormons seems to be based on
their belief that American culture is turning away from God, despite considerable statistical evidence to the contrary. They are
especially concerned by the more realistic portrayal of the Mormon experience by historians, particularly those who write from
within the fold. Their purpose is to build a subculture within
America, with its own mores and social institutions, that would
provide a divine alternative to the dominant secular cultural
ethos. If outsiders perceive this desire to preserve God's ways as
paranoia or, less pejoratively, as "a different world," then that is
something to be proud of, not ashamed of, they believe.

There is no way statistically to measure the number of Mormons in this group. There are no journals or organizations to
publicize the authoritarian views of these Mormons, as there are
for the liberal Mormons. Nevertheless, this authoritarian strain
is frequently commented upon, both by insiders and outsiders,
and does give a certain negative flavor to Utah's culture. Still,
even if roughly 30 to 40 percent of all active Mormons were inclined to be authoritarian in their views they would represent
about 15 percent of the total population of the state. This 15 per-

cent is very powerful, however, because a substantial number of Church leaders are included within this group.

To the left of the orthodox Mormons are the liberal Mormons. Liberals are much more autonomous, independent, pragmatic, and broadminded than the orthodox and openly oppose the authoritarian mentality of their fellow Mormons. Whereas an authoritarian Mormon might be inclined to say the Church is "true" because God said so, a liberal Mormon would more likely affirm the "usefulness" of the Church because the values it teaches are important and worthwhile. Liberal Mormon views are best expressed in *Dialogue*, an independent journal which seeks to bring the Mormon faith "into dialogue with the larger stream of Judeo-Christian thought and with human experience as a whole," and *Sunstone*, a younger and more spritely magazine of the same genre. There are few if any liberals today among the Church's General Authorities and not very many in the second echelon of leadership.

Liberal Mormons exhibit a wide spectrum of belief in the doctrine of Mormonism including the ethical teachings and social activities of the L.D.S. Church, but generally they are more critical of Church leaders and much more pragmatic in their commitments than the orthodox. More autonomous and tolerant of other faiths, liberals are also inclined to accommodate to modern secular culture more than the orthodox. To liberals the Church no longer speaks as the sole voice of authority, so characteristic of Mormonism in the 19th century, but most of them are active participants and have a real affection for their Church. Like the orthodox, liberals like the order and decency of the Mormon community and many believe that God speaks to them through the Church however imperfect.

Liberals emphasize free inquiry, rationality, and personal commitment in their faith. They tend to think in terms of degrees of probability, rather than absolutes, and are skeptical of "faithful" or "official" Church history. Some doubt there was such a man as Adam and many are sure Joseph Smith made a lot of mistakes, especially with regard to polygamy. A few Mormon liberals doubt Joseph Smith had a vision or that the *Book of Mormon* is an authentic, historical record, but their numbers are small. Perhaps it would be more accurate to describe these persons as "heretics" rather than liberals, since belief in the *Book of Mormon* is the sine qua non of membership.

If commitment characterizes the orthodox and certainty the authoritarian Mormon, then broadmindedness and a strong commitment to intellectual freedom are the hallmarks of the liberal. The determination to face history squarely and honestly, and the willingness to be critical of official orthodoxy means, of course, that the Mormon liberal must define himself. Living without certainty while yearning for some sort of religious affirmation also means that the liberal's path is sometimes a lonely and controversial one.

Liberal Mormons can be found among all classes but tend to cluster among the affluent and the well-educated. But as BYU researchers Stan Albrecht and Tim Heaton have shown, unlike those of most other faiths, the more educated a Mormon is the more likely he or she is to attend church, pay a full tithing, and to pray. Accordingly, liberal Mormons tend to be very active and very committed. This might seem strange to an outsider but not to an insider who knows the importance placed on having a "calling" in the Church. Although their numbers are small, perhaps 5 to 10 percent of the population, the ability of Mormon liberals to raise questions and to get their views into the public media is substantial. This liberal characteristic tends to make issues appear to be more significant than they really are, at least in the number of people who really care about them, but then that is the nature of the avant-garde in any society.

All of these different kinds of active Mormons, as well as the third of the state who are non-Mormons and the fourth that are inactive Mormons, are part of the "different world of Utah," but they relate quite differently to their culture and are often in conflict with one another. Like all states, Utah has a diverse population. Generalizations about Utah are therefore risky and should be qualified by whether one is a Mormon or not, and if Mormon, whether one is orthodox, liberal or whatever. It also makes a difference whether one has a rural or urban background, high or low income, and a college or a high school degree. If one is talking about lower-middle-class, moderately educated, elderly Utahns living in a conservative or an especially insular Utah community, many authoritarian adjectives might be justified. If one is talking however about upper-class, well-educated, young Mormons who reside along the eastern foothills of Salt Lake City, more liberal adjectives would probably be required. Mormons attending BYU seem to be much more conservative, but not necessarily more active, than Mormons attending the University of Utah. Mormons who are knowledgeable about the Church's history are perhaps more critical of official Church publications describing that history than those who are not, but they are not necessarily less committed. One simply cannot generalize very easily about Mormons. They come in a wide variety of ideological packages and exhibit a wide range of commitments, but that range is narrower to be sure than it is among Protestants.

The main problem with journalistic accounts about "the different world of Utah" is that they focus on the *Mormons,* when most people in Utah are really not Mormons in any meaningful way. That is, the majority of Utahns do not go to a Mormon church regularly, pay tithing, abstain from stimulants, send their children on missions, do temple work, etc., etc. Additionally, when journalists talk about the state's active Mormon community, they tend to focus on the authoritarian Mormons, who are in the minority, rather than mainstream Mormons, who are much more typical. This approach lends itself to sensationalism and distortion. It is like judging all Muslims by the Shiite sect or all Catholics by the Jesuits or all Protestants by the views of the Southern Baptists. There *is* a "different" and authoritarian subculture in Utah, just as there is a "different" and authoritarian subculture in west Texas, southern California, and eastern Kentucky—but in all of these cases they are just that: subcultures.

Looking more closely at other descriptive characteristics of Utah can also be instructive. Take for example Utah's birthrate. In 1979 it was 29.0 per thousand population, or twice the national average. But by 1984 Utah's birthrate had fallen to 23.8—which is "only" 58 percent above the national average. Rather than being exceptional, Utah's birthrate is now comparable to the birthrates in Alaska and Wyoming, neither of which has any appreciable number of Mormons, and probably no higher than the birthrate for Nazarenes, Pentecostals, and Church of God adherents. Based on the average number of children born to each 1,000 women aged 15–44, Utah's birthrate is only 8 percent higher than that of Arkansas or Mississippi. In out-of-wedlock births however Utah still ranks near the bottom of the list. Moreover, the most recent statements on birth control issued by Mormon authorities stress that the size of a person's family is for the husband and wife to decide, not a matter of doctrine. In recent months Church leaders have also instructed their news editors not to glorify large families. It should also be pointed out that many Church leaders have small families themselves. Clearly, the popular image of Utah's special fecundity needs to be modified.

Twenty-five years ago Thomas O'Dea, a Catholic sociologist who taught for some years at the University of Utah, wrote in *The Mormons* that Mormonism was a "curious combination of typicality and peculiarity." During the 19th century Mormons were certainly more peculiar than typical, but beginning in the early part of this century the shift has been toward typicality. This trend toward the center continued until the 1960s when a reaction to the counter culture trends of that decade set in and there was in Utah a demonstrable shift toward more conservative and authoritarian orientation, as there was in the nation as a whole. This reaction continued into the 1980s and is still in evidence. However, there are several signs that today Utah and the Mormons are again moving toward greater accommodation with American culture.

It was mentioned earlier that all of the state's public university and college presidents and the state's Commissioner of Higher Education are Mormons. But that fact masks how narrow the margin of election was for several of these officials. A change of a vote or two by the Regents could have resulted in the appointment of several non-Mormons, and the appointments of the presidents of the state's major universities were not decided on a strict Mormon/non-Mormon split.

One also needs to know what kind of Mormon holds political office in Utah, not just whether the office is held by a Mormon. The two previous governors who served during the past 20 years were nominal Mormons—neither active nor orthodox—and both were Democrats and extremely popular. Many of Utah's mayors are only nominal Mormons as are many of Utah's school district superintendents. Some prominent and politically important Mormons are really anti-Mormon in their private sentiments. Several examples of this phenomenon could be cited in the state legislature, on the Board of Regents, and in many state agencies. The "Mormon seats" on corporate boards held by Church officials are significant only to the extent that the Mormon who holds that seat is persuasive, and that varies considerably, and to the degree other board members share his assumptions and beliefs.

Utah's congressional delegation is all Republican but that is also true of Wyoming and Alaska. Utah state legislature is also heavily oriented toward the Republican Party but far less so than several other states are toward the Democratic Party. It is true that the Mormon Church exercises considerable political influence behind the scenes, but the Church has not always been successful when it has entered the political arena. In 1954 some Church leaders tried to rig reapportionment of the Utah senate by granting each county one senatorial vote, which would have allowed the Church politically to dominate the state, but that attempt failed. Since then the Church has been much more circumspect—and has lost about as many political battles as it has won. The Church lost its fight for Sunday closing laws, had to compromise on liquor by the drink, and was openly rebuked by Mormon congressmen when it attempted to get them to repeal section 14b of the Taft-Hartley Act. It won its fight in Utah and elsewhere against the ERA and MX missile basing mode, although more credit may be due the governor, one of the Congressional candidates, and a few professors at major universities than the Church for the defeat of the MX.

On the whole, Utah's laws are more typical than different from those of the surrounding states, with the exception perhaps of Utah's liquor laws (which are more liberal than the laws of some south central states). There is little that is distinctive about Salt Lake City or Utah generally when compared with cities or areas of similar size, income, geography, climate, and ethnic distribution. Television, newspapers, movies, music, restaurants, entertainment, and educational activities within the state are pretty much as they are elsewhere, and hardly the "self-contained universe" that journalists describe. The state is conservative, but then so is the West generally, and the residents are remarkably friendly, but that is hardly a characteristic of an isolated religious commonwealth.

The current Mormon leaders as a group are neither especially authoritarian nor are they especially controversial; they are primarily pragmatic businessmen with special expertise in marketing religion. Most of the recently appointed General Authorities were trained at secular universities, have come from the corporate, professional, or academic world, and are indistinguishable from similar leaders in a variety of other fields. Like most businessmen they are conservative, committed to the professional values of their peer group (in this case the corporate world), and appalled by any hint that they might be fanatical or kooky. Respectability is their hallmark and doing anything that would bring disrespect on the Church perhaps their greatest fear. Accordingly, favorable publicity is not only welcomed but also deliberately cultivated by them in order to enhance the acceptability of the Mormon message, both in Utah and around the world. The Tabernacle Choir, *Reader's Digest* ads, visitors' centers, and an army of clean-cut young missionaries teaching family and togetherness are more important and more typical characteristics of current Mormon activity than are the authoritarian characteristics so frequently mentioned in the press.

Mormon semi-annual conference orations are a good guide to official policy and the trend toward greater typicality. These conference speeches are quite moderate compared with 19th century Mormon jeremiads and much more subdued than the rhetoric of many Protestant evangelical preachers. Almost totally lacking in hell-fire and damnation themes, the average conference address is conservative, moderate, and non-controversial— at least among the religiously inclined. Family and personal morality are emphasized far more than conflict with the culture. Mormon leaders still insist on having the final word on religious truth, but so does virtually every other church, although usually with less fervor. Today, mainstream Mormons are puzzled by their founder's treasure hunting, concerned that he would take additional wives without the knowledge of his legal wife, and embarrassed by the even more bizarre events in their past. All Mormons, whatever their philosophical orientation, are hypersensitive about being labeled non-Christian by their fellow Americans.

The one major exception to this trend toward more accommodation is the Church's growing concern about how its history is studied and written. The historical consciousness of the Mormons is "wholly different" from other denominations, David Brion Davis wrote in a recent review of four books on Mormon history in *The New York Review of Books*. "For Mormons the visions and revelations received by Joseph Smith . . . opened a new dispensation in human history and ended 'the Great Apostasy' of some fifteen centuries, during which Catholic and Protestant churches had deluded the world and blocked the way to Christian salvation," he said. God intervened into this mundane history through Joseph Smith, Mormons believe, and established the only true church of Jesus Christ. Traditionally, Mormons rest their belief in a literal interpretation of these sacred events and have attempted to control to some degree the sources and interpretation of their history in order to support their religious goals. Those who criticize the Church—and especially its leaders—are engaged in "evil speaking of the Lord's anointed" Mormons are told. To say "anything bad about the leaders of the Church," Mormons are warned by their leaders, is to act unrighteously. "It does not matter that the criticism is true," a Church leader recently said.

The Church's historians, i.e., those who are professionally trained in the major universities and who are members of the Mormon Church, are constantly subject to scrutiny, occasionally repressed, and inevitably placed in an impossible position. If they are critical of the Church in any way they are suspect in the eyes of the Church and their fellow Mormons; if they do not treat their subject objectively they are suspect in the eyes of their professional colleagues. Either way, they lose.

The recently announced ban on the authors of the award-winning book *Mormon Enigma: Emma Hale Smith* is a case in point. This book examines polygamy from the point of view of the Prophet's legal wife, who until quite recently was not held in high regard in the western branch of the Mormon Church because she opposed polygamy. The authors, both liberal but committed members of the Church, are not to be invited to speak about the subject of their book in Church meetings. The rationale given by the leadership was that the authors were using Church meetings, especially the Relief Society, to promote their book. Many orthodox Mormons write books, of course, and speak in Church but none of them have been banned. This decision is disturbing because the authors were not given a hearing prior to the announcement of the ban, nor were they informed personally that they had been placed under interdict, nor given the opportunity to defend the accuracy of their book. A member of the University of Utah's LDS Institute faculty, a person widely respected by students and faculty alike, was also recently dismissed, apparently for writing in *Dialogue* and *Sunstone,* again without a hearing. The point here is not that the Church does not have the right to dismiss employees or to insist that they support Church doctrine and policy. The point is that this dismissal was handled in an unfair manner. The Church's official historian, a person of considerable professional stature, was dismissed from his office three years ago in a similar fashion, apparently for similar reasons.

In the September issue of *The Ensign*, the Church's official publication, President Gordon B. Hinckley, Second Counselor in the First Presidency stated:

"Fundamental to our [Mormon] theology is belief in individual freedom of inquiry, thought, and expression. Constructive discussion is a privilege of every Latter-Day Saint. But it is the greater obligation of every Latter-Day Saint to move forward the work of the Lord, to strengthen his kingdom on the earth, to teach faith and build testimony. . . . "

This view of how Church members should approach their history is, of course, not new. Salvation history, i.e., acknowledging God's hand in the past, present, and future, is a fairly common approach to history today among Christian and especially Catholic leaders. In this view there is no substitute for proclaiming the gospel and all other acts have only an ad hoc meaning. Since only fully convinced witnesses can proclaim the gospel properly, the role of the inspired General Authorities is central. The major qualification for the historian of Mormonism, in this view, is conviction, not competence. From this perspective the Church's conflict with its secularly-trained historians is really only an echo of a larger battle between God and Satan.

The historian's primary allegiance on the other hand is to truth. Truth is determined through the intellect and supported by empirical data. The constant willingness to follow this ideal—even when it puts him at odds with the culture which nourishes and sustains him—is a measure of the historian's honesty and commitment to his craft. Building the kingdom and producing an accurate and honest record of how the kingdom was built are not always compatible. Indeed, it is this very tension that "keeps sharp the biting edge of the mind" of the historian, just as a similar tension between the church and the world strengthens the spirit.

To the historian's mind, claims by Church leaders, whatever the source of their calling, that they are beyond criticism is an assertion that they are infallible. Averring that "it does not matter that the criticism is true" is nothing less than a denigration of the truth itself. In fact, experience shows that following such advice induces people to disguise their real opinions, or to discuss only trivial matters, and lacking critical insights, to give but dull and torpid assent to the doctrines they espouse. Ultimately such a course also diminishes faith because it diminishes truth.

Since there is no one way to write history, no historical orthodoxy as it were, different approaches are common and acceptable. Great writers can be cited supporting both the "salvation" approach and the "secular" approach, continuity and change, Truth with a capital "T" and relativity, metahistorical data and empirical data. The point is that even in this area of growing tension between Church leaders and Church historians, the Mormons are a part of a fairly typical American phenomenon, clearly evident among the Catholics and evangelicals today, and certainly an important part of America's past. Mormons may be a little late in facing this controversy and a little more strident toward each other, but then they are also relatively new to the game.

Looking back on a century and a half of Mormon experience, the Mormons, for the most part, are no longer a "peculiar" people so much as a typical people with a "peculiar past." The gradual accommodation of the Mormons to national norms has been a slow process with some reversals and many difficult moments. But there is no question that it has occurred. It is clearly not complete and tension points are still evident, particularly with regard to women's issues and historical inquiry. But the longer trend, which started nearly a century ago, is still in the direction of greater similarity between Utah and the nation.

Gone are the practices of polygamy and racial discrimination which so outraged America, the unsuccessful efforts at communal living, the conference tirades by General Authorities against American presidents, the continual treks into the wilderness to escape Babylon, and the widespread belief in the imminence of the Second Coming. Gone, too, is the militancy of an earlier era, including the defiant and decades-long opposition to the whole nation on the polygamy question, the harangues against luxurious living, the crusade for the prohibition of liquor, and opposition to the teaching of evolution in the public schools. Today, Mormons, unlike many evangelicals, are not upset about proscriptions on prayer in the public schools, nor are they agitating for a constitutional amendment to prohibit abortion. It is the Protestant evangelicals who are the prime advocates for a different and more authoritarian world and are the most militant in opposition to modernism. These avowed "fundamentalists" are almost all strict millenarians and insist on Biblical inerrancy. It would be difficult to find a Mormon today who would agree to either of these propositions. Most Mormons do not experience the profound ambivalence toward their surrounding culture that their forebears once did and fundamentalists do today; most embrace it with alacrity.

Rather than a beleaguered minority out of step with the rest of the nation, most Mormons and certainly most Utahns are reasonably comfortable in the modern world. Respectability is the order of the day, not deviance. Most of the younger Mormons participate fully in the business world, dress like businessmen, talk like businessmen, and act like businessmen do elsewhere. Many are comfortable with religious diversity, cultivate friendships outside the Church, and most have a strong desire to succeed in corporate America. Young Mormons differ as a group from their more elderly leaders in the Church just as today's leaders differ from the even more autocratic Mormon leadership at the turn of the century. Each generation is more willing and more able to accommodate and adjust to contemporary norms; each is more willing to put some distance between the present and what earlier Americans called the "barbarous" aspects of 19th century Mormonism.

Rather than "the different world of Utah" the dominant although not always linear direction in Utah today is one of movement along a continuum from peculiarity toward typicality. Utah is not there yet. Like most states it has its idiosyncrasies. The Mormon Church is still of course a "peculiar" religion in that it was founded by a "prophet," offers to the world additional scripture based on a "translation" from golden plates, and shuns all efforts to bring it under the Catholic-Protestant-Jewish umbrella. But Utah as a state is becoming less peculiar, and more typical with each passing decade.

Given the gradual secularization of American culture and within it of Mormon culture as well, and given the rising emphasis on scholarship and the number of new-found historical documents which challenge traditional Mormon teachings about the past, it seems quite probable that Mormons—like those of older faiths—will become less literalistic about their history and more oriented toward contemporary concerns as time goes on.

The Church has gone through and is now experiencing a very rough period in terms of confrontations with its past, as document after embarrassing document, some of which may eventually turn out to be forgeries, has come to light casting doubt on some long-accepted version of what happened during the Church's founding era. Without taking a stand on either the authenticity or the significance of each of these new challenges to Mormon orthodoxy, the total impact has certainly been to make it harder for the *informed* faithful to defend traditional Mormon views of the origin of their Church. Many such views have simply been discarded—like the old Mormon myth that God punished the "mob" who murdered Joseph and Hyrum. Things once denied are now readily admitted—like Joseph's money digging, and the early existence of Mormon avengers called "Danites." More and more Mormons are coming to believe that not all of the American Indians could have descended from the red-skinned half of the Book of Mormon people called Lamanites (as the early Church leaders taught), or that blacks are descendants of Ham and under a divine curse (as Brigham Young taught), or that all negative comment about the Church is meant to demean or comes only from dissidents and apostates.

Some within the Church are suggesting that much of this hassling over the past is a waste of time, and that contemporary Church leaders should begin to move away from the tendency to defend everything every early leader ever did and begin to focus more on the Church's undisputed capacity to bring satisfaction and happiness to its membership here and now. I share this view. We ought to cease trying to defend the excesses of Mormonism and focus on its essence. Whatever happened a hundred and fifty years ago, whatever 19th century Mormons were inclined to believe or practice, there are real spiritual needs that should be addressed *today* by a Church with a demonstrated capacity to make a major and lasting contribution to society. As Sterling McMurrin has said, "the church is not a book, nor is it a collection of books . . . Nor is it simply an ecclesiastical organization. The Church is the people who constitute it and their relationship to one another."

The Church moved out of sacred and into ordinary time when, Jan Shipps has written, it adjusted its doctrine and practices to conform with the limits of permissible dissent in American culture at the turn of the century. It could just as easily shift its focus once again from defending every suspect, often irrelevant, and sometimes outrageous incident in the distant past to supporting present needs. It would not be the first time Church leaders have turned Mormonism away from the course intended by its early leaders; nor will it be the last. Learning to live with a less literalistic and less bizarre past would take time and be traumatic for some, but probably no more traumatic than it was for Mormons 80 years ago who had to give up polygamy and all the theocratic trappings that went with it.

During the 1890s the over-riding challenge for Mormons was whether they were going to continue to practice polygamy and see their church destroyed, or change their course and survive. They chose survival. Today, the primary challenge to Mormons is to come to terms with their past, as most of the older religions have done. By building on the essence rather than defending its excesses, Mormonism will continue to grow and remain the satisfying faith it has traditionally been for the millions who subscribe to its tenets. For non-Mormons the challenge is essentially the same as it was nearly a century ago—to point out the social disadvantages and the ultimate limits of excessive peculiarity, and to expand the limits of what is religiously permissible as much as is humanly possible in our pluralistic and secular society and thereby accommodate what still remains of the different world of Utah.

CIVIL RIGHTS, INDIAN RITES[3]

Religious freedom is a fundamental right in America. The urgency of the Founding Fathers' concern to protect it is seen in that it is first among the rights guaranteed in the Bill of Rights. The First Amendment to the United States Constitution begins: "Congress shall make no law respecting an establishment of religion or prohibiting the free exercise thereof. . . . " However, freedom of religion was actively denied to American Indians for a century and a half following the ratification of the Bill of Rights. Only in recent years has the government given attention to the subject. In 1968 and again in 1978 the United States Congress formally acknowledged that the constitutional guarantee of religious freedom extends to American Indians. Encouraging as this might be, however, American Indians still experience difficulties in freely practicing their religions.

In 1968 the United States Congress extended many of the provisions of the Bill of Rights and the Civil Rights Act to Indians living under tribal jurisdiction. The "Indian Bill of Rights" for-

[3]Reprint of an article by Robert S. Michaelsen, professor of religious studies at the University of California at Santa Barbara. Published by permission of Transaction, Inc., from SOCIETY, vol. 21, no. 4, May/June 1984. Copyright © 1984 by Transaction, Inc.

mally protects Indians from tribal interference in their religion. While this act marked an advance of sorts, Indian tribes are scarcely the most formidable obstacles to the free exercise of religion by Indians. The chief culprit is the United States government itself. Congressional recognition of this fact gave rise to the passage of the American Indian Religious Freedom Act (AIRFA) in 1978.

The American Indian Religious Freedom Act

The AIRFA affirms that religious freedom is "an inherent right" for all people; it also recognizes that religious practices form the basis of Indian identity and value systems and hence are integral to Indian life. The heart of the act is a congressional resolve: "that henceforth it shall be the policy of the United States to protect and preserve for American Indians their inherent right of freedom to believe, express, and exercise [their] traditional religions . . . , including, but not limited to access to sites, use and possession of sacred objects, and freedom to worship through ceremonials and traditional rites."

Congressional hearings and other governmental consultations held in connection with AIRFA revealed the nature and extent of the abridgment of Indian religious freedom by governmental agencies. An impressive list of details is given in a twenty-nine-page appendix to the Department of the Interior's *American Indian Religious Freedom Act Report* (1979) under the headings of land, cemeteries, sacred objects, border crossings, museums, and ceremonies. Following are some examples.

Sacred sites have been destroyed by governmental action. Cherokee burial grounds in the Little Tennessee Valley were flooded by the completion of the Tellico Dam. Sites regarded by the Navaho as sacred, and even as deities, were inundated by the impoundment of Lake Powell. According to Navaho belief, the deities were drowned by this action. Sacred sites have also been desecrated, and access to sites has been denied or severely limited. Hopi and Navaho have persistently protested that the erection and proposed expansion of ski resort facilities on sacred sites in governmentally owned areas of the San Francisco Peaks in northcentral Arizona not only interferes with their religious practices—many of which entail secrecy—but also destroys the sanctity of the sites.

Federal legislation designed to preserve wilderness areas and to protect endangered species sometimes adversely affects important Indian religious practices by preventing access to sacred sites and objects. Congress sought to rectify this situation through AIRFA. Nevertheless, government agents continue to have or to create problems concerning Indian access to sacred objects such as bald eagles and bald eagle feathers. The full list of complaints continues. For example, the sacredness of medicine bundles has been repeatedly violated by the probing of customs officials, and Indian remains have been removed from sacred ground for public display in museums.

The implementation of AIRFA relative to these and similar complaints has been disappointing. While AIRFA contains praiseworthy affirmations, it is basically a toothless resolution. It calls upon federal agencies to reform but provides no way of assuring that reform results. The implementation section of the act called upon the president to direct the relevant federal agencies "to evaluate their policies and procedures in consultation with native traditional religious leaders in order to determine appropriate changes necessary to protect and preserve Native American religious cultural rights and practices." Results of these evaluations were to be reported to the Congress within a twelve-month period along with a report on administrative changes made and a list of recommendations for possible legislative action.

Under the chairmanship of the secretary of the interior a federal agencies task force was formed which, following relatively extensive consultations, produced, within the required time frame, the *American Indian Religious Freedom Act Report*. This report includes some thirty-seven pages of recommendations for federal agency action, uniform administrative procedures, and possible legislation. An executive order was also prepared to facilitate federal implementation of the congressional resolution. Very few of the recommendations for administrative action have been implemented; uniform administrative procedures have not been developed; none of the proposals for legislation have been followed, and the executive order has not been signed. Noting this massive inaction, a frustrated spokesperson for Native American rights called upon the House Subcommittee on Civil and Constitutional Rights to hold oversight hearings regarding Indian religious freedom and the implementation of AIRFA. That was in June of 1982, and nothing has happened since. American

Indian religious freedom has apparently moved off the public agenda once again.

The Continuing Problem

Like the characters in Jean Paul Sartre's *No Exit,* Indians and agents of the federal government have been thrown together in an intimate, continuing, and frustrating relationship from which there is apparently no escape. Each has sought a way out. Congress and various administrations have repeatedly sought to solve "the Indian problem" through one form or another of "the final solution." Despite high (or low) hopes, none of these proposed solutions has worked. Indians, the weaker party in the encounter, have recently sought redress through the courts, and some, giving up on the American system entirely, have appealed to international agencies. Results of Indian freedom-of-religion appeals in the United States courts have been mixed. The effects of appeals to international forums are more difficult to assess.

Some recent governmental approaches to Indian affairs have given increasing prominence to input from Indians. This was intended in AIRFA. It is even more clearly prescribed in such acts as the Indian Education Act of 1972, the Indian Self-Determination and Education Assistance Act of 1975, and the Indian Child Welfare Act of 1978. These acts extend the degree of tribal control over tribal affairs, including tribal education. Control over education of the young can be of critical importance to the free exercise of religion.

Resort to the Courts

Failing to achieve desired results through legislative or executive channels, many Indian groups and individuals have turned to the courts in search of protection of their religious freedom. These efforts have been more successful than results achieved through the other branches of government but less successful than desired. It is most significant that the United States Supreme Court has yet to pronounce directly and decisively on American Indian religious freedom. Therefore, one must look entirely to lower court decisions.

Over the past two decades the Native American Church, an Indian religious group, has achieved increasing judicial and legislative recognition of the legitimacy of the sacramental use of peyote in that church. While peyote is one of the substances subject to control under the Federal Comprehensive Drug Abuse Prevention and Control Act of 1970, federal regulations for the enforcement of that act provide an exempt status for "the nondrug use of peyote in bona fide religious ceremonies of the Native American Church" (21 C.F.R. § 1307.31 [1971]). Nine states also legislatively exempt the use of peyote for religious services from their controlled substance laws: Iowa, Minnesota, Montana, Nevada, New Mexico, South Dakota, Texas, Wisconsin and Wyoming. Case law in three additional states supports such an exemption: Arizona, California and Oklahoma.

In *People* v. *Woody* (1964) the Supreme Court of California reversed, on free exercise grounds, the conviction of several Navahos for illegal possession and use of peyote in a service of the Native American Church. The *Woody* decision has been cited in similar cases in California and in other states. With *Woody* and subsequent decisions, and following the exemption clause to the federal act, Native American Church use of peyote in services has been relatively free of prosecution. However, there have been many court cases involving possession of peyote in contexts other than a Native American Church ceremony.

In *Whitehorn* v. *State* (1977) the Oklahoma Court of Criminal Appeals significantly extended free exercise protection beyond the sacramental use of peyote in a religious service of the Native American Church to "the practice of 'carrying' peyote by members" of that church. If this view were shared by other courts, prosecutions of Native American Church members for illegal possession might be sharply reduced.

Problems remain in the peyote area. Avoiding the consequences of antipeyote legislation typically entails membership in the Native American Church. But what constitutes such membership? Further, what about the sacramental use of peyote by people who are not members of the Native American Church? Exemption clauses do not include them, and court doctrine has ordinarily required that in litigation they must demonstrate good faith as religious practitioners.

Debate also continues concerning the long-range effects of peyote. Is it (or is the mescaline in the peyote cactus) a dangerous drug? Is it addictive? Does persistent use result in adverse long-range effects? Edward F. Anderson has provided a thorough and useful summary of the results of research on these and related questions in *Peyote: the Divine Cactus.* The evidence is inconclusive. A layman might well conclude that since peyote is relatively scarce in the United States, since its use is thus quite limited, and since it is apparently used chiefly for religious purposes, it does not pose a serious threat to public order. Therefore, as an act of good public policy, peyote could even be decriminalized. Such a move would certainly enhance the free exercise of religion.

Another area of considerable litigation involves other objects regarded as sacred which, at the same time, have been given protected status by legislation. These include a variety of game animals, such as deer and moose, species designated as endangered, such as bald eagles and golden eagles, certain species of whales, and selected plants. Here too court results have been mixed, and this continues to be a source of tension between Indians and federal agents. Perhaps the most significant positive developments from the standpoint of Indian religious freedom have been those by which Indians have been exempted on free exercise grounds from certain game laws. For example, following a case in which a Winnebago Indian was exonerated by an appellate court from a conviction for violating a Wisconsin game law concerning deer, the Wisconsin legislature adopted a provision which exempted the taking of deer by Winnebago Indians for religious purposes. The Supreme Court of Alaska noted that provision and recommended a similar one for that state in a case in which it reversed, on free exercise grounds, the conviction of an Athabascan Indian for violating the game laws of Alaska concerning moose. (The case is *Frank* v. *Alaska* 1979.) In both of these instances the importance of religious practices to particular Indian tribes was clearly acknowledged.

Relationships between life-style and American Indian religions have been a central concern in a number of court cases. Indians seeking to wear long hair in keeping with their religious beliefs or traditions have been prevented from doing so by institutional regulations in schools and prisons. Several have sought relief through the courts on free exercise of religion and other grounds. Appellate court decisions have given mixed signals on this issue. Some have seen sufficient connection between life-style and Indian religion to grant claimants' relief; others have not. The most significant case of the former type is *Teterud* v. *Gillman* (1975), in which a federal district court in Iowa upheld the claim of a Cree prisoner in an Iowa penitentiary that the prison's regulations concerning hair violated his First Amendment rights. Teterud maintained that wearing long hair in braids was integrally related to his religion and hence was entitled to First Amendment protection. Both the Iowa district court and the court of appeals supported his claim.

Recent litigation has focused on access to and control of sacred sites. This is the most significant area for measuring the progress of equal protection for American Indian religious freedom. It is the area in which the stakes are the highest as far as public interest is concerned. Furthermore, sacred sites are often critically important to Native American religions and culture. Typically, specific geographical areas are understood to be the places in which the people originated and the loci of other significant events in tribal life. They may also be thought to be points of origin of the world and life in general and axes upon which the world turns. In these locales people relate in a sacred manner to ancestors and relatives, including, perhaps, animal and plant as well as human relatives. Here one relates to all of the most significant sacred powers.

Special relationship to place is essential to the continuing vitality of traditional Indian religions and cultures. This became evident in the most significant and successful access-to-site claim yet to receive public attention—the return in 1970 of Blue Lake and its environs to the Taos Pueblo. As national forest land since 1906 this area had been open to various uses—recreational and commercial, for instance—by nonmembers of the Taos Pueblo as well as by tribal members. The argument that led to the congressional decision to restrict the area to use by the Taos Pueblo was (1) that religion is central to Taos life generally, (2) that Blue Lake and the surrounding areas are crucial to Taos religion, and hence (3) that continued denial of protected access to that lake threatened the very existence of the culture.

Most Indian claims involving sacred sites on governmentally controlled land have not been successful. These include: Cherokee seeking to block the flooding of the Little Tennessee River Valley by the Tellico Dam (*Sequoyah* v. *TVA* 1980); Navaho seeking to have the water level of Lake Powell lowered and tourist traffic restricted in the Rainbow Bridge area (*Badoni* v. *Higginson* 1981); Hopi and Navaho seeking to prevent the expansion of a ski resort in the San Francisco Peaks area of northwestern Arizona (*Wilson* v. *Block* and *Navaho Medicinemen's Association* v. *Block* 1984); Lakota (Sioux) and Tsistsistas (Southern Cheyenne) seeking more protected access to Bear Butte in western South Dakota (*Frank Fools Crow* v. *Gullet* 1983); and Inupiat seeking to preserve an area in the Beaufort and Chuckchi Seas from oil exploration (*Inupiat Community of Arctic Slope* v. *United States* 1982). The free exercise clause has also been appealed to by the Sioux in their claim to the Black Hills of South Dakota, but that appeal has played no role in court decisions in the cases which have been generated by this claim.

The central issue for the courts in dealing with these free exercise claims involving sacred sites has been the nature and extent of access required to protect the Indians' religious rights. Sincerity of view has not been an issue of weight, nor, for the most part, has been the question of whether the contested areas are of some importance to the religious practices of the complainants. The question has been one of degree: *How* important are the sites to those practices? In answering this question the courts have come to rely upon the criteria of *centrality* and *indispensability*. These are the controlling criteria which were first set forth by the Sixth Circuit Court of Appeals in *Sequoyah* v. *TVA*, and they have become predecential for other court decisions in sacred site cases. The sixth circuit acknowledged the historical importance of the Little Tennessee Valley in the life of the Cherokee people and its significance for the "personal preference" of the individual complainants, but it did not see the area as being central and indispensable to the practice of Cherokee religion or in the life of the Cherokee people.

Court imposition of the criteria of centrality and indispensability raises questions of equity. Satisfaction of these criteria is not a simple matter in any religious system, but it may be especially difficult in one in which there are neither formal definitions of orthodoxy nor formally sanctioned promulgators and interpreters of the faith. Such an imposition may require more of Indian free exercise claimants and less of the state than has been required of other free exercise claimants. Nonetheless, these criteria have assumed a significant role in sacred site cases in particular.

Even when these criteria can be satisfied in a court case, the free exercise claim must compete with state interest. Constitutional free exercise doctrine affirms the absolute character of the protection of religious belief but the relative character of the protection of religious practice. For example, even though professedly grounded in religion, practices which seriously threaten public health or safety may be denied the protection of the free exercise clause. Further, even in free exercise cases in which such a threat is not evident and it has been established that certain state actions do impose a burden on claimants' free exercise of religion, the courts must balance the free exercise right against state interest. If that interest is found to be "compelling," and if it can be achieved through no other means, the court may decide for the state.

State interest has been generally well treated in Indian sacred site cases. Indeed, as the Circuit Court of the District of Columbia commented in one case, some courts have even implied that "the Free Exercise Clause can never supercede the government's ownership rights and duties of public management." On the contrary, that court continued in a statement that is both obvious and necessary: "The government must manage its lands in accordance with the Constitution" (*Wilson* v. *Block* 1984).

Sacred site cases typically entail a confrontation between the right to protect property of religious significance and the right to regulate property in the interest of the public. The law for dealing with this confrontation is not well developed in this country, possibly because we are a nation of movers and hence do not tend to invest particular areas with sanctity. The sacred sites of the major religions of the United States are, for the most part, at some distance from this country. The courts have faced the challenge in Indian sacred site cases of balancing constitutional free exercise rights against governmental claims to manage public property in the interest of the larger public. Therefore, representatives of the federal government have argued successfully that the flooding of the Little Tennessee Valley and the Lake Powell areas brought benefits to the larger public which overrode the free exercise claims of the Indians. Similarly, representatives of the state have successfully maintained that public lands such as the San Francisco Peaks and Bear Butte areas should be managed in such a way as to benefit both Indians and non-Indians and to serve recreational and commercial as well as religious interests.

There is one significant case in which the trial court held that the interests of the state were not sufficiently compelling to override Indian free exercise claims: *Northwest Indian Cemetery Protective Association* v. *Peterson* (1983). In this case the United States District Court of Northern California supported the free exercise claims made by and on behalf of the Yurok, Karok, and Tolowa Indians regarding an area in the Six Rivers National Forest. The Indians and various supporters, including the State of California through its Native American Heritage Commission, challenged decisions by the United States Forest Service to complete construction of a paved road—known as the "G-O Road"—and to allow the harvesting of timber in an area known to the Indians as "the high country." The Indians contended that the area is central to their religious beliefs and practices in its present pristine condition and that the construction and use of a road in it would so change the area as to violate their freedom of religion. The district court held that the evidence supported a conclusion that access to and use of "the high country" in its pristine state is "central and indispensable" to the religion of the Yurok, Karok and Tolowa Indians. Indeed, the court concluded that the projected National Forest Service changes in the area would actually pose a "very real threat of undermining" not only the religious practices of the Indians but the tribal communities themselves. Hence, the court concluded that the interests of the federal government in the development of the area were not sufficiently compelling to override such weighty free exercise claims. The Forest Service is appealing this decision.

In general, having examined the status of the free exercise of religion by American Indians through a survey of recent legislation and litigation, public policy and practice have clearly improved since the ratification of the Bill of Rights, especially in recent years. While the effects of the American Indian Religious Freedom Act of 1978 have been disappointing, the fact that it is on record continues to be of some importance. Cases such as *Woody, Whitehorn, Teterud, Frank* and *Northwest* have brought significant advances in selected areas. Still, the United States Supreme Court has yet to pronounce decisively and directly on any aspect of the subject. Failed cases such as *Sequoyah, Badoni, Wilson, Inupiat,* and *Fools Crow,* as well as a host of continuing conflicts over such matters as sacred objects and ceremonies, indicate that the current situation is far from a complete success.

A SINISTER SEARCH FOR "IDENTITY"[4]

"God said what he meant and meant what he said," proclaims Richard Girnt Butler, 66, of the Church of Jesus Christ Christian. Butler sounds like just another Fundamentalist country preacher—until he reveals his peculiar interpretation of God's word. He is one of the leaders of the increasingly troublesome Christian Identity movement, which preaches the most corrosive theology in America, blending hatred of blacks and Jews with visions of an imminent apocalypse and advocating—and sometimes practicing—armed violence to achieve its goals.

Butler's seven-building complex, with its WHITES ONLY sign at the gate, nestles amid towering evergreens near Hayden Lake, Idaho. The tranquil setting contrasts with unnerving events in nearby Coeur d'Alene over the past several weeks: a bombing at the home of a Roman Catholic priest who opposes white racism, then more bombings to divert attention from planned robberies at banks and a National Guard armory. Last week a former security chief of Butler's church, David Door, 35, and two others who attended meetings were charged in the bombings. The church professed shock at the incidents.

Whatever the outcome of the Idaho case, there is no question about violence committed by Identity believers elsewhere. Robert J. Mathews, who left Aryan Nations, Butler's umbrella organization for racists, and formed the Order, died in a 1984 gunfight with federal agents after a crime spree; other Order members drew prison terms of up to 100 years. In Arkansas last year, a heavily armed camp of another Identity group, the Covenant, the Sword and the Arm of the Lord, surrendered to state and federal officers who confiscated a large arms cache and 30 gal. of cyanide. The leader was sentenced to 20 years in prison. In the Midwest, Identity ideas are frequently espoused by groups like Posse Comitatus, the violent tax-protest vigilantes.

In all, experts estimate that the disparate Identity groups count from 2,000 to 5,000 members plus several times that many sympathizers and seem to have particular appeal for bankrupt farmers and the unemployed. A handful of Identity churches,

[4]Reprint of a magazine article by staff writer Richard N. Ostling. *Time*. 128:74. O. 20, '86. Copyright © 1986 Time Inc. All rights reserved. Reprinted by permission from TIME.

like Butler's, hold services in traditional places of worship. But the network includes little-noticed groups that meet in private homes and individuals who regularly receive audiocassettes and publications in the mail. The word is also spread through contacts in prisons, computer bulletin boards and shows on public access channels on TV cable systems, which are required by law to air material from local citizens.

The first thorough analysis of Christian Identity doctrine and history will appear next month in a report by Leonard Zeskind of Kansas City, research director with the Center for Democratic Renewal (formerly the National Anti-Klan Network). Zeskind says the Identity system "provides religious unity for differing racist political groups and brings religious people into contact with the racist movement."

Though Identity has only recently come to public notice, its central concept dates back to the 19th century. In its farfetched "British Israelism" theory, which lacks historical evidence, people of Britain or northern Europe (and hence white Americans) are the descendants of the ten Lost Tribes of ancient Israel. "The Jews have no part in this household," asserts Butler.

British Israelism was popularized among millions of Americans through books, magazines and broadcasts by the late Herbert W. Armstrong and his Worldwide Church of God, although Armstrong had no connection with the Identity movement. The Identity churches stem more directly from the preaching before and after World War II of Gerald L. K. Smith, a notorious anti-Semite. It was Smith's West Coast operative, Wesley Swift, who founded the church that Butler now leads. Later a Swift offshoot in Mariposa, Calif., led by retired Army Colonel William Potter Gale, produced the newsletter *Identity* and solidified the ideology.

Though Identity often sounds Fundamentalist, it is anything but. Identity followers believe they are saved by race rather than grace and welcome followers of Nordic pagan cults alongside Bible believers. The movement scorns Fundamentalism's support for Israel and its opposition to British Israelism. Unlike Fundamentalists like Jerry Falwell, who advocate involvement in the U.S. political system, Identity advocates despise the Federal Government, calling it ZOG (the Zionist Occupation Government).

Most Fundamentalists think believers will be taken to heaven in a "rapture" and escape calamities preceding Jesus Christ's Second Coming. But the Identity movement tells believers they must endure these dire events and prepare by taking military and survival training and stockpiling weapons and food. John Harrell of Louisville, Ill., wealthy head of the Christian Patriots Defense League, who teaches that "Caucasians are the most proven, most capable" of racial groups, recommends that every family of followers "have a 12-gauge shotgun, a .22 rifle and at least 500 rounds of ammunition."

Bruce Hoffman, a Rand Corp. analyst, warns against dismissing such adherents as "kooks or country bumpkins. These people are very adept at using weapons and explosives." The movement would be more dangerous, he says, if an effective leader were to arise. J. Gordon Melton, of Santa Barbara, Calif., and expert on marginal U.S. religions, agrees. "It's not a huge movement, and it's a fairly disorganized movement," he says. "But it doesn't take that many people with guns to do the damage."

WHAT THE FUNDAMENTALISTS WANT[5]

Distinguished social analysts, surveying the complexities of our religious, cultural, and political situation, have offered their considered judgment that: "The Falwells are coming! The Falwells are coming!" The less distinguished have joined in sounding the tocsin, and the alarm is getting louder. We can expect it to get louder still. If alarm is our only response to the public resurgence of religion in American life, there is reason for alarm. Yet among those who speak for the knowledge class, alarm has been the dominant, in some cases the only, response to date. It has been more reaction than response; reaction to alleged reactionaries, and therefore reactionary twice over.

Jerry Falwell, Ed McAteer, Gary Jarmin, Pat Robertson, Jimmy Swaggart, Jim Robison, Tim LaHaye—they are, so we hear, out to take over America and establish a theocracy in which all who disagree will be, at best, second-class citizens. But surely, we may think, nobody really believes such alarmist nonsense. Nonsense or not, reports of the great terror that is upon us are raising

        [5]Reprint of a magazine article by Richard John Neuhaus, a Lutheran pastor and director of the Rockford Institute's Center on Religion and Society. *Commentary*. 79:41–6. My. '85. Copyright © 1985 by the American Jewish Congress. Reprinted from *Commentary*, May 1985, by permission; all rights reserved.

millions of dollars in fund appeals by Planned Parenthood, the
American Civil Liberties Union, the National Organization for
Women, Norman Lear's People for the American Way, and others who claim to believe that the religious Right is the greatest
peril to American democracy since Joe McCarthy. Whatever else
the religious Right may be, it is a bonanza for its opponents. And
if its opponents are right about the "whatever else" the religious
Right may be, the money is well given and well spent in warding
off the threat.

Thus full-page advertisements in prestige newspapers inform
us that the religious Right is determined to abolish the no-
establishment clause of the First Amendment, impose its fundamentalist morality upon all of us through law, put politicians in
our bedrooms, censor what we may read and see, and then, for
good measure, blow up the world in order to force history's de-
nouement in the final act of Armageddon. Truth to tell, it is possible to find statements by leaders of the religious Right who in
spasms of sermonic excess have suggested that they intend to do
all these unpleasant things, and more. But they should not be cari-
catured by their hyperbolic lapses any more than they should caricature their opponents as friends of pornography, incest,
pedophilia, drug-tripping, and treasonous opinion, although
truth to tell again, many of their opponents are on friendly terms
with some or all of these. I have been warned that, by not taking
at face value some of the more bizarre statements issuing from
the religious Right, I am making the same mistake made by those
who brushed aside the "hyperbole" of the Brown Shirts. For solemn reasons, no reference to the Third Reich should be dismissed lightly. For the same solemn reasons, the experience of
the Third Reich should not be trivialized by such facile reference.
But I do believe that those who compare our situation to that of
the Weimar republic or the religious Right to the Nazis have fall-
en victim to polemical heat prostration.

"When I hear the words 'Christian America' I see barbed
wire," a notably liberal Reform rabbi tells me. I do not doubt him,
but then he and a surprising number of others have a curious view
of, among other things, Christianity. In this view the high points,
sometimes the only points, of two millennia of Christian history
are the blood curse upon the Jews, the Crusades, the Inquisition,
and the Holocaust. This way of telling the Christian story is not
unlike telling the story of America exclusively in terms of Salem

witch-hunts, Indian massacres, slavery, the Ku Klux Klan, and alleged preparations for a nuclear first strike. Both stories, while highlighting some important truths, profoundly distort the tales they would tell.

Those who are most vocally anxious about Christian America usually have a special kind of Christian in mind. They do not worry about people who "happen to be" Lutheran, Episcopalian, Methodist, Catholic, or whatever. Even less worrisome are people who add that they happen to be whatever they happen to be "by background." These are the liberally acculturated who do not let their religion stick out or get in the way of living like normal people. They are, as Mort Sahl said of Adlai Stevenson, the sort of people who believe in the "Ten Suggestions" and who would— were they members of the Ku Klux Klan—burn a question mark on your lawn. With Christians like that, Christian America is no problem. But then there are those other Christians who do not just happen to be but really are. And what they really are frequently carries an off-brand name, such as Independent Baptist, Holiness, Pentecostal, or Assemblies of God.

Many of us have never actually met one of these people, and almost nobody we know has ever actually met one, but there they are, millions of them, "out there." And we are inclined to think that we know all about them. In a recent interview Norman Lear explains how People for the American Way got started. After leaving the television comedies, "I was planning to write a film called *Religion*, because I was fascinated with the use of religion as a tax dodge by so many people who become ministers in order to write off a chunk of their living expenses. In order to prepare, I started watching how the reverends were functioning on television . . . and very quickly became concerned about the way they were mixing politics and religion." Lear goes on to suggest that the television evangelists are less interested in religion than in gaining political power. At the same time, he is outraged because they believe that "only those who accept a particular version of Jesus Christ as their savior will go to heaven and all others will go to hell." "In some profound way that we never shake, even Jews—and of course Christians—believe that good people go to heaven and bad people go to hell," says Lear.

Norman Lear is also in this respect typical of the reaction of many to the religious Right. They cannot make up their minds whether these television evangelists are religiously sincere or not.

Even more troubling, they cannot decide whether it would be better if the evangelists were sincere. Ordinarily, sincerity gets a gold star in the kindergarten of contemporary culture, but not when sincerity is "divisive" in its violation of the rules of a pluralistic society. It is worth noting too that in a film titled *Religion* the subject was to be, of course, religious charlatanism.

For the image of Elmer Gantry runs deep in American elite culture and is now frequently and variously invoked in reaction to the religious Right. The leaders of the religious Right are said to be playing upon a nostalgia for an America that never was, but there is nostalgia too among critics who have revived the cast of villains from the 1920's. After the intellectual fads and passions of intervening decades, the world has become simpler again. Our sense of superiority is assured as we take our stand once more with H. L. Mencken against the "booboisie," the Victorians, Puritans, Yahoos, and rednecks, the benighted denizens of Gopher Prairie (now Virginia Beach) and Winesburg (now Lynchburg). Perhaps even the Left Bank and Greenwich Village will come back and, by the inadvertent grace of Jerry Falwell, it will again be possible to be a bohemian.

But such nostalgic fantasies are dispelled as we are recalled to the sure knowledge that this is not the way things were supposed to be in the future that is our present. Etched upon the mind of every educated American is Mencken's acidly brilliant derision of William Jennings Bryan in the company of his "rustic gorillas," utterly discredited and limping off the Tennessee stage to a timely death. There is more than one "teaching of contempt," and this one most of us learned well. But now some of us are no longer so certain, Broadway notwithstanding, that we understand who sowed the wind and who is reaping the whirlwind. Something has gone radically wrong with the script of modernity. We tell ourselves that this religious Right, indeed the more general phenomenon of religion bursting-out all over, is atavistic, a temporary malfunction in the ordering of time. Until we recognize that it is the certitudes of Clarence Darrow which now seem pitiably quaint, while the future is claimed by "high-tech" religious communicators who style themselves the American Coalition for Traditional Values. Little wonder that sectors of our cultural leadership show every sign of having gone into cultural shock.

In fact this new situation is not so new. The American people have always been determinedly, some would say incorrigibly, religious. What is new is the public recognition of this fact and the debate over the problems that attend it. To put it differently, what was thought to be a private and therefore eminently ignorable reality is spilling over into the public arena in most inconvenient ways. The spillover, or inundation, as some would have it, has been most visibly occasioned by the emergence of the religious Right. As it happens, on the map of American religion, politicized fundamentalism is a minority phenomenon. This minority, however, has kicked a tripwire alerting us to the much larger reality of unsecular America. As in 1962 Michael Harrington alerted public opinion to the forgotten minority of "The Other America," so the religious Right has thrown open the closet door to expose the beliefs, fears, and aspirations shared by an overwhelming majority of Americans of almost every description.

In high schools and colleges across the country students are reading textbooks that state in a taken-for-granted manner that America is, or is rapidly becoming, a secular society. If religion is mentioned at all, it is said that people once found answers to their problems in religious teaching, but, of course, that is no longer possible in "our increasingly secular and pluralistic society."

Yet the proposition that America is, or is becoming, a secular society has everything going for it except the empirical evidence. The proposition is tied to a two-part dogma which has exercised an intellectual hegemony for nearly two hundred years. The dogma states that as people become more enlightened (read, more educated) religion will wither away. The second part of the dogma states that, to the extent religion endures, it is a residual phenomenon that can be hermetically sealed off in the "private sphere" of life, safely removed from the public arena where, by the canons of secular "rationality," we debate and decide the ordering of our life together. This is a hypothesis about historical development. As such it is subject to historical confirmation or falsification. At least in America, it has been historically falsified.

Survey research does not tell the whole story, but it tells an important part of it. It matters little whether one consults Gallup, Roper, or some other study; on some questions the answers are as close to unanimity as allowed by margins of error. For example, 94 percent of the American people profess belief in God, 88 percent say the Bible is the inspired word of God, 90 percent identify themselves religiously with a specific Christian denomination or as Jews, 89 percent of us say we pray regularly, and so forth. Why do some otherwise thoughtful people go on insisting that there is no frame of reference for a moral consensus among the American people? With near unanimity Americans say that morality is derived from the Jewish and Christian traditions (the Bible, the Ten Commandments, the Sermon on the Mount, the teachings of the Church, etc.). There is in fact a shared world of moral reference, a common vocabulary, that can be drawn upon in public discourse.

I said that with "near unanimity" Americans believe that moral judgment is derived from our Jewish and Christian traditions. The problem is with the "near." The civil libertarian immediately, and rightly, asks about those who dissent from that view—the religiously indifferent, the atheist, the declared "secular humanist," as well as the Buddhist or Muslim.

For one answer, we can turn to the massive "Middletown III" study of Muncie, Indiana, directed by Theodore Caplow of the University of Virginia and sponsored by the National Science Foundation, which is pertinent to the question both of religious resurgence and religious tolerance. In *All Faithful People* (University of Minnesota, 1983), Caplow and his colleagues demonstrate that, contrary to the expectations of Robert and Helen Lynd who did the original Middletown study in the mid 20's, the people of Muncie are dramatically more religious today than they were then. Comparisons of the Muncie data with national surveys convincingly show that Muncie is not an exception on this score. Of course one can be skeptical about the authenticity, however defined, of this religiousness; survey research cannot search the interstices of the human heart. But it can measure the social reality. It can measure what people say they believe (for example, in Muncie 97 percent say the Bible is inspired and 86 percent "have no doubt" about the divinity of Jesus). It can measure churchgoing, rites of passage (marriages, funerals, etc.) under religious auspices, the time and money given to religious purposes, and numerous other facts of behavior. The farther back we go in time the less scientifically rigorous are the data, but on the evidence available Caplow thinks it reasonable to conclude that Americans are more religious today than they were, say, a hundred years ago.

Studies such as Middletown III have caused a remarkable turnaround among social theorists who had supposed there to be a necessary connection between increased modernity and increased secularization. As Peter L. Berger, arguably America's premier sociologist of religion, remarked at a recent conference, the evidence had been accumulating for some years, "but the Caplow study has put the final nail in the coffin of the theory that modernity means secularity."

On the question of tolerance, Caplow says that, "In a liberal perspective, these findings are almost too good to be true." But rechecking and rechecking again only reinforces the conclusion that, as the people of Muncie have become more religious, they have also become more tolerant. "We cannot turn up a group whose religious chauvinism comes anywhere near the level that was normal in 1924," Caplow reports. In this connection it is important to note that the research includes the fundamentalist Christians who are thought to be least tolerant of others. Of this "extraordinary ecumenicism" Caplow ventures the suggestion that "such a situation may never before have existed in the long history of Christianity." A clear and positive correlation between religious commitment and religious tolerance would seem to turn the conventional wisdom on its head.

Caplow offers several speculations on "why Middletown people are so reluctant to lay down the law or to expound the prophets for the benefit of their neighbors." One reason, Caplow suggests, is that religious people tend to think they are in the minority. They believe "the stereotyped misreading of social change" promulgated by television and other media which persuades them that religion is weaker than it is. The result is that "Devout Christians in Middletown, like happily married couples there, regard themselves as exceptional: surrounded by people just like themselves, they think they stand quite alone."

Another explanation is that the people of Middletown believe it is wrong, *morally* wrong, for anybody, and most especially for the state, to mess around with other people's souls. In other words, it is the will of God that we be tolerant of those who disagree with us about the will of God. Respect for those who believe differently or do not believe at all stems not from religious indifference but from religious commitment. If this interpretation is correct, it is very good news indeed for the future of religious freedom in America.

II

The public resurgence of religion is hardly limited to fundamentalism, but fundamentalists are the main focus of the public debate. The key leaders of the American Coalition for Traditional Values (ACTV—pronounced "active"), for example, are fundamentalists. This does not mean that all fundamentalists support the religious Right, and it certainly does not mean that the religious Right is exclusively fundamentalist. Many, perhaps most, fundamentalists still adhere to the maxim that was almost universal among fundamentalists only a few years ago: "Religion and politics don't mix." Jerry Falwell of the Moral Majority was eloquent in arguing that proposition against Martin Luther King, Jr. and other clergy in the civil-rights movement. The pattern in the media and elsewhere is to use the term fundamentalist in a careless way that refers to anything we deem religiously bizarre or fanatical. Thus journalists refer to Islamic fundamentalists and polemicists compare Jerry Falwell with the Ayatollah Khomeini. The pattern reflects intellectual laziness mixed with an unseemly measure of bigotry.

Fundamentalism derives its name from *The Fundamentals*, twelve paperback books issued from 1910 to 1915 which received enormous circulation. Written by conservative American and British writers, these books constituted a frontal assault upon religious "modernism." Modernism, in turn, was the confident liberal doctrine that there is an almost perfect congruence between God's will and the inevitable progress of civilization, especially American civilization. The fundamentalists believed that this was a false religion and that most of the Protestant churches in America had sold out to it. (It is of more than passing interest that, while today millions of Americans call themselves fundamentalists, almost nobody calls himself a modernist.)

In its early years fundamentalism had some formidable intellectual leadership. For instance, J. Gresham Machen, professor of New Testament at Princeton Theological Seminary, made an impressive case in *Christianity and Liberalism* (1923) that religious liberalism was in fact not Christianity but a new religion that, while using Christian symbols and language, replaced faith in God with faith in humanity and historical progress. Most fundamentalists boiled their case down to insistence upon five "fundamentals": the inerrancy of Scripture (the Bible contains no errors in any subject on which it speaks); the virgin birth of Jesus (the Spirit of God conceived Jesus in Mary without human intervention); the substitutionary atonement of Jesus Christ (on the cross he bore the just punishment for the sins of the entire world); his bodily resurrection; the authenticity of the biblical miracles; and pre-millennialism.

The last point touches on the question of, among other things, Armageddon, a question which erupted in, of all places, the 1984 presidential campaign. All orthodox Christians believe in the return of Jesus in glory and the establishment of the kingdom of God as the consummation of history. Some Christian groups are pre-millennialist, others are post-millennialist, and some do not take a position on the question. Both post- and pre-millennialists believe there will be on earth a thousand-year-reign of perfect peace, justice, and harmony with God's will. Pre-millennialists believe that Jesus will return first and then there will be that millennium; post-millennialists say the millennium will be established first and then Jesus will return in glory. The debate turns upon the interpretation of some marvelously obscure passages in the prophets Daniel and Ezekiel and the last book of the Christian Scriptures, Revelation.

In the past it was generally thought that pre-millennialist Christians would be politically passive, because there wasn't much point in trying to change the world before Jesus returns to set everything right. The important thing was not social reform but saving individual souls. At the end of the last century, before the fundamentalist-modernist split was formalized, evangelist Dwight L. Moody set forth the pre-millennialist thesis: "I look upon this world as a wrecked vessel. God has given me a lifeboat and said to me, 'Moody, save all you can.'" Post-millennialists, on the other hand, were avid social reformers, eager to put the world in order, establish the millennium, and thus hasten the return of Jesus. (The more modernist among them thought the last point to be an inspiring metaphor not to be taken literally.) But today the most aggressive political activism is being pushed by pre-millennialists.

The change is causing considerable consternation within the fundamentalist world. Fundamentalism is magnificently fissiparous. The local churches jealously protect their independence from any larger association. Leaders can cooperate in groups such as ACTV and the Moral Majority because, it is repeatedly emphasized, they are not religious but political organizations. If non-fundamentalists worry about what fundamentalists say about them, it is as nothing compared with what they routinely say about one another. Bob Jones (of Bob Jones University) has declared that Jerry Falwell is the greatest instrument of Satan in America today. While they are partners in a moral crusade, off the platform one partner does not hesitate to announce that one or more of the other partners is surely going to hell. That God will not hear their prayers is the least of it. The public platform and the pulpit platform engage two quite different worlds of discourse. The Moral Majority advertises and carefully nurtures its support from Catholics, Jews, and non-believers. But membership in the Moral Majority, it is made unmistakably clear, is not to be confused with membership in the company of the truly saved.

Jews are notably and understandably interested in their part in fundamentalist scenarios for the End Time. These scenarios are closely linked, of course, to the fundamentalists' impassioned support for the state of Israel. They involve the Rapture, Armageddon, the final war with the Soviet Union, and other items of high drama which cannot delay us here. Suffice it to say that, while all orthodox Christians say Jesus will return, most fundamentalists are "dispensationalists" who derive from "Bible prophecy" a quite precise blueprint and timetable for the return. There are, they believe, dispensations or ordered events and time periods predicted in the Bible. Jews are critical to the final act. There is considerable confusion over whether this means that the Jews will finally be converted to Christianity. The alternative way of putting it, which is increasingly accepted, is that Jews will be fulfilled in their Jewishness in welcoming their long-awaited messiah, who will turn out to be Jesus of Nazareth. He will not be the "Christian" messiah but most definitely the Jewish messiah, as he has been the Jewish messiah for Christians all along. As one rabbi has told me, "I can't get exercised over this dispute. If and when all this happens, we will see whether the one who comes is coming for the first time or the second time. I only hope that when we meet we'll be glad to see one another."

Christians of all persuasions have had a difficult time finding a secure theological place for living Judaism. There is little problem with the Jews of the Hebrew Scriptures (the Old Testament, as Christians say) and dispensationalists have an important role

for Jews in the End Time, but Judaism between the biblical
prophets and the eschaton is something of an anomaly. Today
this may be changing as Christians are reflecting in a new way
upon Paul's explorations (Romans 9 through 11) into the
"mystery" of living Judaism and what it means that God will never
break His covenant with the people of Israel. Fundamentalists too
are increasingly insistent that this mystery means that the nation
that blesses the Jews will be blessed and the nation that curses
them will be cursed. It is less a sense of guilt over the Holocaust—
which is viewed as something perpetrated by other people in a
distant land—than of Divine purpose that gives Judaism and the
state of Israel such a special place in the fundamentalist world
view.

Of course some Jews protest that it is demeaning to be fitted
into a theological system to which they do not subscribe. This, I
believe, may be a mistake. Acceptance of Jews, which means also
resistance to anti-Semitism, is better secured when it is religiously
grounded. Some Jews take a more pragmatic view in welcoming
fundamentalist support for Israel in particular. Irving Kristol recently noted, "It is their theology, but it is our Israel." To that
sage observation I would add that Israel is more firmly supported
because it is their theology and not simply their prudential geopo-
litical judgment.

If a previously apolitical pre-millennialist fundamentalism has
now turned in an activist direction, fundamentalist leaders did
not just get together one day and decide to go political. They felt,
and they feel, that they are responding to an assault upon their
religious freedom. As Seymour Martin Lipset has put it, their activism may be viewed as an "aggressive defense." Their defense
is against what they perceive as governmental actions dictated by
the "secular humanists" in control of American public life. Ten
years ago, before the religious Right was a major factor, Leo Pfef-
fer (then of the American Jewish Congress) saw the dynamic that
would produce this response. "Matters which have long been considered private," he wrote, "are increasingly becoming the concern of government." He added, "The thirst for power is a potent
force even in a democracy, and the state will be tempted and will
yield to the temptation of seeking to exercise dominion over religion for no other reason than because it is there."

There were several flashpoints that contributed to the political activation of fundamentalism. Of enormous importance was the outlawing of prayer in the public schools in the early 1960's. These court decisions sent a seismic shock that traveled far beyond the worlds of fundamentalism. Whatever one may think of the merits of school prayers, their removal was understandably seen as a major step toward the secularization of public space. An incorrigibly and increasingly religious society simply does not understand why children cannot publicly acknowledge God in the classroom, nor why, as another court ruling determined, the Ten Commandments cannot be posted on the classroom wall.

As important as these court rulings were, the religious Right was activated by the increasing aggressiveness of the Internal Revenue Service and other government agencies in "interfering" with the free exercise of religion. During the 1960's and 1970's the IRS moved in the direction of treating tax exemption for religion as a tax subsidy. The reasoning here is that money exempted from taxation is in fact a governmental expenditure, and what the government spends the government should control. It is again understandable that fundamentalists, and not only fundamentalists, believe that implicit in this reasoning is a massive, even totalitarian, expansion of state control over religion and other exempt forms of voluntary activity. Moreover, fundamentalists in particular found themselves in collision with state educational authorities over the control of their Christian day schools. They believe, rightly or wrongly, that some state requirements for the certification of teachers and curricula exceed any legitimate public purpose and threaten to dissolve the religious distinctiveness of the alternative education they have elected for their children.

In discussing the "assaults" that sparked the defensive reaction of the religious Right, I have not mentioned the 1973 *Roe* v. *Wade* decision and abortion on demand. It is generally acknowledged that abortion was not that important in the generating passions of the religious Right. Until a very few years ago it was merely included in the catalogue of our society's "decadence," along with drugs, pornography, homosexual activism, and an exploding divorce rate. Today, of course, the limiting of abortions (or, as they prefer, the protection of unborn life) is high on the agenda of the religious Right, and of many millions of Americans who in no way identify with the religious Right.

Even those who try to understand the religious Right sympathetically find themselves asking, "Yes, but what else do they want?" One useful answer is ACTV's list of ten issues in its campaign to "restore traditional moral and spiritual values" to American life. The list includes prayer and Bible reading in public schools, a "pro-life" amendment (or some other instrument for overruling *Roe* v. *Wade*), legal restrictions on pornography, an end to state "harassment" of Christian schools, resistance to feminist and gay-rights legislation, increased defense spending, and terminating social programs that, it is believed, only increase the dependency of the poor. Even some of the committed opponents of the religious Right might concede that most, if not all, of these items are legitimate issues for debate in a democratic society. Yet many people are alarmed, for they thought that all these issues had been "settled." Only now has it become evident that, at least on some of these issues, a majority of the American people had not consented to the settlement.

Leaders of the religious Right have expressed surprise at what they view as the hysterical reaction to their enterprise. Jerry Falwell and some others increasingly try to calm the reaction by expressing devotion to the rules of liberal democracy (yes, *liberal* democracy) and by distancing themselves from the antidemocratic theocrats who are attracted to the cause. Falwell and others are publicly insistent that they are not advocating an officially "Christian America." Beneath the public gloating over their triumphs recent and portending is evidence of a deep insecurity about the power they are believed to possess. These people are not accustomed to being viewed with such intense fear and loathing. With loathing, yes. During their half-century in the religious, cultural, and political wilderness, fundamentalists knew that they were the object of deepest contempt, and that knowledge reinforced their determination to have nothing to do with the "principalities and powers" of the American establishments. But the sensation of being feared is something new. They find it hard to believe that the "northeasternliberalestablishment" (one word) could be so easily intimidated, as some who are of that establishment may also find it hard to believe. Finding it hard to believe, some of us try to persuade ourselves of what it is almost impossible to believe, namely, that the religious Right and the conservative trend of which it is part are but a passing aberration and tomorrow morning we will wake up to discover that America has returned to "normalcy."

The activist fundamentalists want us to know that they are not going to go back to the wilderness. Many of them, being typical Americans, also want to be loved. They explain, almost apologetically, that they did not really want to bash in the door to the public square, but it was locked, and nobody had answered their knocking. Anyway, the hinges were rusty and it gave way under pressure that was only a little more than polite. And so the country cousins have shown up in force at the family picnic. They want a few rules changed right away. Other than that they promise to behave, provided we do not again try to exclude them from family deliberations. Surely it is incumbent on the rest of us, especially those who claim to understand our society, to do more in response to this ascendance of fundamentalism—and indeed of religion in general—than to sound an increasingly hysterical and increasingly hollow alarm.

BIBLIOGRAPHY

An asterisk (*) preceding a reference indicates that the article or part of it has been reprinted in this book.

BOOKS AND PAMPHLETS

Adler, Margot. Drawing down the moon: witches, Druids, goddess-worshippers, and other pagans in America today. Beacon Press. '86.

Alley, Robert S. James Madison on religious liberty. Prometheus Books. '85.

Barthel, Diane L. Amana: from Pietist sect to American community. University of Neb. Press. '84.

Boyer, Ernest. A way in the world: family life as spiritual discipline. Harper & Row. '84.

Brewer, Priscilla. Shaker communities, Shaker lives. University Press of New England. '86.

Brown, Joseph Epes. The spiritual legacy of the American Indian. Crossroad. '82.

Caplow, Theodore, Bahr, Howard M., and Chadwick, Bruce A. All faithful people: change and continuity in Middletown's religion. University of Minn. Press. '83.

Cox, Harvey Gallagher. Religion in the secular city: toward a postmodern theology. Simon & Schuster. '85.

Kennedy, Eugene C. The now and future church: the psychology of being an American Catholic. Doubleday. '84.

Levy, Leonard Williams. The establishment clause: religion and the First Amendment. Macmillan. '86.

Marty, Martin E. Protestantism in the United States: righteous empire. Scribner's. '86.

McCall, Emmanual L. Black church life-styles, Black Christian experience. Broadman Press. '86.

Mead, Frank Spencer, and Hill, Samuel S. Handbook of denominations in the United States. Abingdon Press. '85.

Melton, J. Gordon. The encyclopedia of American religions (first edition, Supplement). Gale Research Co. '85.

Melton, J. Gordon. The encyclopedic handbook of cults in America. Garland Pub. '85.

Miller, William Lee. The first liberty: religion and the American republic. Knopf. '86.

Moore, R. Laurence. Religious outsiders and the making of Americans. Oxford University Press. '86.

Newman, Jay. Foundations of religious tolerance. University of Toronto Press. '82.

Ochs, Carol. Women and spirituality. Rowman & Allanheld. '83.

Peshkin, Alan. God's choice: the total world of a fundamentalist Christian school. University of Chicago Press. '86.

Robbins, Thomas, and Anthony, Dick. In gods we trust: new patterns of religious pluralism in America. Transaction Books. '81.

Robbins, Thomas, Shepherd, William C., and McBride, James. Cults, culture, and the law: perspectives on new religious movements. Scholars Press. '85.

Ruether, Rosemary Radford. Womanguides: readings toward a feminist theology. Beacon Press. '85.

Shepherd, William C. To secure the blessings of liberty: American constitutional law and the new religious movements. Crossroad Pub. Co/Scholars Press. '85.

Shipps, Jan. Mormonism the story of a new religious tradition. University of Illinois Press. '85.

Silberman, Charles E. A certain people: American Jews and their lives today. Summit Bks. '85.

United States Commission on Civil Rights. Religion in the constitution, a delicate balance. U.S. Commission on Civil Rights. '83.

PERIODICALS

RELIGIOUS PLURALISM

Transformations: American religion in the 1980s. Martin E. Marty. Annals of the American Academy of Political and Social Science. 480:11+. Jl. '85.

*Denominational America and the new religious pluralism. Wade Clark Roof and William McKinney. Annals of the American Academy of Political and Social Science. 480:24+. Jl. '85.

Members of Congress hold ties to 21 religious groups. Christianity Today. 29:61–4. Ja. 18, '85.

*Religion in post-Protestant America. Peter L. Berger. Commentary. 80:41–5. My. '86.

America's return to prayer. Kenneth A. Briggs. The New York Times Magazine. 106+. N. 18, '84.

*In the name of God. Mary Ann Meyers. The Pennsylvania Gazette. 85:14–21. D. '86.

To walk in balance with the earth. Archie Fire Lame Deer. The Center
Magazine. 17:41. S./O. '84.

Does liberal Protestantism have an American future? William R. Hutchison. The Center Magazine. 18:9-16. N./D. '85.

*Hawaii's domestication of Shinto. James Emerson Whitehurst. The
Christian Century. 101:1100-1. N. 21, '84.

Revitalized religion (Other Realities: New Religions and Revitalization
Movements conference in Lincoln, Neb.). Martin E. Marty. The
Christian Century. 102:650-2. Jl. 3-10, '85.

Marty's invitation: the mysteries of Catholic identity (An invitation to
Catholic history). Garry Wills. The Christian Century. 103:715-17.
Ag. 13-20, '86.

Spiritual renewal brings booming growth to three Episcopal churches in
Northern Virginia. Beth Spring. Christianity Today. 28:38-9. Ja.
13, '84.

American Indian spiritual politics. Christopher Vecsey. Commonweal.
111:203-8. Ap. 6, '84.

*Spiritual explorers: recovering the lost wisdom of women-led religions.
Karen Lindsey. Ms. 14:38+. D. '85.

Feeling the spirit: books, rituals, action. Toby Axelrod. Ms. 14:79+. D.
'85.

*Children of the Hutterites. Gertrude Enders Huntington. Natural History. 90:34+. F. '81.

*The new Orthodox: a Jewish revival on the Upper West Side. Cathryn
Jakobson. New York. 19:52-60. N. 17, '86.

*The cloistered life. Julia Lieblich. New York Times Magazine. 88:12+.
Jl. 10, '83.

American Jews rediscover Orthodoxy. Natalie Gittelson. The New York
Times Magazine. 40-1+. S. 30, '84.

Portrait of a small black church. David Bradley. New York Times Magazine. p16+. Je. 30, '85.

The Mormons—growth, prosperity and controversy. Robert Lindsey.
The New York Times Magazine. 18-22+. Ja. 12, '86.

American Catholic in Rome. Barbara Grizzuti Harrison. The New York
Times Magazine. 56-7+. Mr. 16, '86.

Utah: helping thy neighbor (flood assistance organized by Mormons)
George Raine. Newsweek. 101:27. Je. 20, '83.

Shaker bicentennial: is the end near? George Hackett. Newsweek.
102:24+. N. 21, '83.

Jews in a soulful debate (views of C. E. Silberman). Kenneth L. Woodward. Newsweek. 106:77. S. 23, '85.

*The Holy Ghost people. Michael Watterlond. Science '83. 4:50+. My. '83.

Hispanic Catholics (Archdiocese of New York). Society 20:2-3. Mr./Ap. '83.

Many seek faith along other paths. U.S. News & World Report. 94:42-3. Ap. 4, '83.

After 5 centuries, Protestants show renewed vitality. James Mann. U.S. News & World Report. 95:81-3. N. 14, '83.

*On the different world of Utah (address, October 31, 1985). James L. Clayton. Vital Speeches of the Day. 52:186-92. Ja. 1, '86.

RELIGIOUS FREEDOM

The Supreme Court and religious freedom. Robert F. Drinan. America. 152:254-5. Mr. 30, '85.

The wall of separation. Richard B. Morris. American Heritage. 35:77-9. Ag./S. '84.

*The bicentennial of the Virginia Statute (Virginia Statute for Religious Freedom). William Lee Miller. The Christian Century. 102:1171-5. D. 18-25, '85.

Freedom to shape not to control. James M. Wall. The Christian Century. 103:227-8. Mr. 5, '86.

An exchange on religious freedom. Ronald Reagan and Norman Lear. Harper's. 269:15-18+. O. '84.

*Voices of reason, voices of faith. Time. 124:28-9. S. 17, '84.

*The faith of the Founding Fathers. Robert P. Hay. USA Today. 114:80-3. My. '86.

Our common heritage. Paul O. Sand. Vital Speeches of the Day. 50:530-2. Je. 15, '84.

*Religion and a neutral state: imperative or impossibility? (address, April 5, 1984). Carl H. Esbeck. Vital Speeches of the Day. 50:548-53. Jl. 1, '84.

*Religious freedom for all: a Jewish perspective (address, September 6, 1984). Samuel Rabinove. Vital Speeches of the Day. 51:59-62. N. 1, '84.

CONFLICTS AND CONTROVERSIES

Fundamentalism and the Hispanic Catholic. Allan Figueroa Deck. America. 152:64-6. Ja. 26, '85.

Catholics and Jewish prayer. Daniel J. Harrington. America. 152:306-7, Ap. 13, '85.

Ten commandments of the electronic church. Robert Abelman. Channels of Communications. 4:64+. Ja./F. '85.

Comparative study of religions: a theological necessity. Ivan Strenski. The Christian Century. 102:126-8. F. 6-13, '85.

Mennonites and politics. Sue C. Steiner. The Christian Century. 102:463-4. My. 8, '85.

Science and religion: getting the conversation going. William H. King. The Christian Century. 103:611-14. Jl. 2-9, '86.

Church apologizes to Native Americans. Jim Cairney. The Christian Century. 103:852-3. O. 8, '86.

Historic peace churches seek a new evangelistic emphasis (Anabaptist denominations). Timothy K. Jones. Christianity Today. 29:44-5. My. 17, '85.

White supremacists take on trappings of religion. Eva Simson. Christianity Today. 30:30-1. Ag. 8, '86.

*What the fundamentalists want. Richard John Neuhaus. Commentary. 79:41-6. My. '85.

The Baptist schism. Michael Berryhill. The New York Times Magazine. 90-5+. Je. 9, '85.

Why people join cults. Steven Strasser. Newsweek. 104:36. D. 3, '84.

Bible-Belt confrontation (fundamentalists vs. Mormons). Kenneth L. Woodward. Newsweek. 105:65. Mr. 4, '85.

Is fundamentalism addictive? Kenneth L. Woodward. Newsweek. 106:63. Ag. 5, '85.

Radical departures. Saul V. Levine. Psychology Today. 18:20-7. Ag. '84.

*Civil rights, Indian rites. Robert S. Michaelsen. Society. 21:42-6. My./Je. '84.

*Marginal movements. Thomas Robbins. Society. 21:46+. My./Je. '84.

*A sinister search for "Identity." Richard N. Ostling. Time. 128:74. O. 20, '86.

A unisex Bible? Reformers run into a storm. Michael Doan. U.S. News & World Report. 97:70. D. 17, '84.

When a state takes aim at faith healing. Muriel Dobbin. U.S. News & World Report. 100:22. Mr. 24, '86.